theatrical seasonings

Cover Design by Steve A. Unger

Illustrations by Robert G. Raymonda

Stage Guild Publications
Syracuse, New York

THEATRICAL SEASONINGS, ENCORE!

For additional copies, use order forms in back of book or write to:
Stage Guild Publications
Stage Guild to Syracuse Stage
820 East Genesee Street
Syracuse, New York 13210

Checks should be made payable to Stage Guild Publications for the amount of $9.95 plus $1.50 postage and handling per book. For sales tax (applicable if delivered in New York State), add $.70 per book. Gift wrap is available at $.50 per book.

THEATRICAL SEASONINGS, ENCORE! may be obtained for fundraising projects or by retail outlets at special rates. Write above address for further information.

First Printing	November, 1983	4,000 copies
Second Printing	February, 1984	4,000 copies

International Standard Book Number: 0-9612330-0-1

Library of Congress Catalog Card Number: 83-50926

The proceeds from the sale of this book will benefit Syracuse Stage.

Printed in the United States of America
by
Salina Press, Inc.
Syracuse, New York

Setting the Stage

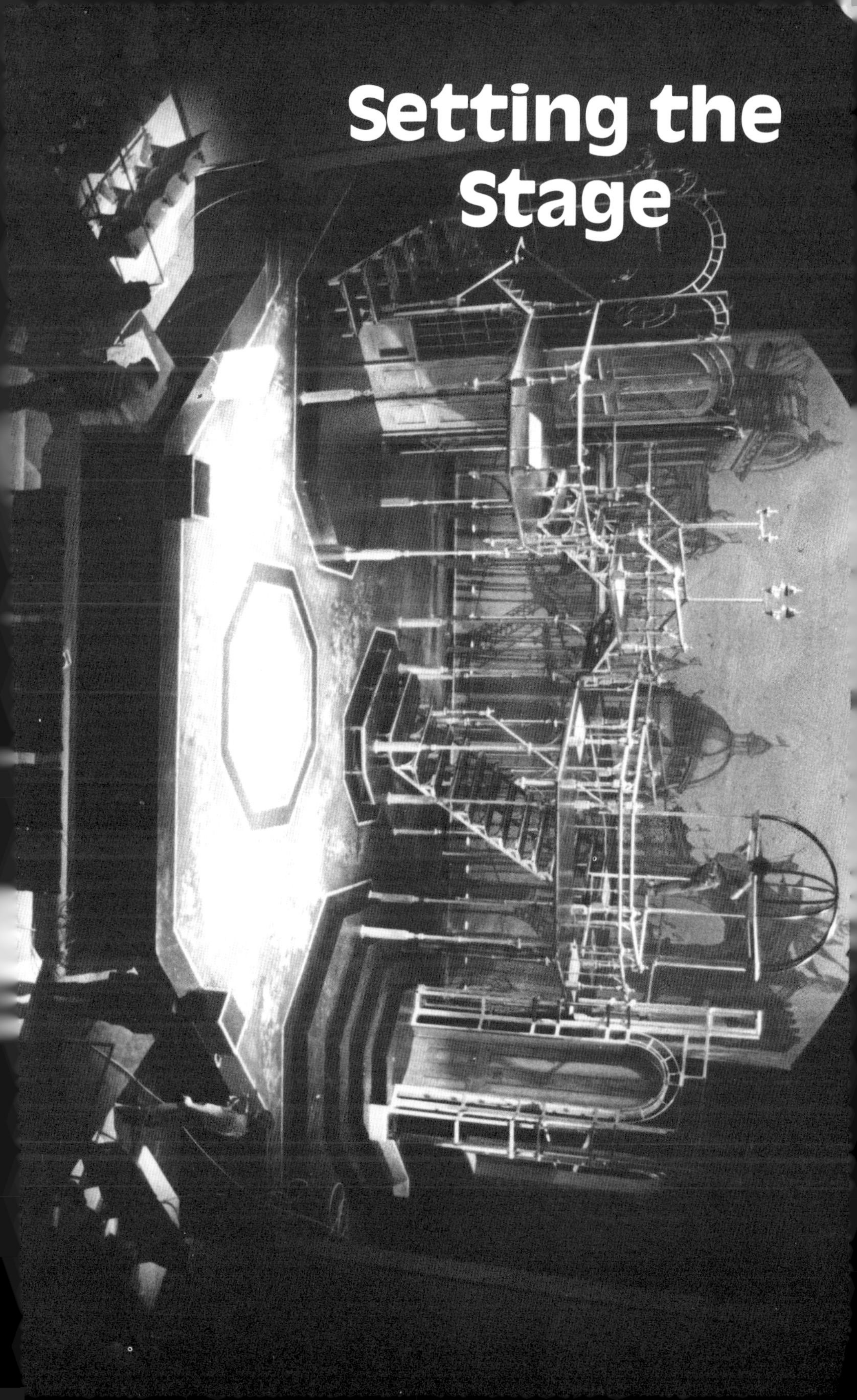

A Word from the Director

I had always stood plate in hand in awe of cooks. Lady cooks, or should I say women as cooks? A complacent participant in a sexist society, I passively accepted woman's role with *kinder, kirche, kuche* -- particularly *kuche.* When I was thrown on my own resources in the advanced stages of middle age I thought I faced a burnt out future of T.V. dinners and an unending array of canned goods. Hesitantly, I ventured into the world of cooking with trepidation and a crock pot. After a number of experiments yielded black potatoes, rubbery chicken and a roast that bounced, I was ready for Burger-King. In other words, I was suicidal. It was a cookbook that saved me. The breakthrough was M.F.K. Fisher's "The Art of Eating." In lucid prose Ms. Fisher charmingly set forth how easy it is to cook and eat well. (There's a cookbook title!) She demystified the whole process and brought light and clarity. After that "ah-hah!" it became as easy as spaghetti carbonara (page 219).

So, dear eater, here is yet another cookbook -- a treasure chest of tested, scrumptious, easy recipes to tempt you. Add them to your collection. I'm sure I can squeeze one more into my four foot shelf of cookbooks.

Eat in good health!

Arthur Storch

Arthur Storch
Producing Director of Syracuse Stage

Photo on front cover:

A Christmas Carol, 1981 - Christopher Doane (Peter Cratchit), Mike Champagne (Bob Cratchit), Michael Eller (Tiny Tim), Yolanda Childress (Mrs. Cratchit), Emily Goodpaster (Martha Cratchit), Susan Keill (Belinda Cratchit)

Photo on p. 3:
Set, 1980 - *The Comedy of Errors*

Notes & Cues

"When I am in trouble, eating is the only thing that consoles me. Indeed, when I am in really great trouble, as anyone who knows me intimately will tell you, I refuse everything except food and drink." Thus our friend Algernon of *The Importance of Being Earnest* cues us on gastronomy and its magical effect on the character of man, his imagination, his wit, his courage, his perceptions -- whether awake or asleep, active or resting.

There is a certain kinship of theater and gastronomy: one nourishes the body, the other uses the body as its exclusive instrument; one might be called the first art, the other the first science; with each the script or recipe may be the same, but the actors and director or the cooks and chef will make it different; both must in the end have an audience.

Unlike Minerva, this book did not spring fully prepared from the brain of Jupiter. From the Spring of 1974 when Stage Guild gave its first Saturday Night Supper for cast and crew, which has grown into a weekly tradition during the theater season, hostesses have been enthusiastically swapping recipes and menus. Our first cookbook, *Theatrical Seasonings*, was such a success, that we are back by popular demand for our brand new book -- *Theatrical Seasonings, Encore!*

Originally known as Theatre Guild, the Stage Guild was founded in 1973 when Arthur Storch became the Producing Director of Syracuse Stage. Fundraising activities range from the annual appeal to the community -- the Angel Appeal -- to a fashion show, house tour, costume collection, gift gallery and of course, this cookbook. Service projects include transportation for our actors while they are in Syracuse, guided tours of the theater complex and the preparation of dinner every Saturday night for cast and crew.

The cookbook committee applauds Arnold Poltenson and his staff at Salina Press, Steve Unger of Syracuse China, Charles Pascale of Pascale Wine Bar and Restaurant, and Nancy Craig of Grand Design, who have given us invaluable assistance in the production of this book. We also thank Robert Raymonda, Thomas Krizka, John Kuhn, JZ Typography, the committee volunteers and the many recipe contributors.

Photos by Susan Piper Kublick: pp. 47, 153, 175, 301, 324
Photos by Robert Lorenz: cover, pp. 3, 9, 15, 57, 83, 113, 123, 213, 223, 265, 309, 322
Photo by James vanPatten: p. 189
Illustrations on pp. 30, 64, 170: Sharon Drinkwine

Committee

Chairman and Editor	Joan M. Good	
Co-chairmen & Editors	Karen E. Goodman Sally G. Tully	
Assistant Chairmen	Sheila Goldie Joan Shay	Cynthia Evans Marilyn Sechrist
Testing Chairman	Ann R. Pierce	
Testers	Ellen Agnew Rosemary Armstrong Suzanne Beeching Karen A. Berg Linda Berger Abigail E. Beutler Mary Jane Bisesi Barbara Black Kathy Brown Pamela Burdick Frances Campbell Susan Cobb Jessica Cohen Connie Colleran Irene B. Collins Patricia Covell Ellen Daniels Carol Decker Kathy Demore Mary Durkin Hannah Dushay Cynthia Evans Liz Fabel Isabelle Fleming Jacqueline Fox Phyllis Gammon Nan Gartner Marilyn Giancola Susan Glotzer Sheila Goldie Patricia S. Haggerty Helen F. Hale Gay Henegar Marilyn Husted June Jesmain Frances Knapp Doris Kuckhoff Wendy Larkin	Janet Lower Anne Maier Marie Margosian Maralee Martin Marie Matchuk Judith L. McCumber Barbara C. McGill Ann Melvin Marjorie Merle Jeanne Morris Betty Murray Diane A. O'Brien Elizabeth A. Palmer Nancy Palumbo Bonnie Percival Judith Poltenson Dilys Port Carlye Redderoth Shannon Roscini Ruth Sager Rosanne Sammons Betty Schmidt Mary Jayne Schneider Sheila Schwartz Helen Schwarzer Joan Shay Elaine Shende Sylvia Slater Sara Smiley Carol Stewart Eileen Thompson Inez Thompson Sara Townsend Sally Tully Chris Turner Connie Vianese Kathy Vogel Dorothy Weber Hazel Zogg
Typists	Ellen Agnew Mary Durkin Hannah Dushay Pat Druger Jean Mulligan	Bonnie Percival Carol Porter Marilyn Sechrist Carole Taylor Sandra Wells
Index	Patricia Druger	

Table of Contents

Wine

The wine suggestions in this book have been selected by Charles Pascale, noted Central New York restauranteur and wine merchant. Mr. Pascale studied viticulture and viniculture in California, France, Germany, Italy and Australia and has acted as a wine judge in a number of major wine competitions. With his brother, Neal Pascale and associate Etienne Merle, he owns Pascale Wine Bar and Restaurant in Syracuse, New York, which specializes in fine French cuisine and features one of the first wine bars in the country. Mr. Pascale is a member of the Ordre Mondial des Gourmets and the Grand Ordre International des Academiciens.

It has been my pleasure to select wines
for the entrees in this book.

Good luck and much success!

Charles A Pascale

Magic Time

Beverages

Photo on p. 9:
Old World, 1980 - Lawrence Hugo (Dr. Nikolayevich), Shirin Devrim Trainer (Lidya)

bloody mary

1 drink

- 1 tsp. lemon juice
- 1 drop Tabasco
- 2 drops Worcestershire sauce
- 1 tsp. dill sauce *or* chopped fresh dill
- 1/4 tsp. horseradish
- 2 shots Vodka
- Salt, pepper
- V-8 juice

Put all ingredients, except V-8 juice, into an 8-ounce glass. Mix thoroughly. Fill the glass with V-8 juice. Add ice, if desired.

opening night champagne punch

35 servings

- 6 oz. lemon juice
- 6 oz. pineapple juice
- 6 oz. orange juice
- 12 oz. brandy *or* rum
- 3 bottles (fifths) Sauterne
- 3 bottles (fifths) champagne

Chill all ingredients. Mix everything except champagne. Pour over block of ice in punchbowl. Add champagne just before serving.

deadly juice

Great for fall outdoor parties, after skiing, etc.

- 1 gallon apple cider (without preservatives)
- 1/2 quart cranberry juice
- 1 box of stick cinnamon
- 1 bottle (fifth) rye whiskey
- 1 Tbsp. butter
- Nutmeg and ginger to taste

In saucepan, combine all ingredients except whiskey. Simmer 2 to 3 minutes. Add whiskey; heat only 2 minutes more. Remove from heat. Serve hot.

**"What's drinking?
A mere pause from thinking!"**
Lord Byron

"I'm only a beer teetotaler, not a champagne teetotaler."
George Bernard Shaw

syracuse's irish cream

Serves: 10

- **3 eggs**
- **1 Tbsp. chocolate syrup**
- **1 tsp. vanilla**
- **10 oz. rye, Scotch *or* bourbon**
- **1 tsp. white creme de cacao *or* coconut extract**
- **1 14-oz. can sweetened condensed milk**

In a blender, mix all ingredients well. Serve as a liqueur.

kahlua

2 quarts

- **4 cups sugar**
- **2 cups water**
- **9 Tbsp. instant coffee**
- **1 quart 100 proof Vodka**
- **1 Tbsp. vanilla**

Stir sugar and water together; bring to a boil. When sugar is dissolved, stir in coffee. Add vodka and vanilla; cool. Pour into bottles and let stand 72 hours before drinking.

melon colada

Serves: 2

- **2 oz. cream of coconut**
- **4 oz. pineapple juice**
- **3 oz. Midori melon liqueur**
- **1 cup chipped ice**
- **Whipped cream**

Combine all ingredients except cream in blender. Blend well; strain. Pour into two 7 or 8-ounce stemmed glasses, about ¾ full. Top with whipped cream. Serve with a straw.

orange julius

Serves: 4

Great drink all year round.

- **1 6-oz. can frozen orange juice concentrate, thawed**
- **¼ cup sugar, *or* to taste**
- **1 cup water**
- **1 cup milk**
- **1 tsp. vanilla**

Put all ingredients into blender; fill container to top with ice. Blend until ice is finely chopped. Serve in chilled glasses.

rum slush

Serves: 20

Serve in old-fashioned glasses, garnished with a maraschino cherry. Add a short straw!

3 6-oz. cans frozen limeade concentrate, thawed
40 oz. 7-Up
Fifth of light Bacardi rum
Green food coloring (few drops)

Mix all ingredients in large bowl. Place in freezer for 24 hours, stirring every few hours. When slushy and not too watery, scoop out a drink.

summer slush

Serves: 15-18

Refreshing on a hot summer day.

1 12-oz. can frozen orange juice concentrate, thawed
1 12-oz. can frozen lemonade concentrate, thawed
2 tea bags, steeped in 2 cups boiling water and cooled
1½ cups sugar
2 cups whiskey
7 cups water
7-Up *or* gingerale
Cherries *or* lemon wedges (opt.)

Mix together orange juice, lemonade, tea, sugar, whiskey and water. Place in freezer for at least 24 hours (mixture will freeze to "slush"). To serve, fill serving glass ¾ full with slush. Add mixer of 7-Up or gingerale to fill glass. Garnish with cherry or lemon wedge, if desired.

Director's note: *Slush must be kept in freezer until serving time.*

strawberry-banana cooler

Serves: 6

Delicious and nutritious!

2 cups fresh *or* frozen whole strawberries
2 bananas, mashed
2 Tbsp. honey
2 cups cold milk
1 cup plain yogurt
Grated nutmeg

Combine all ingredients except nutmeg in blender. Blend until smooth. Serve in chilled glasses, garnished with nutmeg and whole strawberry, if desired. Serve with a straw.

hot mulled wine

Serves: 8

- **2 oz. apple brandy**
- **2 oz. apricot brandy**
- **Handful of raisins**
- **12 cloves**
- **6 cinnamon sticks**
- **Pinch of nutmeg**
- **6 oz. honey**
- **2 lemon wedges**
- **14 oz. water**
- **2 quarts Burgundy wine**

In saucepan, combine all ingredients except Burgundy. Bring to a boil; simmer until liquid is reduced by 1 cup. Strain. Add to Burgundy wine. For individual servings, add 2 ounces brandy mixture to 8 ounces wine.

whiskey sour punch

Serves: 26-30

This one will really bring the house down.

- **1 quart whiskey**
- **1 cup sugar**
- **18 oz. pure lemon juice**
- **27 oz. unsweetened orange juice**
- **20 oz. ginger ale**

Mix all ingredients except ginger ale. Pour over block or ring of ice in punchbowl. Add ginger ale just before serving.

john's hangover cure

Contributed by John D. Archbold.

1. First pull off the blankets, then remove (a) paper hat, (b) false nose, (c) dinner suit, (d) shoes. Next reach for your bottle of Eau de Pippleparrot. But Eau de Pippleparrot, miracle water though it be, is not enough to work the miracle required for today. You must mix yourself a tonic. Take:

   - **Two eggs**
   - **Powdered Ivory**
   - **Crushed rose petals**
   - **A pint of vinegar**
   - **A noggin of old brandy**
   - **Pulverized beeswax**

2. Mix and stir gently. Pour the mixture out of the window, and yourself into a cold bath. Repeat on New Year's Day.

Teasers

Hot Appetizers

Cold Appetizers

Photo on p. 15:
Tartuffe, 1978 - Nancy Reardon (Elmire), Munson Hicks (Tartuffe)

sugared bacon

Thick sliced bacon
Dark brown sugar

Cut bacon slices in half. Dredge in sugar. Bake at 200° for 2 hours. Drain on paper towels.

artichoke hearts with clam dip

Serves: 16-20

2 17-oz. cans artichoke hearts
8 oz. cream cheese, softened
3 oz. cream cheese, softened
2 6½-oz. cans minced clams
3 Tbsp. cooking sherry
Tabasco to taste

Cut artichokes in half; dry on paper towels. Mix remaining ingredients. Top each artichoke half with ½ teaspoon of clam mixture. Broil for 5 minutes. Serve immediately.

buffalo chicken wings

4 lbs. chicken wings
Salt (opt.)
Freshly ground pepper
4 cups peanut *or* vegetable oil
4 Tbsp. butter
2 to 5 Tbsp. Frank's Louisiana Red Hot Sauce
1 Tbsp. white vinegar
Blue cheese dressing
Celery sticks

Cut off and discard small tip of each chicken wing. Cut main wing bone and second wing bone at joint. Sprinkle with salt and pepper to taste. Heat oil in deep fryer or Dutch oven. Add ½ of wings and cook 10 minutes, stirring occasionally to brown well. When golden and crisp, remove and drain on paper towels. Deep fry remaining wings; drain well. Melt butter; add hot sauce to taste and vinegar. Place chicken wings on warm platter; pour butter mixture over them. Serve with blue cheese dressing and celery sticks. Dip both wings and celery into dressing, if desired.

chicken curls

1 whole chicken breast, boned
Mayonnaise
½ cup butter, melted
1 stack saltine crackers, crushed
Garlic salt

Cut chicken into 2-inch long pieces. Coat lightly with mayonnaise. Combine melted butter, crushed saltines and garlic salt. Roll chicken in mixture. Place on greased cookie sheet. Bake at 350° for approximately 40 minutes.

curried chicken tidbits

4 dozen

Tidbits

36 French Onion crackers, rolled into 1 cup fine crumbs
4 tsp. curry powder
¾ tsp. salt
¾ tsp. ground cardamom
3 Tbsp. flaked coconut
2 large whole chicken breasts, cut into bite-size pieces
2 eggs, beaten
Vegetable oil

Combine crumbs, curry powder, salt, cardamom and coconut. Roll chicken in crumb mixture, then in beaten egg and in crumbs again. Fry in 1½ inches oil, heated to 325°, about 3 minutes or until golden. Serve with Chutney Dip.

Chutney Dip

1 tsp. cornstarch
⅓ cup orange juice
½ cup finely chopped chutney

Blend cornstarch into orange juice; stir over low heat until thickened and clear. Stir in chutney. Heat, stirring occasionally, until mixture comes to a boil. Cool.

Director's note: *These can be frozen after cooking. To serve: place frozen pieces on cookie sheet. Bake at 400° for 10 minutes.*

drunken dogs

1 lb. hot dogs, cut diagonally into bite-size pieces
¾ cup bourbon *or* rye whiskey
½ cup catsup
⅓ cup brown sugar
1 Tbsp. grated onion

In saucepan, combine bourbon, catsup, brown sugar and onion. Simmer, uncovered, for 40 minutes to 1 hour until thick and rich. Meanwhile, braise hot dog pieces in frying pan until lightly browned; add to sauce. Serve in chafing dish.

"exposition" meatballs

4 lbs. sausage meat
1 1-lb. pkg. light brown sugar
2 8-oz. cans crushed pineapple
2 Tbsp. catsup
2 Tbsp. sirloin steak sauce
¼ cup apple cider vinegar
2 Tbsp. hamburger relish

Shape sausage meat into small balls; brown in frying pan. Drain on paper towels. Combine remaining ingredients; simmer for 5 to 10 minutes. Place meatballs in baking dish; pour sauce over top. Bake at 350° for 45 to 50 minutes.

Director's note: *Can be frozen; reheat at 350° until bubbly.*

stage manager's mushrooms

Serves: 10

2 lbs. large fresh mushrooms, cleaned
2 Tbsp. butter *or* margarine, melted
3 Tbsp. Worcestershire sauce
½ to ¾ cup finely chopped Italian sausage
1 cup herb-seasoned stuffing mix
⅛ tsp. celery seed
¼ tsp. celery salt

Remove stems from mushrooms, leaving caps whole. Finely chop stems; saute in butter and Worcestershire sauce; remove and set aside. Saute sausage in same pan; remove and drain. Combine mushroom stems, sausage, stuffing mix, celery seed and celery salt. Mix well. Stuff each mushroom cap with sausage mixture. Place in greased shallow pan.* Bake at 300° for 20 to 30 minutes.

Director's note: **Can be prepared to this point, refrigerated and baked just before serving.*

mushrooms casino

1 dozen

- 1 dozen medium-size fresh mushrooms
- 1 Tbsp. butter
- 1 Tbsp. Roquefort cheese
- ½ tsp. Worcestershire sauce
- 1 tsp. minced green pepper
- 1 tsp. minced onion
- Bacon

Remove stems from mushrooms. Place caps, stem side up, on cookie sheet. Melt butter with cheese; add Worcestershire sauce, green pepper and onion. Fill each cap with ½ teaspoon of mixture; top with a bit of bacon. Place under broiler on low heat for 15 minutes. Serve at once.

mushroom rolls

7-8 dozen

- 1 lb. mushrooms, finely chopped
- ½ cup butter
- 6 Tbsp. flour
- 1½ tsp. salt
- 2 cups light cream
- 2 tsp. lemon juice
- 1 tsp. onion salt
- 1½ loaves sliced bread
- Melted butter

Saute mushrooms in butter for 5 minutes; cool. Add flour and blend well. Add salt. Stir in cream; cook until thick, stirring constantly. Add lemon juice and onion salt; cool. Remove crusts from bread; roll slices flat. Spread mushroom mixture on each slice and roll up. Freeze rolls slightly to make them easier to slice. Cut each roll into thirds.* Dip into melted butter; bake at 375° for 15 to 20 minutes.

Director's note: **Can be frozen at this point. Place pieces in plastic bag; freeze until needed. Do not dip into butter until ready to bake.*

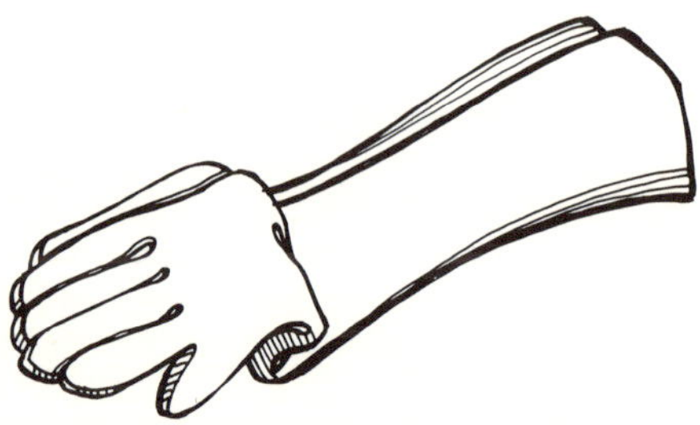

olive pecan rolls

3 dozen

- 1½ cups flour
- ¾ tsp. salt
- ½ tsp. paprika
- ½ cup butter *or* margarine
- ½ cup sour cream
- ¾ cup chopped pecans
- ¾ cup grated Cheddar cheese
- ¾ cup chopped pimiento-stuffed green olives
- 2 Tbsp. mayonnaise

Sift flour with salt and paprika. Cut in butter. Add sour cream; mix well.* Cover and chill dough ½ hour. Mix pecans, cheese, olives and mayonnaise.** Divide dough into 2 balls. Roll each into an 8 x 15-inch rectangle; cut each lengthwise into two 4-inch wide strips. Spread olive filling down the center of each strip. Bring long sides together; pinch to seal. Pinch ends together. Place on baking sheet, seam side down. Bake in preheated 400° oven for 20 minutes or until brown and crisp. Cool and slice.

Director's notes: **Dough may be mixed in food processor using plastic blade. **Filling may be mixed using steel blade.*

"slow fade" puffs

4 dozen

- ½ cup butter *or* margarine
- 1 cup boiling water
- 1 cup sifted flour
- ½ tsp. salt
- 4 eggs
- ½ cup grated Parmesan cheese

Preheat oven to 425°. In saucepan, melt butter in boiling water. Add flour and salt all at once. Cook over medium heat, stirring constantly, until mixture leaves sides of pan and is smooth and compact, about 2 minutes. Remove from heat; cool about 1 minute. Blend in eggs, 1 at a time, beating vigorously after each addition until mixture is smooth and glossy. Add cheese; mix well. Drop by teaspoonfuls onto greased baking sheet.* Bake for 18 to 20 minutes. Serve immediately.

Director's note: **Puffs may be refrigerated at this point until baking. Dough may be covered and stored in refrigerator up to 3 days.*

mini quiches

24-30

- 1 $17\frac{1}{4}$-oz. pkg. Pepperidge Farm frozen puff pastry dough
- 4 slices bacon
- ¼ cup thinly sliced onion
- ¼ cup shredded Swiss cheese
- 1 egg, beaten
- ½ cup heavy cream
- 2 Tbsp. grated Parmesan cheese
- 2 Tbsp. grated Mozzarella cheese
- ¼ tsp. nutmeg
- ¼ tsp. white pepper

Preheat oven to 375°. Grease 2 mini-muffin tins. Divide dough into fourths; roll out. With cookie cutter, cut circles big enough to cover each mini-muffin cup. Place dough in cup; shape up the sides with thumb. Cook bacon; set aside. Saute onion in bacon fat until golden. Mix crumbled bacon and onion with remaining ingredients; place about 1 tablespoonful in each muffin cup. Bake for 20 minutes.

Director's note: *Can be frozen after baking. Reheat at 375° for 5 minutes.*

spinach bites

6 dozen

- 2 10-oz. pkgs. frozen spinach, cooked and squeezed dry
- 2 cups packaged stuffing mix (small crumbs)
- 1 cup grated sharp Cheddar cheese*
- 6 eggs, well beaten
- ¾ cup butter, softened
- ½ tsp. garlic powder
- Salt and pepper to taste
- ½ tsp. thyme

Combine all ingredients; let stand until moisture is absorbed. Roll into 1-inch balls; place on cookie sheet and freeze. While still frozen, bake at 400° for 15 to 20 minutes. Flip spinach bites once while baking, if desired.

Director's notes: **One-half cup each of Romano and Parmesan cheese can be substituted for Cheddar cheese. Extra spinach bites can be stored in freezer until needed.*

mini reubens

2 dozen

- 24 slices party-size rye bread, toasted lightly
- ½ cup Thousand Island dressing
- 1 16-oz. can sauerkraut, drained and chopped
- 12 thin slices corned beef, halved
- 12 thin slices Swiss cheese, halved

On each toast slice, spread dressing, sauerkraut, corned beef and cheese. Place on cookie sheet and broil until cheese melts.

norwegian roquefort pastry

16 pieces

Crust

- ½ cup butter *or* margarine
- 2 cups flour
- ½ tsp. salt
- 1 egg yolk
- 2 Tbsp. heavy cream (more if needed to hold ingredients together)

Blend mixture into flour and salt. Mix egg yolk and cream; add to flour mixture. Place ⅔ of mixture on lightly floured board; roll to ⅛-inch thickness. Press onto bottom of 9-inch square pan and 1 inch up sides. Roll remainder of dough to rectangle. With pastry wheel or knife, cut into ½-inch strips. Pour Filling into lined pan. Crisscross lengths of crust over top, lattice-fashion. Brush with slightly beaten egg white; dust with paprika. Bake in preheated 350° oven for 45 minutes or until lightly browned. Cut into 16 squares; serve warm (not hot).

Filling

- 3 eggs
- ½ cup plus 2 Tbsp. heavy cream
- 2 Tbsp. brandy *or* whiskey
- 2 Tbsp. sherry
- 4 to 6 oz. Roquefort cheese
- 1 egg white, slightly beaten
- Paprika

In top of double boiler, beat eggs slightly; add cream. Cook over simmering water, stirring constantly, until thickened and smooth. Cool. Add brandy, sherry and finely crumbled Roquefort.

"A man hath no better thing under the sun, than to eat, and to drink, and to be merry."
Ecclesiastes 8:15

o'hara's appetizer

Pate Sucree

- **1¾ cups flour**
- **1 tsp. salt**
- **2 Tbsp. sugar**
- **10 Tbsp. butter *or* margarine**
- **2 Tbsp. shortening**
- **⅓ cup cold water**

Combine flour, salt and sugar; cut in butter and shortening until crumbly. Add water; form a firm ball. Knead dough briefly to uniformly mix butter. Wrap in plastic wrap and refrigerate at least 1 hour before rolling.* Roll out chilled dough to 3/16-inch thickness. Trim to 12-inch square; transfer to baking sheet. Spread ½ of dough with Cheese-Nut Filling, leaving a 1-inch margin around edge. Moisten edges lightly with cold water. Turn top of dough over filling; crimp edges to seal. Lightly brush turnover with egg glaze. Cut parallel slashes completely through top layer of dough, ¾ inch apart. Bake in preheated 350° oven for 30 minutes or until golden brown. Serve warm.

Cheese-Nut Filling

- **1¼ cups grated Swiss cheese**
- **½ cup chopped walnuts**
- **1 egg**
- **½ tsp. Worcestershire sauce**
- **⅛ tsp. garlic powder**
- **⅛ tsp. onion powder**
- **¼ tsp. each oregano, thyme and basil**
- **⅛ tsp. dry mustard**
- **1 egg**
- **1 tsp. cold water**

Combine cheese, nuts and egg. Add seasonings to taste. In separate bowl, beat egg with water to form egg glaze.

Director's note: **Can be frozen at this point.*

spanish shrimp (gambas al ajillo)

- **1½ lbs. medium-size shrimp, raw**
- **¾ cup olive oil**
- **2 or 3 whole cloves garlic**
- **1 Tbsp. chopped parsley**
- **½ tsp. salt**

Shell and devein shrimp, leaving tails intact. In a bowl, combine olive oil, garlic, parsley and salt. Add shrimp and let stand for at least 1 hour. Transfer shrimp and oil mixture to a shallow 5-cup baking dish. Bake at 450° for 5 to 7 minutes, or until shrimp is pink. Discard garlic and serve shrimp hot, using picks for spearing.

spanikopita

40 puffs

Absolutely delicious and simple to do once you are used to handling Phyllo dough.

½ lb. Phyllo dough
½ lb. fresh Ricotta cheese
3 eggs
Dash nutmeg
1 cup butter, melted

Cut Phyllo dough into 6 x 9-inch strips. Cover with tea towel to prevent drying. Combine cheese and eggs in bowl; whip until smooth and creamy. Add nutmeg. Brush 1 strip of Phyllo with butter.* Place small teaspoonful of cheese filling on left end of dough. Fold Phyllo up ⅓ from long side closest to you. Brush dry surface with butter. Fold down top side of Phyllo, resulting in about a 2-inch strip. Brush top surface with butter. Fold lower left corner up so short left end is parallel to top. (The dough will be taking a triangular shape.) Continue folding triangle over and over to the end of Phyllo strip. Place resulting triangle end side down on greased cookie sheet. Repeat for each strip. Brush tops with melted butter. Bake in preheated 350° oven for 15 to 20 minutes or until light golden brown. Serve immediately.

*

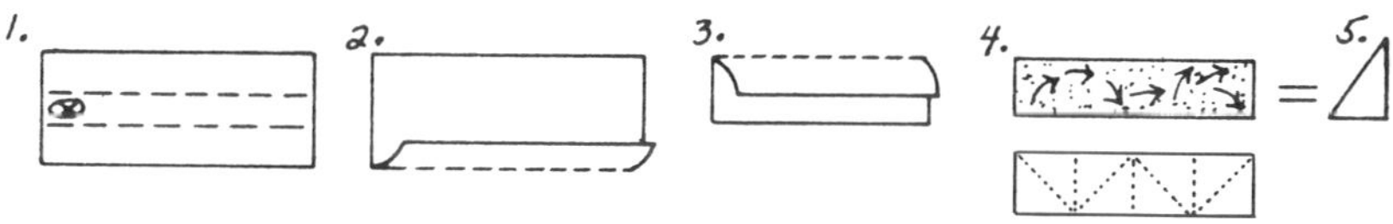

Spinach Filling

½ cup vegetable oil
1 lb. frozen chopped spinach, thawed
1 tsp. freeze dried dill weed *or* 1 Tbsp. fresh dill
1 clove garlic (opt.)
Small tomato, chopped
½ lb. Feta cheese, crumbled
6 oz. cream cheese, softened
1 tsp. garlic salt
Freshly ground pepper

In oil, saute spinach, dill, garlic and tomato until tender. Add cheeses, garlic salt and pepper. Mix thoroughly until ingredients are hot. Cool slightly and substitute for cheese filling in Phyllo dough triangles, proceeding as above.

Director's note: *Both kinds can be frozen unbaked.*

sauerkraut balls

4-5 dozen

- **½ cup chopped onion**
- **3 Tbsp. butter *or* margarine, melted**
- **1 cup diced cooked corned beef**
- **1 cup diced cooked ham**
- **½ clove garlic, crushed**
- **6 Tbsp. flour**
- **1 egg, beaten**
- **1½ tsp. dry mustard**
- **⅛ tsp. seasoned salt**
- **2 tsp. chopped fresh parsley**
- **¼ tsp. Worcestershire sauce**
- **½ cup beef bouillon**
- **2 cups well drained sauerkraut, finely chopped**
- **2 cups milk**
- **2 to 2½ cups flour**
- **2 cups fine dry bread crumbs**

Saute onion in butter until soft. Stir in corned beef, ham and garlic. Mix well. Cook 8 to 10 minutes, stirring occasionally. Blend in the 6 tablespoons flour and egg. Stir in dry mustard, seasoned salt, parsley, Worcestershire sauce, bouillon and sauerkraut. Cook slowly, stirring occasionally, until mixture thickens. Chill. Shape into 1-inch balls. Combine milk and flour. Dip balls into mixture; roll in bread crumbs. Fry in deep fat for 2 to 3 minutes, until deep golden brown. Place on paper towels to absorb grease. Serve warm.

Director's notes: *These can be refrigerated after frying and reheated in oven before serving. They can be frozen before frying. Remove from freezer 1 hour before frying and partly thaw at room temperature. Add 1 minute to frying time.*

water chestnuts and bacon

4 dozen

- **2 6-oz. cans whole water chestnuts**
- **1 lb. bacon, cut in half**
- **1 cup catsup**
- **1 4½-oz. jar strained baby food, apricots *or* peaches**
- **4 Tbsp. brown sugar**
- **1 Tbsp. Worcestershire sauce**

Wrap chestnuts in bacon halves; secure with toothpicks. Mix remaining ingredients. Dip bacon rolls into sauce; bake at 350° for 30 minutes.* Broil 4 inches from heat for a few minutes until bacon is cooked.

Director's note: **Can be done to this point ahead of time and refrigerated.*

sausage balls

Serves: 8-12

1 lb. pan sausage
8 oz. Cheddar cheese, shredded
1 onion, chopped
2 cups Bisquick

Mix all ingredients together with hands. Form into bite-size balls. Bake at 375° for 20 minutes. Can be frozen after baking.

crispy potato skins

Serves: 2

2 medium-size baking potatoes
2 Tbsp. butter, melted
½ cup grated Cheddar *or* **Parmesan cheese**
¼ cup bacon, crumbled

Scrub potatoes. Pierce each one with fork to prevent bursting while baking. Bake at 375° for 1 hour, or until done. Remove from oven. While cooling, cover each potato with damp paper towel to prevent skin from drying out. Cut potatoes in half lengthwise. Scoop out insides, leaving ¼-inch potato next to skin. Brush with melted butter. Sprinkle inside of each potato half with ¼ of cheese. Sprinkle bacon evenly over top. Bake at 375° for 30 minutes or until brown and crispy.

Pauline, *The Seagull*

bacon swiss rounds

3 dozen

8 oz. Swiss cheese, shredded
½ cup crumbled crisp bacon
½ cup chopped ripe olives
¼ cup chopped scallions
2 tsp. Worcestershire sauce
½ tsp. salt
1 cup mayonnaise

Mix ingredients a day before serving. Spread on party rye. Bake at 350° for 10 minutes.

cheese and bacon tempters

2 dozen

1 cup mayonnaise
½ cup grated Cheddar cheese
2 tsp. drained horseradish
1 Tbsp. sherry
Crumbled crisp bacon, *or*
½ cup Bacos

Mix all ingredients together. Spread on crackers. Broil until golden and bubbly. Watch carefully so they don't burn.

crab and cheese canapes

12 dozen

2 6-oz. pkgs. frozen crab meat
2 5-oz. jars Old English cheese spread
½ cup butter *or* **margarine, softened**
1 Tbsp. minced onion
½ tsp. garlic salt
½ tsp. celery salt
12 English muffins, split in half

Rinse and drain crabmeat. Combine with cheese, butter, onion, garlic and celery salts. Spread on muffins. Place muffins on cookie sheet and freeze. Cut each into 6 pieces. Place pieces in plastic bag in freezer. When ready to serve, place frozen pieces on cookie sheet and broil until bubbly.

"The cook was a good cook, as cooks go; and as cooks go she went."
Saki (Hector Hugh Munro)

croghan hot appetizer

Croghan Bologna is a smoked prepared meat whose closest cousins are salamis and sausages. It was brought to northern New York State in the late 1800's by a Swiss immigrant and is still being enjoyed by everyone who tastes it.

Place thin slice of Croghan Bologna on a cracker; top with thinly sliced Cheddar cheese. Broil 2 inches from heat until cheese is melted. Serve warm.

onion party puffs

40 puffs

- **1 7½-oz. pkg. refrigerator biscuits**
- **⅓ cup Onion Butter***

Preheat oven to 400°. Cut each biscuit into quarters. Place on ungreased cookie sheet; dot with Onion Butter. Bake 8 minutes or until brown.

Onion Butter*

- **1 env. onion soup mix**
- **1 cup butter**

Blend soup mix and butter thoroughly.

Director's note: *Recipe makes 1 cup Onion Butter. It keeps well in refrigerator.*

salami squares

4 dozen

- **12 slices white bread**
- **½ lb. ground salami**
- **1 to 2 Tbsp. mayonnaise**
- **8 oz. cream cheese, softened**
- **½ tsp. baking powder**
- **1 egg yolk**
- **2 Tbsp. grated onion**
- **Paprika**

Remove crusts from bread. Grind salami and mix with enough mayonnaise to make a spreading consistency. Spread thin layer on each slice of bread. Mix together cream cheese, baking powder, egg yolk and grated onion. Spread a thin layer of this mixture on top of salami layer. Cut bread slices into quarters; place on cookie sheet; sprinkle with paprika. Place under broiler until slightly brown and cheese mixture ***just begins*** to melt, about 1 minute.

snails in roquefort cream sauce

Serves: 4-6

1 15½ oz. can snails, drained
4 Tbsp. butter
3 Tbsp. white wine
2 scallions, chopped
½ pt. heavy cream
4 oz. or more crumbled Roquefort cheese
Freshly ground black pepper
1 medium tomato, peeled, seeded and chopped
Fresh parsley, chopped (opt.)

Saute drained snails in melted butter and wine for 3 minutes and remove. Add scallions; stirfry 1 minute. Add cream and bring to a slow simmer. Add cheese and pepper; heat through. Taste and adjust cheese and pepper, if desired. Add snails; heat through. Add tomato and parsley just before serving. Serve over patty shells.

Director's note: *Also delicious served over noodles. Toss with Parmesan cheese. Serves 2.*

An Officer, *Tartuffe*

actors' appetizer

9 dozen

- **2 6-oz. jars marinated artichoke hearts**
- **1 clove garlic, minced**
- **¼ cup chopped onion**
- **4 eggs, well beaten**
- **¼ cup bread crumbs**
- **¼ tsp. salt**
- **⅛ tsp. oregano**
- **8 oz. Cheddar cheese, grated**
- **2 Tbsp. minced parsley**

Drain marinade from artichokes into frying pan. Chop hearts; set aside. Add garlic and onion to pan; saute until limp. Combine eggs, bread crumbs, salt, oregano, cheese and parsley. Add chopped artichoke hearts and sauteed mixture. Pour into well greased 9 x 13-inch baking dish. Bake at 325° for 30 minutes or until set. Cool and cut into 1-inch squares.

appetizer pie

Serves: 8-12

- **8 oz. cream cheese, softened**
- **2 Tbsp. milk**
- **1 4-oz. pkg. dried beef, finely chopped**
- **2 Tbsp. chopped onion**
- **2 Tbsp. finely chopped green pepper**
- **½ tsp. pepper**
- **½ cup sour cream**
- **¼ cup chopped walnuts**

Blend cream cheese with milk. Mix with other ingredients except walnuts. Pat into 9-inch quiche pan or pie plate. Top with walnuts.* Bake at 350° for 15 minutes. Serve with Triscuits or other crackers.

Director's note: **Can be prepared to this point and refrigerated.*

cheese onion appetizer

- **1 cup mayonnaise**
- **¼ cup finely chopped onion**
- **1¼ cups shredded Cheddar cheese**

Mix together and spoon into baking dish. Bake at 400° for 10 to 15 minutes or until cheese is melted. Serve with raw vegetables or crackers.

hot artichoke spread

Serves: 10

- 1 14-oz. can plain artichokes, not marinated
- 1 cup mayonnaise
- 1 cup grated Parmesan cheese
- 1 tsp. grated onion
- 1 Tbsp. sherry
- Dash garlic powder
- Paprika

Drain and chop artichokes; mix with other ingredients. Place in shallow baking dish; sprinkle with paprika.* Bake at 350° for 15 to 20 minutes until bubbly, ***do not overbake.*** Serve with crackers.

Director's notes: **Can be prepared to this point and refrigerated. Variation: for onion, sherry and garlic powder, substitute dash of Worcestershire sauce and dash of lemon juice.*

clam and cheese spread casino

Serves: 15-30

- 4 6½-oz. cans minced clams (more if desired)
- 4 tsp. lemon juice
- 2 medium onions, quartered
- 2 small green peppers, quartered
- ½ cup chopped parsley
- Clam juice
- 1 cup butter
- 2 Tbsp. oregano
- 2 tsp. hot pepper sauce
- ½ tsp. salt
- Pepper to taste
- 1½ cups canned bread crumbs
- American cheese slices
- Parmesan cheese, paprika

Simmer the clams in their juice for 15 minutes. Drain; reserving juice. Add lemon juice to clams. In a blender, blend onions, green peppers, parsley and enough clam juice to allow mixture to spread evenly. Add to clams with butter and oregano. Heat until butter melts; add hot pepper sauce, salt, pepper and bread crumbs. Mix until the consistency of oatmeal, adding more clam juice if necessary. Do not make it too watery. Turn into two 8-inch pie plates.* Spread with slices of American cheese. Sprinkle with Parmesan cheese and paprika. Bake at 350° for 15 to 20 minutes or until golden brown and bubbly. Serve immediately with Triscuits.

Director's note: **At this point, can be refrigerated or frozen. Before baking, bring to room temperature. Proceed with recipe.*

fantan

2½ cups

Delicious hot or cold, especially hot. Raw carrots make good "dippers".

½ cup chopped pecans
2 Tbsp. butter, melted
½ tsp. salt
8 oz. cream cheese, softened
2 Tbsp. milk
¼ tsp. pepper
½ tsp. garlic powder
¼ cup minced onion
⅛ cup minced green pepper
2½ oz. dried beef, chopped
½ cup sour cream

Mix pecans with butter and salt. Bake at 350° for 15 minutes; set aside. Mix together all other ingredients except sour cream. Fold in sour cream; pour into 9-inch square baking dish. Sprinkle with nut mixture; bake at 350° for 20 minutes.

creamy mushrooms

This could be served in pastry cups, as well.

8 oz. mushrooms, sliced
¼ cup butter *or* **margarine**
2 Tbsp. flour
1 cup sour cream
½ to 1 env. onion soup mix
8 oz. Cheddar cheese, grated

Saute mushrooms in butter. Stir in flour; cook 1 minute. Add sour cream and onion soup; blend. Place in shallow 9-inch square baking dish. Cover with cheese. Bake at 400° for 10 minutes or until bubbly. Serve with Melba Toast Rounds.

"When men drink, then they are rich and successful and win lawsuits and are happy and help their friends.
Quickly, bring me a beaker of wine, so that I may wet my mind and say something clever."
Aristophanes

mushrooms with sour cream

Serves: 10

- **1 lb. fresh mushrooms, sliced**
- **1 clove garlic, minced**
- **6 Tbsp. butter**
- **2 Tbsp. chopped fresh parsley *or* 1 tsp. parsley flakes**
- **¼ tsp. salt**
- **¼ tsp. pepper**
- **1 cup sour cream**
- **1 Tbsp. flour**

Saute mushrooms and garlic in butter; stir in parsley, salt and pepper. Stir frequently until mushrooms are cooked. Blend sour cream and flour. Stir into mushrooms. Blend until heated through. Place in chafing dish and serve with Melba toast rounds or plain crackers.

Director's note: *If made in advance, heat* ***very slowly*** *when rewarming.*

mexican dip

Serves: 8-12

This is the first thing to go at a party.

- **1 lb. ground beef**
- **½ cup chopped onion**
- **½ cup hot catsup**
- **1 tsp. chili powder**
- **1 tsp. salt**
- **1 1-lb. can kidney beans, partly drained**

Brown ground beef and onions in a frying pan. In blender, puree catsup, chili powder, salt and kidney beans. Add pureed mixture to browned meat and onion; simmer 15 minutes. Spoon into chafing dish and arrange Garnishes in circular fashion on top. Serve with Fritos.

Garnishes

- **1 cup grated Cheddar cheese**
- **1½ cups chopped green olives**
- **½ cup chopped onion**

Director's note: *Double the meat mixture and pureed mixture for a crowd. Garnish remains the same.*

cheese crisps

6 dozen

- ½ cup butter, softened
- ½ cup margarine, softened
- 8 oz. sharp Cheddar cheese, grated
- ½ tsp. cayenne pepper
- 2 cups flour
- 1 tsp. salt
- 2 cups Rice Krispies

Preheat oven to 350°. Cream butter, margarine, cheese and pepper. Add flour, salt and Rice Krispies. Stir by hand like mixing meatloaf. Roll into large, marble-size balls. Place on an ungreased cookie sheet and with a fork that has been dipped into ice water, flatten each ball in criss-cross pattern. Bake for 15 to 20 minutes or until crisp and golden brown. Serve warm or cold.

ha'pennies

3 dozen

- 1 cup flour
- ½ cup butter *or* margarine, softened
- ½ tsp. salt
- ½ env. onion soup mix
- 8 oz. sharp Cheddar cheese, grated

Blend together flour and butter. Add remaining ingredients; mix thoroughly. Form into a ball; wrap in foil and refrigerate. Shape dough into large marble-size balls; place on ungreased cookie sheet. Flatten a little. Bake in preheated 350° oven for 8 to 10 minutes or until crisp. Store in airtight container.

puffballs

3 dozen

- 8 oz. cream cheese, softened
- 1 cup diced cooked chicken
- 1 cup blanched slivered almonds
- 2 Tbsp. mayonnaise
- 1 Tbsp. curry powder
- 1 Tbsp. chopped chutney
- ½ tsp. seasoned salt
- Grated coconut

Combine all ingredients thoroughly except coconut. Chill. Form into small balls; roll in grated coconut. Chill again, about 2 hours. Serve on toothpicks.

crab and ham roll-ups

12 dozen

- **1 7½-oz. can crabmeat, rinsed and drained**
- **1 Tbsp. lemon juice**
- **8 oz. cream cheese, softened**
- **¼ cup finely chopped celery**
- **2 Tbsp. chopped parsley**
- **¼ cup diced toasted almonds**
- **Salt and pepper, to taste**
- **12 slices lean boiled ham**

Drain and chop crabmeat. Sprinkle with lemon juice. Blend softened cream cheese with crabmeat, celery, parsley and almonds. Spread on slices of ham and roll up, securing with toothpicks if necessary. Chill well. Cut into ½-inch pieces. Large ham slices yield approximately 12 pieces per roll-up.

boursin stuffed mushrooms

- **16 medium-size mushrooms**
- **Fresh lemon juice**
- **1 5-oz. pkg. Herb and Garlic Cheese, softened**
- **1 tsp. chopped parsley**

Wash mushrooms; pat dry. Remove stems and finely chop. Sprinkle mushroom caps with lemon juice. Beat cheese in small bowl until fluffy; mix in chopped stems. Fill caps with mixture. Garnish with parsley.

gravlax

Serves: 8-10

Serve as an appetizer or main dish, garnished with lemon wedges and accompanied with Mustard Sauce.

3 to 3½ lbs. fresh salmon, cut in half lengthwise and with bones removed
1 large bunch fresh dill weed, chopped
¼ cup salt
¼ cup sugar
2 Tbsp. white peppercorns, crushed
Lemon wedges

Place ½ of the fish, skin side down, in deep dish. Sprinkle with dill. Combine salt, sugar and pepper; sprinkle evenly over dill. Top with other half of fish, skin side up. Cover fish with foil and on it set a heavy platter slightly larger than the fish. Weight the platter. (Several cans of food make convenient weights.) Refrigerate 48 hours or up to 3 days. Turn fish every 12 hours and baste with the marinade that accumulates, basting between the sections as well. Replace platter and weights each time.

When gravlax is finished, remove from marinade. Scrape away dill and seasonings and pat dry with paper towels. Place skin side down on carving board. Slice salmon thinly on the diagonal, detaching each slice from the skin.

Mustard Sauce

4 Tbsp. dark, highly seasoned prepared mustard
1 tsp. dry mustard
3 Tbsp. sugar
2 Tbsp. white vinegar
⅓ cup vegetable oil
3 Tbsp. chopped fresh dill weed

Mix the 2 mustards, sugar and vinegar to a paste. Slowly beat in the oil until it forms a thick mayonnaise-like emulsion. Stir in chopped dill.

Director's note: *Leftovers make wonderful sandwiches or are great for breakfast with scrambled eggs.*

Suggested wine: California Fume Blanc

"Cookery is become an art, a noble science; cooks are gentlemen."
Robert Burton

sugared pecans

3 cups

- 2 cups pecan halves
- 2 egg whites
- ½ cup sugar
- 2 tsp. cinnamon
- 1 tsp. freshly grated nutmeg
- ¼ tsp. ginger

Preheat oven to 350°. Combine pecan halves with egg whites; stir mixture until nuts are well coated. Combine sugar, cinnamon, nutmeg and ginger. Transfer pecans to the sugar mixture with a slotted spoon; toss to coat thoroughly. Arrange pecans ½ inch apart on lightly oiled cookie sheet. Bake for 8 minutes, or until brown and crisp. Let pecans cool on cookie sheet for ***1 minute.*** Using a spatula, transfer them to a rack to cool completely.

"tormentor" pecans

Who can stop at one?

- 2 Tbsp. butter
- ½ tsp. seasoned salt
- 2 dashes Tabasco
- 1 lb. pecan halves
- 3 Tbsp. Worcestershire sauce

Combine butter, salt and Tabasco in 8 x 12-inch baking dish; place in 300° oven. When butter is melted, add pecans and stir to coat. Bake for 20 minutes, stirring now and then. Sprinkle with Worcestershire sauce and bake another 10 minutes.

Director's note: *These may be frozen. When ready to use, heat and serve.*

blue cheese ball

3 balls

- 2 8-oz. pkgs. cream cheese
- 2 2 to 3-oz. wedges blue cheese
- 2 3-oz. pkgs. chive cheese
- Dash Worcestershire sauce
- 1 4-oz. Cheddar cheese spread
- ½ cup chopped walnuts
- ½ cup chopped pecans

Have all cheeses at room temperature. Combine all ingredients except nuts; mix thoroughly. Form into 3 balls; roll each in chopped nuts. Wrap well to freeze.

beef-olive ball

Great and improves with age.

8 oz. cream cheese, softened
2 Tbsp. butter *or* margarine
1 tsp. instant minced onion
1 3-oz. pkg. smoked beef, finely snipped
1 Tbsp. dry sherry
¼ cup chopped green olives with pimiento
Crushed nuts *or* pretzel crumbs

Beat cream cheese and butter together. Add onion, snipped beef, sherry and olives; blend thoroughly. Shape into ball. Roll in crushed nuts or pretzel crumbs. Good with crackers and celery sticks.

boursin ball

8 oz. cream cheese, softened
½ tsp. garlic salt
1 tsp. caraway seed
1 tsp. basil
1 tsp. dill weed
1 tsp. chopped chives
Lemon pepper

Mix everything but lemon pepper. Shape into a ball. Roll in lemon pepper. Serve with plain crackers.

salmon ball

1 16-oz. can salmon, drained and flaked
8 oz. cream cheese, softened
1 Tbsp. fresh lemon juice
2 tsp. chopped onion
4 tsp. chopped fresh parsley
1 tsp. horseradish
½ cup chopped pecans

Thoroughly combine all ingredients except pecans. Form into a ball; roll in nuts. Chill 2 to 3 hours. Serve with crackers.

boursin — homestyle

2 cups

Great with Triscuits or apple slices.

16 oz. cream cheese, softened
1 clove garlic, minced *or* **¼ tsp. garlic salt**
¼ cup mayonnaise
2 tsp. Dijon-style mustard
2 Tbsp. minced fresh chives *or* **2 tsp. dried chives**
2 Tbsp. minced fresh dill weed *or* **2 tsp. dried dill weed**

Beat cream cheese until smooth. Add other ingredients; beat well. Spoon into any container; cover and refrigerate. Bring to room temperature before serving.

cream cheese pate with chutney

8 oz. cream cheese, softened
1 tsp. curry powder
¼ tsp. onion juice
¼ tsp. Worcestershire sauce
1 9-oz. jar chutney

Combine cheese, curry powder, onion juice and Worcestershire sauce; mix well. Shape into a flat 6-inch circle on flat serving dish. Drain chutney, if juicy. Cut up any large pieces and spread chutney on cheese. Serve with bland or unsalted crackers.

cheese with jezebel sauce

1 18-oz. jar apple jelly
1 12-oz. jar pineapple preserves
1 5-oz. jar horseradish
1 1½-oz. can dry mustard
8 oz. cream cheese

Combine apple jelly, pineapple preserves, horseradish and dry mustard. Blend thoroughly; store in refrigerator indefinitely. To serve, place bar of cream cheese in shallow serving dish; spread sauce over top. Serve with crackers.

"Appetite comes with eating.....but the thirst goes away with drinking."
Francois Rabelais

hot green pepper jelly

1½ cups sliced green bell pepper
1½ cups cider vinegar
6½ cups sugar
1 bottle Certo
¼ cup cayenne pepper
Few drops green food coloring

Finely grind green pepper in blender or grinder. Mix all ingredients; boil for 5 minutes. Add food coloring. Cool slightly; pour into hot jelly jars. Seal with ⅛ inch paraffin. After paraffin hardens, add another ⅛ inch. To serve, spread crackers with a thin layer of cream cheese and a thin layer of jelly.

Director's note: *This is "hot". The cayenne pepper may be reduced as desired.*

cocktail mystery

Contributed by Dee Victor who played in PLOUGH AND THE STARS (1977) and TARTUFFE (1978).

1 12-oz. jar Raffetto Chut-Nut chutney
1 lb. Cheddar cheese, grated
Unsalted butter, (if desired)

Mince the chutney very finely, reserving the syrup. Mix with grated cheese, softening to a spreadable consistency with reserved syrup and a little butter, if desired. Serve garnished with parsley or cucumber slices. Spread on crackers.

Director's note: *If refrigerated, remove in time to soften to proper consistency.*

Dee Victor

fancy chicken log

Serves: 12

16 oz. cream cheese, softened
1 Tbsp. bottled steak sauce
½ tsp. curry powder
1½ cups minced cooked chicken
⅓ cup minced celery
¼ cup chopped parsley
½ cup chopped almonds *or* walnuts

Beat together cream cheese, steak sauce and curry powder. Blend in chicken, celery and 2 tablespoons of the parsley. Shape into log or ball. On plastic wrap, mix almonds and remaining parsley. Wrap log in plastic wrap and refrigerate overnight.

chicken liver pate

2½ cups

5 oz. lean bacon
8 oz. chicken livers
Salt and pepper to taste
¼ cup port wine
½ cup butter
3 egg whites

Chop bacon in food processor until smooth paste. Add remaining ingredients. Process until mixture is smooth and creamy. Turn into a terrine or other crock-like oven-proof dish. Place terrine in baking pan; pour water into pan until it comes half-way up the sides of terrine. Bake at 325° about 40 minutes. Cool; refrigerate.

"leading lady" pate

2½ cups

Elegant, but easy.

1 lb. chicken livers
1 cup butter
4 shallots, cut-up
¼ cup brandy
Freshly ground black pepper
Salt
Nutmeg

Saute chicken livers in butter; do not overcook. Let cool. Put into blender with shallots, brandy, lots of good freshly ground black pepper, a little salt and about 8 to 10 grinds of nutmeg. Blend until shallots are ground fine. Pour into crock and ***let sit overnight.***

"rehearsal" pate

2 cups

1 lb. chicken livers
2 hard-boiled eggs, chopped
1 cup chopped onion
2 Tbsp. butter *or* **margarine**
Salt and pepper to taste
1 jigger bourbon

Drop livers into lightly salted and peppered boiling water; simmer until just tender. Drain, cool and finely chop. Add eggs to liver. Saute onion in butter until golden. Add to liver mixture; grind to a fine paste. Season with salt, pepper and bourbon. Serve with plain crackers or rye rounds.

Director's note: *This will keep in refrigerator, covered, for 2 weeks.*

caviar pie

For those special occasions!

- 11 oz. cream cheese, softened
- 2 Tbsp. mayonnaise*
- 2 Tbsp. sour cream*
- ½ cup minced onion
- 4 Tbsp. lemon juice
- 1 4-oz. jar caviar
- 2 hard-boiled eggs, riced
- Parsley, finely chopped
- Melba toast rounds

Mix cream cheese, mayonnaise, sour cream, onion and lemon juice until mixture is of thick spreading consistency. Shape into round, mounded pie shape on serving plate. Top with caviar, riced eggs and parsley. Chill thoroughly. Serve with Melba toast rounds.

Director's note: **If mixture is too thick, add a little more mayonnaise or sour cream.*

smoked oyster roll

- 16 oz. cream cheese, softened
- 1 to 2 Tbsp. mayonnaise*
- ⅛ tsp. garlic powder
- ¼ cup finely chopped onion
- 1 to 2 tsp. Worcestershire sauce*
- Dash salt and pepper
- 2 tins smoked oysters, drained and chopped (DO NOT chop in blender or food processor - easier if cold)

Blend all ingredients except oysters. Spread in thin layer on aluminum foil. Spread oysters on top. Refrigerate 1 hour, then roll like jelly roll. Serve with crackers or party breads.

Director's note: **Do not make cheese mixture too thin or it will not roll.*

hummus

- **1 16-oz. can garbanzo beans, drained (chick peas)**
- **2 cloves garlic, minced**
- **¼ cup lemon juice**
- **1 tsp. salt**
- **¼ cup vegetable oil**
- **1 Tbsp. fresh parsley**
- **2 Tbsp. Tahini* (sesame paste)**
- **1 Tbsp. soy sauce**

Blend all ingredients in blender or food processor until smooth. Serve as a spread with pita bread or crackers.

Director's note: **Tahini can be purchased in a natural food store or gourmet section of grocery store.*

artichoke dip

Serves: 10

- **1 17-oz. can artichoke hearts, drained**
- **1 cup mayonnaise**
- **1 env. Italian salad dressing mix**

Blend all ingredients in food processor or blender. Refrigerate. Good with raw vegetables.

diablo dip

Serves: 12-15

A delicious and different party spread!

- **1 can of bean *or* avocado dip**
- **1 cup sour cream**
- **2 Tbsp. taco seasoning dip**
- **½ lb. Monterey Jack, Swiss *or* Mozzarella cheese, grated**
- **2 *or* 3 tomatoes, finely chopped**
- **½ lb. medium sharp Cheddar cheese, grated**
- **4 scallions, diced**
- **1 can ripe olives, diced**

Make a round mound, layering ingredients in order listed, starting with bean dip and ending with olives. Serve with tortilla chips and Triscuits. Scoop from bottom to top to get a taste of all layers.

dried beef dip in black bread

- 1 lb. round loaf dark rye bread
- 2 loaves rye *or* Italian bread
- 1 7 to 8-oz. jar dried beef*, cut into slivers
- 2 cups real mayonnaise
- 2 cups sour cream
- 1 to 2 tsp. minced onion
- 2 tsp. Beau Monde spice
- Pickle relish (opt.)

Scoop out the center of the round loaf of bread. Cut the bread from the hollow, plus the 2 rye or Italian loaves of bread into "dipper"-size pieces. Combine remaining ingredients; refrigerate. Serve in the hollowed loaf of bread with "dippers" around it.

Director's note: **Corned beef can be substituted for dried beef.*

liptauer cheese

- 2 8-oz. pkgs. cream cheese
- 1 3-oz. pkg. cream cheese
- 6 oz. sharp Cheddar cheese
- 5 Tbsp. unsalted butter, softened
- 1½ to 2 tsp. Dijon mustard
- 2 Tbsp. chopped onion
- ½ tsp. white pepper
- Sweet Hungarian paprika
- Round loaf Pumpernickel bread, 14 to 16-inch diameter

Bring cheeses and butter to room temperature. Blend all ingredients until smooth. Scoop out center of loaf. Cut center section into small squares. Place cheese mixture in hollowed loaf and arrange bread squares around it. Spread cheese and Garnishes as desired on bread squares.

Garnishes

- 2 2-oz. cans anchovy fillets, chopped
- ⅔ cup chopped scallions
- ⅔ cup diced radishes
- ⅔ cup diced cucumber
- ½ cup drained capers

cheddar beer dip

- 1 10-oz. pkg. extra-sharp Cheddar cheese, shredded
- ½ cup beer
- 1 tsp. caraway seeds
- ¼ tsp. salt
- ¼ cup mayonnaise
- 1 tsp. Worcestershire sauce
- ¼ tsp. ground red pepper

In blender or food processor with knife blade, blend all ingredients until smooth. Cover and refrigerate. Serve with unsalted crackers or vegetables.

Director's note: *Prepare at least 30 minutes before using to blend flavors, even the day before.*

double shrimp dip

- 1 10¾-oz. can cream of shrimp soup
- 3 oz. cream cheese, softened
- 1 env. unflavored gelatin
- ¼ cup chopped celery
- ¼ cup chopped onion
- 1 cup mayonnaise
- 1 4 to 5-oz. can shrimp, rinsed and drained

Blend soup and cream cheese. Add gelatin; heat and stir until dissolved. Add celery, onion, mayonnaise and shrimp. Mix well. Place in serving dish or lightly oiled 4-cup mold. Chill until set. Unmold, if desired.

triple cheese dip

2 cups

- 8 oz. whipped cream cheese
- ¼ cup mayonnaise
- ¼ tsp. salt
- ⅛ tsp. ground pepper
- 3 to 4 drops Tabasco
- 1 Tbsp. milk
- ¼ cup grated Cheddar cheese
- 2 Tbsp. grated Parmesan cheese
- 2 Tbsp. diced stuffed olives

Mix ingredients thoroughly. Refrigerate for at least ½ hour.

Stock Characters

Soups

Photo on p. 47:
We Won't Pay, We Won't Pay, 1982 - Valery Daemke (Margherita), Judy Scarpone (Antonia)

blender avocado cream soup

Serves: 4-6

- **1 large avocado**
- **1 tsp. lemon juice**
- **1 tsp. salt**
- **4 tsp. chopped chives***
- **Dash pepper**
- **8 oz. plain yogurt**
- **1½ cups half-and-half**
- **3 tsp. lemon juice**

At least 2 hours before serving, peel and quarter avocado. Cube 1 avocado quarter; place in small bowl. Sprinkle with the 1 teaspoon lemon juice; toss gently. Cover and refrigerate. Place remaining 3 avocado quarters, salt, chives, pepper, yogurt, half-and-half and the 3 teaspoons lemon juice in blender. Blend at low speed until smooth. Pour blended mixture into medium bowl. Cover and refrigerate until well chilled, at least 1½ hours. Before serving, combine blended mixture with cubed avocado and juice. Serve chilled.

Director's note: **¼ teaspoon dill weed can be substituted for chives.*

bouillon a l'indienne

Serves: 8-12

- **2 quarts turkey, chicken, duck *or* goose stock**
- **12 scallions, chopped**
- **1½ tsp. Tandoori spice***
- **3 eggs, beaten**
- **Freshly ground pepper**
- **Garlic salt**
- **Chopped parsley**

Place stock in large kettle with scallions; bring to a boil. Add Tandoori spice. Remove from heat. Stirring briskly, slowly add a small amount of hot liquid to the beaten eggs. Return to pan and cook over low heat, stirring constantly, until slightly thickened. Add pepper and garlic salt to taste. Garnish with parsley.

Director's note: **Tandoori spice can be purchased in gourmet sections of supermarkets.*

"Unquiet meals make ill digestions."
Comedy of Errors, Shakespeare

chicken-broccoli soup

Serves: 6-8

- **1 20-oz. pkg. frozen chopped broccoli**
- **2 chicken bouillon cubes**
- **1½ cups milk**
- **2 cups heavy cream**
- **2 10¾-oz. cans cream of chicken soup**
- **½ tsp. oregano**
- **Pepper**

Cook broccoli according to package directions; drain and reserve liquid. In large saucepan, add bouillon to drained liquid; stir until dissolved (heat if necessary). Add milk, cream, soup, oregano, pepper and broccoli.* Blend thoroughly and heat through. Serve warm or cold.

Director's note: **Variation - combine all ingredients except broccoli. Put 1½ to 2 cups milk mixture and broccoli into blender; blend for a few seconds. Add to rest of soup in saucepan.*

upstate clam chowder

Serves: 12

Better than New England; much, much better than Manhattan!

- **6 medium potatoes, pared and diced**
- **3 medium onions, diced**
- **2 stalks celery with tops, diced (opt.)**
- **6 6½-oz. cans minced clams with juice, more if desired**
- **12 cups milk***
- **Salt and pepper to taste**
- **Tabasco to taste (opt.)**
- **½ cup butter**
- **1 cup heavy cream**
- **Cold milk**
- **4 Tbsp. cornstarch**
- **Paprika**
- **Chopped fresh parsley**

Barely cover potatoes, onions and celery with water; cover and simmer until tender. Do not pour off water. Add clams and their juice, milk, salt, pepper and Tabasco. Bring to a boil, stirring constantly. Add butter and cream. Stir a little cold milk into cornstarch, making a smooth, thick paste. Add gradually to chowder. Stir until thickened. Garnish with paprika and parsley.

Director's note: **This is a thin chowder. For a thicker chowder, reduce milk to 6 cups and thicken to desired consistency.*

french chicken soup with vegetables

Serves: 6

- Chicken pieces to serve 6*
- 2 Tbsp. butter
- 2 Tbsp. vegetable oil
- Salt and pepper
- 4 medium potatoes, cut into eighths
- 4 carrots, sliced
- 4 medium onions, thickly sliced
- 4 stalks celery, cut into bite-size pieces
- 2 green peppers, cut into strips
- 2 bay leaves, crushed
- 3 cloves garlic, minced
- 1 tsp. salt
- ½ tsp. pepper
- 1 tsp. sugar
- 1 tsp. oregano
- 2 Tbsp. parsley
- Juice and grated rind of 1 orange
- 2 10¾-oz. cans chicken broth
- ½ cup water (approx.)
- 1 28-oz. can Italian tomatoes

Heat butter and oil in frying pan; remove skin from chicken and saute skin about 5 to 7 minutes. Discard skin and reserve ¼ cup of the fat. In Dutch oven, arrange vegetables in layers, beginning with potatoes. Combine bay leaves, garlic, salt, pepper, sugar, oregano and parsley; sprinkle over vegetables. Combine orange juice and rind with reserved fat; pour over vegetables. Add broth and enough water just to cover carrots. Add tomatoes; top with uncooked chicken pieces, meaty side down. Cover; bring to a boil. Immediately place in preheated 350° oven for 1 hour or until tender.

Director's note: **Do not bone chicken — bones add flavor to soup.*

corn chowder

Serves: 8

Great while watching football games!

- **8 oz. diced salt pork**
- **½ cup chopped onion**
- **½ cup chopped celery and celery tops**
- **1 bay leaf, crumbled**
- **2 Tbsp. flour**
- **4 cups water**
- **3 cups cooked diced potatoes**
- **2 cups cream style corn**
- **2 cups evaporated milk**
- **Salt and pepper to taste**
- **Chopped fresh parsley**
- **Paprika**

Cook salt pork in large kettle until crisp and brown. Pour off all but 3 tablespoons fat. To pork, add onion, celery and bay leaf; cook 5 minutes. Blend in flour. Add water and potatoes; bring to a boil. Cover and simmer 15 to 20 minutes. Add corn and milk; heat through, but ***do not boil***. Season to taste. Serve in mugs or bowls, garnished with parsley and paprika.

cream of cucumber soup

Serves: 6

- **3 large cucumbers**
- **½ cup minced shallots** *or* **scallions**
- **3 Tbsp. butter**
- **6 cups chicken broth**
- **1½ tsp. wine vinegar**
- **¾ tsp. dried dill weed**
- **4 Tbsp. quick cooking cream of wheat**
- **1 cup sour cream**
- **2 Tbsp. minced parsley** *or* **dill weed**

Peel cucumbers. Cut 18 to 20 paper-thin slices; reserve for floating on soup when serving. Cut remainder of cucumbers into ½-inch chunks. Cook shallots slowly in butter until tender. Add cucumber chunks, chicken broth, vinegar and dill weed. Bring to a boil; slowly stir in cream of wheat. Simmer, partially covered, 25 minutes. Puree in blender. Don't over-blend.* Before serving, bring soup to simmer and beat in ½ cup of the sour cream. Ladle soup into warmed soup bowls. Add a dollop of sour cream to each bowl. Decorate with reserved cucumber slices. Sprinkle fresh parsley or dill weed over top.

Director's note: **May be prepared in advance to this point.*

fish chowder

Serves: 8

- **1 lb. fresh white flaky fish**
- **1 large onion, chopped**
- **2 strips bacon**
- **2 medium potatoes, pared and diced**
- **1½ cups water**
- **1 tsp. salt**
- **¼ tsp. pepper**
- **4 cups milk***
- **2 Tbsp. flour**
- **2 Tbsp. minced fresh parsley**
- **2 Tbsp. lemon juice**

In 3-quart saucepan, fry bacon until crisp; remove. Add onion and cook until soft. Add potatoes, water, salt and pepper; simmer. While potato mixture is simmering, cut fish into bite-size pieces. Add fish to mixture; simmer, covered, 10 minutes. Stir flour into milk. Add to chowder along with parsley and lemon juice. Heat to serving temperature, but ***do not boil.***

Director's note: **2 cups half-and-half can be substituted for 2 cups of the milk.*

gazpacho andaluz

Serves: 6

Contributed by William Putch of Totem Pole Playhouse, Fayetteville, Pennsylvania, who directed THAT CHAMPIONSHIP SEASON (1978) and THE SHOW OFF (1983).

- **4 to 6 tomatoes, peeled and quartered**
- **2 to 3 cucumbers, pared and chopped**
- **2 large onions, chopped**
- **1 to 2 green peppers, chopped**
- **1 Tbsp. vegetable oil**
- **1 Tbsp. Worcestershire sauce**
- **3 to 4 drops hot sauce**
- **1 chicken bouillon cube**
- **Salt, pepper**
- **Oregano, garlic powder**

Mix ingredients in blender. Add salt, pepper, oregano and garlic powder to taste. Serve in bowls with Garnishes as desired.

Garnishes

- **Diced green pepper**
- **Chopped tomatoes**
- **Chopped cucumber**
- **Croutons**

onion bisque

Serves: 4

- **4 cups sliced onion**
- **½ cup butter**
- **½ tsp. salt**
- **2 cups chicken broth**
- **¼ tsp. thyme**
- **1 large bay leaf**
- **2 Tbsp. cream of wheat**
- **1 cup milk**
- **¼ tsp. nutmeg**
- **Dash white pepper**

Saute onion in butter and salt; cook about 15 minutes until clear. Add chicken broth, thyme and bay leaf. Bring to a boil. Dissolve cream of wheat in milk; add to broth. Cover and simmer 20 minutes. Remove bay leaf. Pour into blender; blend until smooth. Just before serving, add nutmeg and pepper.

soup san miguel

Serves: 4-6

Wonderful first course for roast duck.

- **2 10½-oz. cans beef consomme**
- **1 cup finely chopped walnuts**
- **1 cup heavy cream**
- **Pinch nutmeg**
- **Salt and pepper to taste**

Bring consomme to a boil. Stir in walnuts and cream. Heat, but ***do not boil.*** Add nutmeg; season with salt and pepper.

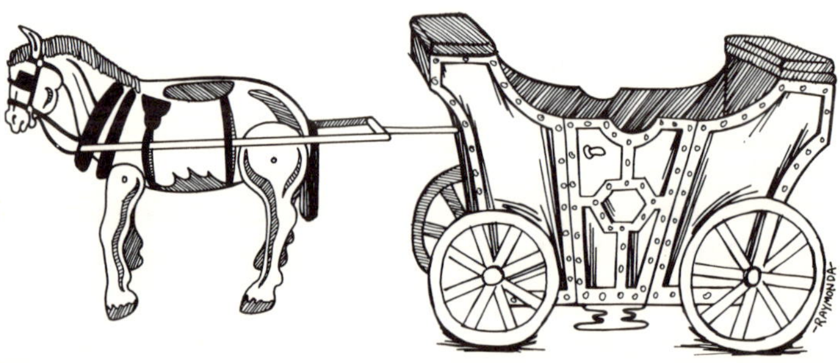

She Stoops to Conquer

cheesy tuna chowder

Serves: 4

- **1 Tbsp. finely chopped onion**
- **2 Tbsp. butter *or* margarine**
- **1 10¾-oz. can Cheddar cheese soup**
- **½ cup milk**
- **1 16-oz. can tomatoes, cut-up**
- **1 7-oz. can tuna fish, water-packed***
- **1 Tbsp. snipped parsley**
- **Dash freshly ground pepper**

In saucepan, cook onion in butter until onion is tender but not brown. Add cheese soup; gradually blend in milk. Add ***undrained*** tomatoes, ***undrained*** tuna, parsley and pepper. Cover and simmer 10 minutes.

Director's note: **A 7½-oz. can minced clams can be substituted for tuna fish.*

vichyssoise

Serves: 6-8

A soup for all seasons - serve either hot or cold.

- **4 leeks**
- **4 Tbsp. unsalted butter**
- **4 medium potatoes, thinly sliced**
- **4 cups chicken broth**
- **½ tsp. salt**
- **1 tsp. white pepper**
- **1 cup heavy cream**
- **Chopped fresh chives**

Saute white part of leeks in butter until translucent. Add potatoes, broth, salt and pepper. Bring to a boil; reduce heat and simmer 40 minutes. Pour soup into blender and blend until smooth; add cream. To serve hot, reheat without boiling. To serve cold, chill thoroughly. May be garnished with a sprinkling of chives.

"Soup of the evening, beautiful soup!"
Alice's Adventures in Wonderland, Lewis Carroll

all american vegetable soup

8 cups

Even better the second day!

- 1 large onion, chopped
- ½ to 1 lb. ground beef
- 3½ cups water
- 1 env. tomato-vegetable soup mix*
- 1 cup chopped celery with leaves
- 1 1-lb. can baked beans in tomato sauce
- 1 cup tomato juice

Brown onion and ground beef together. Add water, bring to a boil. Add soup mix and celery. Boil 10 minutes. Add beans and tomato juice. Heat through.

Director's note: **Lipton's Country Vegetable Soup mix can be used as a substitute.*

vodka soup

Serves: 4-6

Contributed by John D. Archbold for whom our theater is named. His Hangover Cure can be found on page 14.

- 1 10¾-oz. can green pea soup
- 1 10¾-oz. can chicken broth
- 1 16-oz. carton yogurt
- Thyme
- 4 oz. Vodka

Blend soup, broth and yogurt. Heat mixture; add plenty of thyme. Add Vodka. Serve hot and enjoy.

zucchini bisque soup

Serves: 4-6

- 2 medium to large zucchini
- 2 cups chicken broth
- 1 medium onion, sliced
- 1 clove garlic, mashed
- Few sprigs parsley
- Pinch crushed oregano
- 1 cup heavy cream *or* whole milk
- Salt and pepper

Wash and slice unpeeled zucchini. Combine with chicken broth, onion and garlic. Boil gently until zucchini is tender. Add parsley and oregano. Put a little at a time into blender; blend until smooth. Add cream; season to taste.

Supporting Cast

Fruit Salad

Vegetable Salads

*A good luncheon dish

Chicken/Meat/Seafood Salads

Salad Dressings

Photo on p. 57:
A Christmas Carol, 1981 - Joyce Krempel (Charwoman), Fred Lopez (Joe), Gerardine Clark (Charwoman)

avocado salad mold

Serves: 6

- 3 env. unflavored gelatin
- 1½ cups water
- 3 medium oranges
- 2 small ripe avocados
- 3 Tbsp. lime juice
- 2 Tbsp. sugar
- 2¼ tsp. salt
- 1 Tbsp. red wine vinegar
- 1 tsp. grated onion
- ¼ tsp. hot pepper sauce

In saucepan, sprinkle gelatin over water. Cook over low heat until gelatin is dissolved, stirring constantly. Peel and section oranges;* chop orange sections. Mash avocados with fork; stir in oranges, gelatin and remaining ingredients until well mixed. Spoon into lightly oiled, 6-cup mold. Cover mold and refrigerate until set.

Director's note: **Hint - to section oranges, cut along both sides of each dividing membrane; lift out sections from center.*

blueberry gelatin salad

Serves: 15

- 2 3-oz. pkgs. blackberry gelatin
- 1½ cups boiling water
- 1 cup chopped walnuts
- 1 20-oz. can blueberry pie filling
- 1 20-oz. can crushed pineapple, including juice

Dissolve gelatin in boiling water. Add remaining ingredients. Pour into lightly-oiled 9 x 13-inch glass dish. Let set at least 3 hours. Spread with Topping. Refrigerate until set. Cut into squares to serve.

Topping

- 8 oz. cream cheese, softened
- ½ cup sour cream
- ½ cup sugar
- 1 tsp. vanilla

Blend cream cheese and sour cream thoroughly. Add sugar and vanilla. Mix well.

cranberry mold

Serves: 8-10

- **1 3-oz. pkg. raspberry gelatin**
- **1 3-oz. pkg. lemon gelatin**
- **1½ cups boiling water**
- **1 cup cranberry sauce**
- **1 10-oz. pkg. frozen raspberries, thawed**
- **1 cup lemon-lime soft drink**

Dissolve gelatins in boiling water. Stir in cranberry sauce and thawed raspberries with juice. Chill until cold but not set. Carefully stir in soft drink. Chill again until partially set. Pour into lightly oiled 6-cup mold; chill until set. Unmold.

flagstone fruit compote

Serves: 10

A Vermont favorite!

- **1 1-lb. can sliced peaches**
- **1 1-lb. can sliced pears**
- **1 1-lb. can pitted dark sweet cherries**
- **1 8-oz. can pineapple chunks**
- **¾ cup jellied cranberry sauce**
- **3 large bananas**

Drain and reserve juice from peaches, pears and pineapple. Drain cherries. Combine fruits; drain well. Chill overnight. Whip cranberry sauce with mixer until jello-like; fold into well-drained fruit. Refrigerate. Slice bananas; soak in reserved fruit juices. Drain and add to fruit just before serving. Pass Dressing separately.

Dressing

- **½ pint heavy cream**
- **½ cup mayonnaise**
- **¾ cup confectioners sugar**
- **1½ tsp. vanilla**
- **6 drops lemon juice**

Whip cream lightly; fold in remaining ingredients.

frosted fruit salad

Serves: 6-8

1 3-oz. pkg. lime gelatin
1 cup boiling water
1 cup lemon-lime carbonated beverage
1 8¾-oz. can crushed pineapple
1 banana, sliced
¼ cup sugar
1 Tbsp. flour
1 egg, slightly beaten
½ cup heavy cream, whipped
¼ cup shredded sharp American cheese
2 Tbsp. grated Parmesan cheese

Dissolve gelatin in boiling water; cool. Add carbonated beverage; chill until partially set. Drain pineapple; reserve syrup. Fold drained pineapple and banana into gelatin mixture. Turn into 8-inch square pan. Chill until firm. In saucepan, combine sugar and flour. Stir in reserved pineapple syrup and the egg. Cook and stir over low heat until mixture thickens. Chill. Fold whipped cream into egg mixture. Spread over gelatin. Sprinkle with cheese. Cut into squares.

pasta fruit salad

Serves: 12

Deliciously different!

1 cup P & R #27, Gioia #34 *or* **Gioia #37 pasta**
1 20-oz. can crushed *or* **chunk pineapple**
1 11-oz. can mandarin oranges
¾ cup sugar
2 eggs, beaten
2 Tbsp. flour
Dash salt
4 to 8-oz. non-dairy whipped topping

Cook pasta according to package directions; rinse, drain and cool. Drain and reserve juices from pineapple and oranges. Cook juices, sugar, eggs, flour and salt until thick, stirring constantly. Pour over pasta; blend well. Refrigerate overnight. Chill drained fruits. Combine pasta mixture and fruits with thawed topping. Chill until serving time.

"fast curtain" salad

Serves: 6-10

1 lb. cottage cheese
1 16-oz. container non-dairy whipped topping
1 3-oz. pkg. gelatin (any flavor)
1 11-oz. can mandarin oranges, well-drained
1 8-oz. can crushed pineapple, well-drained

Blend cottage cheese and topping well with fork. Sprinkle in gelatin; add oranges and pineapple; mix well. Chill before serving.

Director's note: *More fruit may be added if desired.*

lemon-orange surprise salad

Serves: 15

2 3-oz. pkgs. orange gelatin
2 cups boiling water
1 6-oz. can frozen orange juice concentrate, thawed
2 11-oz. cans mandarin oranges, drained
1 15-oz. can crushed pineapple, undrained

Dissolve gelatin in boiling water. Add orange juice, oranges and pineapple. Pour into 9 x 13-inch glass dish; refrigerate until set. Spread Topping over set gelatin mixture. Chill. Cut into squares to serve.

Topping

1 3 to 4-oz. pkg lemon *instant* **pudding mix**
1 env. whipped topping mix
1½ cups milk

Combine pudding mix, topping mix and milk. Beat until thick.

Director's note: *If in a hurry, make topping while bottom layer is setting in refrigerator. Pour on topping, even if the bottom layer hasn't completely set. The two layers may blend a little, but it will still look pretty.*

rosy pear mold

Serves: 8

Very good with baked ham.

- **1 32-oz. jar cranberry-apple drink**
- **3 Tbsp. sugar**
- **1 Tbsp. lemon juice**
- **½ tsp. salt**
- **3 env. unflavored gelatin**
- **2 medium pears**

In saucepan, combine 2 cups of the cranberry-apple drink, sugar, lemon juice and salt. Sprinkle gelatin over mixture; cook over low heat until gelatin is completely dissolved, stirring constantly. Stir in remaining drink; refrigerate until mixture mounds slightly when dropped from a spoon, about 1 hour. Pare, core and dice pears. Fold pears into gelatin mixture; pour into lightly oiled 6-cup mold. Cover and refrigerate until set. Unmold.

pistachio salad

Serves: 8-10

- **1 3-oz. pkg. instant pistachio pudding mix**
- **1 20-oz. can crushed pineapple**
- **1¾ cups miniature marshmallows**
- **1 8-oz. container non-dairy whipped topping**
- **1 cup ground pecans**
- **Whole pecans**

Add ***dry*** pudding mix to ***undrained*** pineapple. Add marshmallows, topping and ground pecans; blend thoroughly. Transfer to serving dish. Garnish with whole pecans. Refrigerate overnight.

ENCORE!

raspberry gelatin salad

Serves: 8

- **1 10-oz. pkg. frozen raspberries, thawed**
- **½ cup currant jelly**
- **2 cups water**
- **1 6-oz. pkg. raspberry gelatin**
- **½ cup sherry**
- **¼ cup lemon juice**
- **1 1-lb. can pitted dark sweet cherries, drained**

Drain raspberries and reserve syrup. In saucepan, combine jelly and ½ cup of the water; heat and stir until melted. Add remaining 1½ cups water and gelatin. Heat and stir until dissolved. Remove from heat; add sherry, lemon juice and reserved raspberry syrup. Chill until partially set. Fold in berries and cherries. Pour into oiled 6-cup mold. Chill until set. Unmold.

strawberries and cream

Serves: 15

- **2 8-oz. cans crushed pineapple**
- **2 3-oz. pkgs. strawberry gelatin**
- **2 cups boiling water**
- **2 10-oz. pkgs. frozen strawberries, thawed**
- **1 pint sour cream**

Drain pineapple and reserve ½ cup juice. Dissolve gelatin in boiling water. Add reserved pineapple juice, crushed pineapple and undrained strawberries. Pour ½ of gelatin mixture into large glass bowl or 9 x 13-inch glass baking dish. Chill. Leave remaining gelatin at room temperature. When chilled gelatin is set, spread sour cream on top. Spoon remaining gelatin over sour cream, arranging a few berries on top. Refrigerate until set. Cut into squares to serve.

Director's note: *For faster preparation, pour all gelatin mixture into serving dish. When set, spread sour cream on top and decorate with a few berries.*

Anne Whitefield, *Man and Superman*

wine jelly with fruits

Serves: 8

Beautiful if molded in deep, patterned mold rather than in ring mold.

3 cups water
1 3-inch piece stick cinnamon
3 whole allspice
1 6-oz. pkg. lemon gelatin
1 cup dry white wine
1 11-oz. can mandarin oranges, drained
1 1-lb. can purple plums, drained and pitted
Maraschino cherries
1 1-lb. can apricot halves, drained

Heat water with cinnamon and allspice to boiling; remove spices. Dissolve gelatin in spiced boiling water; stir in wine; ***keep gelatin at room temperature.*** Place lightly oiled 8-cup mold in pan of ice and water; pour 1 cup gelatin into mold; refrigerate until as thick as unbeaten egg white. Arrange orange segments in gelatin; chill until slightly firm. Pour 1½ more cups of gelatin into mold; chill again until unbeaten egg white consistency. Arrange plums in gelatin; chill until slightly firm. Pour remaining gelatin into mold; chill as before. Place maraschino cherries in apricot halves; arrange in gelatin with cherries to the outside. Chill at least 4 hours. To unmold, loosen gelatin around edges with knife dipped into hot water. Dip mold very quickly into pan of hot water. Shake gently to loosen. Cover with serving plate; invert; shake gently; lift off mold.

sweet and sour asparagus salad

Serves: 6

1 lb. fresh asparagus spears
6 slices bacon
¼ cup wine vinegar
2 tsp. sugar
Dash salt
Dash freshly ground pepper
2 scallions, diced
Lettuce
2 hard-boiled eggs, sliced

Cook asparagus in lightly salted water 8 to 10 minutes until crisp-tender; drain. Cook bacon in frying pan until crisp; remove, drain and crumble; set aside. Add vinegar, sugar, salt, pepper and scallions to drippings in frying pan; stir to mix thoroughly. Add asparagus; heat through. Arrange lettuce in 6 salad bowls, top with asparagus and egg slices. Pour hot bacon dressing over each salad. Sprinkle with crumbled bacon.

"entracte" ice

Serves: 8-10

For the adventurous hostess!

1 pint lemon sherbet
2 to 3 Tbsp. finely crumbled blue cheese
Bibb lettuce
Artichoke hearts

Stir sherbet to soften; mix in blue cheese. Pour into ice cube tray or freezer dish; freeze. Just before serving, place on lettuce; garnish with artichoke hearts.

ENCORE!

three bean salad

Serves: 10

1 1-lb. can cut green beans
1 1-lb. can whole yellow beans
1 1-lb. can red kidney beans
1 cup apple jelly
⅓ cup cider vinegar
4 tsp. cornstarch
1 tsp. salt
2 cups sliced celery
½ cup sliced scallions

Drain beans. In saucepan, combine jelly, vinegar, cornstarch and salt. Cook until thickened. In large bowl, pour over beans; toss until well coated. Refrigerate for 1 to 2 hours. Add celery and onion. Serve on salad greens or as an accompaniment.

egg and broccoli salad

Serves: 4-6

2 env. unflavored gelatin
1½ cups hot water
1 10¾-oz. can chicken broth
1 cup real mayonnaise
Dash Worcestershire sauce
Salt and pepper to taste
1 10-oz. pkg. frozen broccoli, cooked
3 hard-boiled eggs, coarsely chopped

Dissolve gelatin in hot water. Add chicken broth, mayonnaise, Worcestershire sauce, salt and pepper. Chop broccoli coarsely; place with chopped egg in lightly oiled 6-cup mold. Pour liquid mixture over top. Refrigerate overnight. Unmold.

cauliflower-broccoli salad

Serves: 6-8

1 medium head cauliflower
1 to 2 bunches broccoli
1 16-oz. pkg. Hidden Valley Original Ranch House Dressing
½ cup sour cream
½ cup real mayonnaise

Cut vegetables into florets. Sprinkle dry Ranch House Dressing over vegetables; cover with plastic wrap and refrigerate overnight. Just before serving, mix sour cream and mayonnaise. Add to salad; toss thoroughly.

old fashioned cole slaw

Serves: 8-10

1 3-oz. pkg. lime *or* pineapple-orange gelatin
½ tsp. salt
1 cup boiling water
2 Tbsp. vinegar
½ cup cold water
½ cup mayonnaise
½ cup sour cream
1 tsp. grated onion
1 Tbsp. prepared mustard
1 tsp. sugar
3 cups shredded cabbage
2 Tbsp. chopped pimiento
1 Tbsp. chopped parsley

Dissolve gelatin and salt in boiling water; add vinegar and cold water. Stir in remaining ingredients, blending well. Refrigerate until slightly thickened. Pour into lightly oiled 1½-quart mold. Refrigerate until firm. Unmold.

waldorf slaw

Serves: 6-8

4 cups shredded green *or* Chinese red cabbage
½ cup diced unpared apple
¼ cup broken nut meats
½ cup grapes

Toss above ingredients with Dressing which has been mixed well.

Dressing

½ cup mayonnaise
Salt to taste
¼ tsp. pepper
Dash paprika
½ tsp. sugar
1 Tbsp. vinegar
1 Tbsp. milk

cucumber-lime salad

Serves: 6

Wonderful with beef or pork.

- **1 3-oz. pkg. lime gelatin**
- **¾ cup boiling water**
- **6 oz. cream cheese, softened**
- **1 cup mayonnaise**
- **1 tsp. horseradish**
- **¼ tsp. salt**
- **2 Tbsp. lemon juice**
- **¼ cup finely chopped onion**
- **¾ cup shredded** *unpeeled* **cucumber,** *drained**

Dissolve gelatin in boiling water; cool slightly. Add cream cheese to warm gelatin; stir to blend thoroughly. Add mayonnaise, horseradish, salt and lemon juice. Beat until smooth. Chill until slightly thickened. Fold in chopped onion and cucumber. Place in oiled 4-cup mold. Chill until set. Unmold.

Director's note: **Place shredded cucumber on paper towels to absorb moisture.*

"scene shop" salad

Serves: 6-8

- **1 8-oz. bottle Italian salad dressing**
- **3 cups cooked shells**
- **2 cups tomato wedges**
- **1½ cups zucchini slices**
- **¼ cup chopped parsley**
- **2 Tbsp. chopped scallions**
- **2 avocados, peeled and sliced**
- **Lettuce**

Pour Italian dressing over shells, tomato wedges, zucchini slices, parsley and scallions. Cover and refrigerate for 2 hours. Drain and reserve marinade. Arrange avocado slices on lettuce covered platter. Top with pasta mixture. Serve with reserved marinade.

"Things are seldom what they seem,
Skim milk masquerades as cream."
William Schwenck Gilbert

delicatessen potato salad

Serves: 10-12

This is a real delicatessen potato salad, different from the usual picnic varieties. ***Do not add anything else to it.***

5 lbs. large potatoes
2 large sweet Bermuda onions
¼ cup freshly squeezed lemon juice
2 tsp. sugar
1 tsp. salt
1½ cups *real* mayonnaise, (approx.)

Boil potatoes until ***just tender. Do not overcook.*** Peel and thinly slice. Mince onions; add to potatoes. Mix remaining ingredients well. Gently fold mayonnaise mixture into potatoes and onions. Serve in bowl or on large platter.

Director's note: *Keeps well, refrigerated, for several days.*

ham and potato salad

Serves: 8-12

Ham Layer

1½ cups diced cooked ham
¼ cup chili sauce
1 Tbsp. chopped onion
2 tsp. prepared mustard
1 tsp. horseradish
1 env. unflavored gelatin
½ cup cold water
½ cup mayonnaise *or* **salad dressing**

Combine ham, chili sauce, onion, mustard and horseradish. In saucepan, soften gelatin in cold water. Cook over low heat, stirring until gelatin is dissolved, being careful not to boil. Stir ¼ cup of the gelatin mixture into mayonnaise. Add to ham mixture, mixing well. Turn into 6 x 10-inch dish. Chill until set. Keep remaining gelatin at room temperature. Spoon potato mixture over firm ham mixture in dish. Chill until firm. Cut into serving portions.

Potato Layer

2 cups diced cooked potatoes
½ cup diced celery
2 Tbsp. chopped green pepper
1 Tbsp. chopped onion
2 tsp. vinegar
1 tsp. salt
⅛ tsp. pepper
½ cup mayonnaise *or* **salad dressing**

Combine all ingredients except mayonnaise. Stir remaining ¼ cup gelatin mixture into mayonnaise. Add to potato mixture; mix well.

"proppy" pin wheel

Serves: 6

A luncheon or light supper dish.

- 2 8-oz. pkgs. refrigerated crescent rolls
- 3 oz. cream cheese, softened
- 1 6½-oz. can tuna, drained
- 1 Tbsp. mayonnaise
- 1 Tbsp. horseradish
- ¼ cup chopped onion
- ¼ tsp. garlic powder
- ½ head raw broccoli florets
- ¼ to ½ lb. fresh mushrooms, sliced
- 2 tomatoes, chopped *or* 8 cherry tomatoes, halved
- ½ can pitted olives, halved

Spread crescent roll dough on pizza baking pan. Bake according to package directions; cool. Combine cream cheese, tuna, mayonnaise, horseradish, onion and garlic powder. Spread on "pie" crust. In a circular fashion, starting at the outer edge, make rows of broccoli, mushrooms, tomatoes and olives. Continue to decorate the pinwheel until entire pie is covered. Chill. Fifteen minutes before serving, remove from refrigerator to allow flavors to ripen.

untossed salad

Serves: 8-10

- 1 pkg. fresh raw spinach, washed and torn
- Salt and pepper to taste
- 6 slices bacon, cooked and crumbled
- 4 to 6 hard-boiled eggs, chopped
- 1 cup frozen peas, thawed
- ½ red onion, sliced
- ½ cup chopped green pepper
- ½ cup chopped celery
- ½ cup sliced fresh mushrooms
- Parmesan *or* Cheddar cheese, grated (opt.)
- Sliced almonds (opt.)
- Ham, cheese (opt.)

In large salad bowl, layer salad ingredients in the order given. Frost salad as you would a cake. Refrigerate at least 12 hours. Before serving, top with sliced almonds or julienne strips of ham or cheese, if desired.

Frosting

- 1 cup Miracle Whip salad dressing
- 2 cups sour cream
- 1 env. Hidden Valley Ranch *or* Harvest Onion dressing

Blend frosting ingredients well.

summer salad all year round

Serves: 2

1 cup grated cabbage
1 pink grapefruit, sectioned
1 tomato, sectioned
2 scallions with tops, chopped
2 white radishes, sliced
1 slice American cheese, thinly sliced
½ cup roasted soybeans *or* nuts
Lettuce
1 hard-boiled egg, quartered
Olives for garnish
Fresh parsley
Paprika

In large bowl, mix grated cabbage, grapefruit sections, tomato, scallions, radishes, cheese and soybeans. Chill. A few minutes before serving, pour dressing over chilled salad and toss together well. Refrigerate 15 minutes. Serve on lettuce leaves, garnished with egg, olives, parsley and paprika.

Dressing

¼ cup fresh lime juice
2 Tbsp. honey
¼ cup sunflower seed oil
⅛ tsp. dried garlic
1 tsp. dried parsley
Salt and pepper to taste

Put all dressing ingredients into a jar and shake well.

Emmy, *A Doll's House*

harvest antipasto salad

Serves: 6-8

Great for picnics or as an appetizer.

- **1 small head cauliflower, cut into bite-size pieces**
- **1 green pepper, cut into ½-inch strips**
- **½ cup sliced carrots**
- **½ cup sliced mushrooms**
- **½ cup sliced stuffed green olives**
- **½ cup sliced celery**
- **½ cup wine vinegar**
- **½ cup olive oil**
- **¼ cup lemon juice**
- **¼ cup water**
- **2 Tbsp. sugar**
- **1 tsp. salt**
- **½ tsp. basil leaves, crumbled**

Place all ingredients in large skillet or Dutch oven. Bring to a boil. Reduce heat; simmer, covered, for 5 minutes. Cool; refrigerate overnight. Drain before serving.

Director's note: *Can be increased easily - amounts don't have to be exact, but cauliflower is the largest percentage.*

hearty summer salad

Serves: 6-8

Always a hit, summer or winter.

- **1 cup macaroni, cooked**
- **1 cup diced ham**
- **1 cup diced sharp cheese**
- **1 28-oz. can Brick Oven beans, drained**
- **1 cup thinly sliced celery**
- **½ cup chopped green pepper**
- **1 small red onion, sliced and separated**
- **3 cups finely shredded cabbage**
- **Mayonnaise (enough to bind the salad)**
- **½ tsp. dry mustard**
- **¼ tsp. dill weed**
- **¼ tsp. pepper**
- **1 tomato, cut into wedges**
- **Fresh parsley**

Mix all ingredients together, except tomato wedges and parsley. Chill ***at least*** 3 hours. Serve in large bowl or lettuce cups. Garnish with tomato wedges and parsley.

It's certain that fine women eat
A crazy salad with their meat."
William Butler Yeats

"green room" salad

Serves: 6

- 1 lb. raw spinach, washed and torn into pieces
- 5 slices bacon, cooked and crumbled
- 3 to 4 hard-boiled eggs, sliced
- ¼ red onion, thinly sliced

Dressing

- 1 small onion, quartered
- 1 cup vegetable oil
- ½ cup sugar
- ¼ cup brown sugar
- ⅓ cup cider vinegar
- ¼ cup catsup
- 1 Tbsp. Worcestershire sauce

Put dressing ingredients into blender; blend until smooth. Dress salad.

mandarin spinach salad

Serves: 6-8

- 1 bag fresh spinach
- 1 11-oz. can mandarin oranges, drained
- ½ cup walnut pieces
- 1 cup sliced mushrooms
- 3 Tbsp. sliced scallions
- 6 slices bacon, cooked and crumbled (opt.)
- 3 Tbsp. frozen orange juice concentrate
- 6 Tbsp. real mayonnaise

Combine all ingredients except orange juice concentrate and mayonnaise. Mix concentrate and mayonnaise; pour over salad just before serving.

"stand-in" salad

Serves: 4-6

- 2 cups cubed cooked chicken
- 2 cups cooked rice
- ½ cup white grapes, sliced
- ½ cup chopped celery
- ½ cup toasted slivered almonds
- ½ cup mayonnaise
- 1 Tbsp. lime juice
- Pepper to taste

Mix ingredients well; chill at least 1 hour. Serve on lettuce leaves.

chicken-curry salad

Serves: 6

Absolutely delicious for a luncheon.

2 to 3 lbs. chicken, cooked and chilled
4 tsp. flour
¾ tsp. salt
1 tsp. sugar
¼ to ½ tsp. curry powder
⅛ tsp. pepper
½ cup chicken broth
½ cup milk
2 tsp. cider vinegar
1 small clove garlic, crushed
2 medium zucchini, cut into match-stick like strips (about 2 cups)
Small bunch scallions, cut same way as zucchini

Three hours before serving, remove chicken from bones and cut into match-stick like strips; refrigerate. In small saucepan, combine flour, salt, sugar, curry powder and pepper. With wire whisk stir in broth, milk, vinegar and garlic; cook over medium-low heat, stirring until dressing is thickened. Cover and refrigerate until well chilled. In large serving bowl, combine chicken, zucchini and scallions. Just before serving, toss well with dressing. Serve on lettuce leaves.

salad oliver

Serves: 6-8

1 whole chicken breast *or* **small frying chicken**
3 boiled potatoes, sliced
2 to 4 small dill pickles, chopped
2 Tbsp. chopped parsley
1 Tbsp. Worcestershire sauce
3 Tbsp. real mayonnaise
1 tomato, cut into wedges
6 large olives
2 hard-boiled eggs, cut into wedges

Boil chicken until cooked; allow to cool; shred. Combine chicken, potato slices, pickle and parsley. Mix Worcestershire sauce and mayonnaise; combine with chicken mixture. Turn into serving dish; decorate with tomato wedges, olives and egg wedges. Refrigerate.

Director's note: *Prepare several hours ahead of serving to allow flavors to blend.*

ENCORE!

chicken salad a l'orange

Serves: 4

- 2 cups cut-up cooked chicken
- ½ cup chopped celery
- ½ cup sliced ripe olives*
- ¼ cup real mayonnaise
- 3 Tbsp. vegetable oil
- 3 Tbsp. frozen orange juice concentrate, thawed
- 1 Tbsp. sugar
- 1 Tbsp. vinegar
- ⅛ tsp. dry mustard
- Dash hot pepper sauce

Mix all ingredients together; chill well. Serve on greens in the center of large platter or on individual plates with sections of fruit such as oranges, grapefruit, avocado, peaches and pears around salad.

Director's note: **Blueberries may be substituted for olives.*

oriental chicken salad

Serves: 12-15

Great summer luncheon salad.

- 5 cups cubed cooked chicken
- 2 Tbsp. vegetable oil
- 2 Tbsp. orange juice
- 2 Tbsp. vinegar
- 1 tsp. salt
- 1 cup pineapple chunks, drained
- 3 cups cooked rice
- 1 11-oz. can mandarin oranges, drained
- 1½ cups chopped celery
- 1 cup slivered almonds
- 1½ cups mayonnaise
- Lettuce

Marinate chicken in oil, orange juice, vinegar and salt. Refrigerate for 3 hours. After marinating, mix thoroughly with remaining ingredients. Chill, preferably overnight. Serve on lettuce leaves.

melon chicken salad

Serves: 4

1 cantaloupe
2 cups cut-up cooked chicken
1 cup sliced celery
½ cup sliced radishes
Celery leaves (opt.)

Pare cantaloupe and cut into 4 crosswise rings. Remove seeds and cut out inside of cantaloupe rings to leave a ½-inch ring. Reserve cut-out melon; cut into cubes. Combine melon cubes, chicken, celery and radishes. Mix with Blue Cheese Dressing. Cover and chill several hours. To serve, place melon rings on salad plates and spoon chicken salad into middle of each ring. Garnish with celery leaves.

Blue Cheese Dressing

½ cup sour cream
½ cup mayonnaise
1 Tbsp. lemon juice
2 Tbsp. chopped fresh chives
2 Tbsp. crumbled blue cheese
1 tsp. Worcestershire sauce
½ tsp. salt *or* to taste
¼ tsp. dry mustard

Mix ingredients well.

ham mousse

Serves: 4-6

2 cups cubed cooked ham
1 env. unflavored gelatin
2 Tbsp. cold water
½ cup boiling water
1 Tbsp. prepared mustard
1 tsp. salt
1 Tbsp. horseradish
½ tsp. brown sugar
¼ tsp. paprika
Dash cayenne pepper
1 cup heavy cream, whipped

Finely grind ham; set aside. Soften gelatin in cold water. Add boiling water, stirring until completely dissolved. To this mixture, add ham and remaining ingredients, except cream. Fold in whipped cream last. Turn into lightly oiled 1-quart mold. Chill until firm. Unmold.

Director's note: *Good accompaniments: chilled asparagus spears, deviled eggs, tomatoes, melon slices.*

landing salad

Serves: 4-6

Excellent with roast beef - comes via Pittsburgh.

4 hard-boiled eggs
½ cup real mayonnaise
1 Tbsp. prepared mustard
2 Tbsp. plain white vinegar
1 tsp. salt (opt.)
Freshly ground pepper
½ tsp. sugar
1 head iceberg lettuce
1 red onion, thinly sliced
Crumbled bacon

Chop ***only the whites*** of the hard-boiled eggs. Combine whites, mayonnaise, mustard, vinegar, salt, pepper and sugar. Tear washed lettuce into pieces; dry. In large serving bowl, combine lettuce, onion and bacon with dressing. Crumble egg yolks over top.

mushroom shrimp salad dijon

Serves: 4

Perfect for a summer luncheon or for dinner when it's too hot to cook!

2 cups sliced fresh mushrooms
½ lb. shrimp, cooked
⅓ cup vegetable oil
3 Tbsp. red wine vinegar
2 Tbsp. lemon juice
5 tsp. Dijon-style mustard
½ tsp. salt
1 cup sliced cucumber
Crisp watercress

Arrange mushrooms and shrimp in shallow glass dish. In a jar, combine oil, vinegar, lemon juice, mustard and salt; shake well. Pour over mushrooms and shrimp. Cover and refrigerate 1 hour. Drain marinade into cruet for dressing. Arrange mushrooms, shrimp and cucumber on plates lined with watercress. Pass dressing separately.

"My salad days, when I was green in judgement."
Antony and Cleopatra, Shakespeare

shrimp salad

Serves: 6

6 oz. midget bows (pasta)
2 4-oz. cans shrimp, rinsed
6 hard-boiled eggs, chopped
1 cup diced celery
1 Tbsp. chopped chives
⅛ tsp. black pepper*
½ tsp. salt*
½ tsp. celery salt*
½ cup Miracle Whip*
Fresh parsley (opt.)

Cook pasta according to package directions; drain, rinse and cool. Toss and mix all ingredients thoroughly; garnish with parsley. Chill.

Director's note: **These ingredients are approximate; adjust to personal taste.*

salmon mousse

Serves: 10-12

Contributed by Maxine Taylor-Morris who played in GOODNIGHT GRANDPA (1981).

1 env. unflavored gelatin
3 Tbsp. lemon juice
1 thick slice onion, chopped
½ cup boiling water
1 cup mayonnaise
1 large can salmon, drained and cleaned
Dash salt, pepper, paprika
½ cup sour cream

Dissolve gelatin in lemon juice. Place in blender with onion. Add boiling water; blend. Add mayonnaise; blend. Add salmon; blend. Add salt, pepper and paprika; blend. Add sour cream; scrape sides of blender and mix well. Oil a 1-quart mold with the oil from bottled Italian or Caesar salad dressing. Pour mousse into mold; chill until set. Unmold.

tuna basil mold

Serves: 4-6

1 15-oz. can tuna fish
1 1-lb. can chopped tomatoes
2 Tbsp. finely chopped basil
1 Tbsp. finely chopped onion
1 tsp. ginger
2 env. unflavored gelatin
¼ cup cold water
8 oz. plain yogurt
Salt
Freshly ground pepper

Drain tuna fish; flake with fork. Place tomatoes, basil, onion and ginger in saucepan; heat, but do not boil. Soften gelatin in cold water. Stir into tomato mixture; heat and stir until dissolved. Remove from heat; fold in yogurt and flaked tuna fish. Add salt and pepper to taste. Turn into lightly oiled 6-cup mold. Chill until set. Unmold.

tuna mousse

Serves: 6-8

1½ env. unflavored gelatin
½ cup cold water
¼ cup lemon juice, (little less)
½ cup mayonnaise
½ cup sour cream
½ cup cottage cheese
½ cup chopped pared cucumber
½ cup thinly sliced celery
2 6½-oz. cans white tuna fish in water, drained
¼ cup sliced green olives
1 Tbsp. chopped scallions
1½ tsp. horseradish
¼ tsp. salt
¼ tsp. paprika

In saucepan, soften gelatin in cold water. Add lemon juice. Heat and stir over medium heat until gelatin is dissolved. Combine mayonnaise, sour cream and cottage cheese; stir in gelatin mixture. Add remaining ingredients. Pour into lightly oiled 6-cup mold or 5 x 9-inch loaf pan. Chill until firm. Unmold.

bacon dressing

Good for spinach salad or any combination of greens

½ lb. bacon
¼ cup sugar
½ tsp. salt
1 tsp. dry mustard
1 Tbsp. finely grated onion
⅓ cup cider vinegar
1 cup vegetable oil (scant)
1 Tbsp. poppy seeds (opt.)

Fry bacon; cool and crumble. Combine remaining ingredients except poppy seeds. Blend in blender or shake thoroughly in jar. Add poppy seeds to the amount used each time. Store extra in refrigerator up to 2 weeks. Add bacon to greens; toss well with dressing.

blue cheese dressing

Serves: 6-8

Delicious for coleslaw.

1 4-oz. pkg. blue cheese
1 tsp. salt
⅓ cup vinegar
1 cup sour cream
2 Tbsp. minced parsley (opt.)

Combine ingredients. Cover and chill 1 hour or more before serving. Enough dressing for 6 cups shredded cabbage (1 medium head).

creamy egg & mustard dressing

1¼ cups

2 hard-boiled eggs, mashed *or* chopped
1½ tsp. salt
1½ tsp. sugar
1 Tbsp. chopped parsley
1 Tbsp. Dijon mustard
1 clove garlic, crushed
½ cup olive oil
5 Tbsp. heavy cream
¼ cup wine vinegar

Blend ingredients in the order listed. Serve on combination of greens. Add sliced mushrooms if desired.

garlic dressing

2 cups

- **⅔ cup olive oil**
- **⅔ cup vegetable oil**
- **½ cup cider *or* wine vinegar**
- **2 Tbsp. chili sauce**
- **2 tsp. salt**
- **1 tsp. sugar**
- **1 tsp. horseradish**
- **1 tsp. prepared mustard**
- **½ tsp. paprika**
- **¼ tsp. pepper**
- **2 cloves garlic, crushed**

Combine all ingredients well. Store in refrigerator.

low sodium salad dressing

1½ cups

- **¼ cup red wine vinegar**
- **¼ tsp. garlic powder**
- **¼ tsp. dry mustard**
- **½ tsp. fructose**
- **¼ cup water**
- **¼ tsp. freshly ground black pepper**
- **2 Tbsp. fresh lemon juice**
- **1 cup corn oil**

Combine vinegar, garlic powder, dry mustard and fructose; stir until all dry ingredients are completely dissolved. Add water, ground pepper and lemon juice. Mix well. Slowly stir oil into mixture. Pour into jar with tight fitting lid. Shake vigorously for 2 minutes. Store in refrigerator and use as dressing for salad greens.

low salt creamy dressing

1½ cups

Very subtle flavor.

- **1 cup plain yogurt**
- **½ cup low-salt mayonnaise**
- **1 tsp. chopped chives**
- **⅛ tsp. curry powder**
- **Freshly ground pepper**
- **½ cup low sodium chili sauce, *or* catsup**

Combine all ingredients; chill. Delicious served over salad of spinach, fresh mushrooms, onion, tomatoes and cucumbers.

Director's note: *Dressing can be prepared up to 2 days in advance.*

salad dressing for spinach salad

4 Tbsp. red wine vinegar
⅔ cup olive oil
½ tsp. pepper
1 tsp. salt
1 clove garlic, crushed *or* minced

Combine ingredients; pour over fresh, uncooked spinach leaves. Add crumbled bacon, fresh sliced mushrooms and sliced hard-boiled eggs.

honey dressing

2 cups

Good with both fruit salad and cole slaw.

¼ to ⅔ cup sugar
1 tsp. dry mustard
1 tsp. paprika
1 tsp. celery seed
¼ tsp. salt
⅓ cup honey
⅓ cup vinegar
1 Tbsp. lemon juice
1 tsp. grated onion
1 cup vegetable oil

Combine sugar, mustard, paprika, celery seed and salt. Add honey, vinegar, lemon juice and onion. Pour oil into mixture very slowly, beating constantly.

poppy seed dressing

2 cups

A fruit salad dressing.

½ cup sugar
⅓ cup honey
1 tsp. grated onion
6 tsp. tarragon vinegar
3 Tbsp. lemon juice
1 cup vegetable oil
1 tsp. dry mustard
1 tsp. paprika
¼ tsp. salt
2 tsp. poppy seeds

Place all ingredients in a jar and shake thoroughly until well blended. Will stay fresh at least 2 weeks in refrigerator.

Amplifiers

Quick Breads

Yeast Breads

Spread

Photo on p. 83:

That Championship Season, 1978 - Robert Fields (Phil), Thomas Connolly (James), Edmund Lyndeck (The Coach), David Forsyth (George), Stephen Bradbury (Tom)

apple date bread

1 loaf

- 1 egg
- 1½ cups milk
- 1 tsp. vanilla
- ¼ cup vegetable oil
- 3 cups flour
- 1 cup sugar
- 1 Tbsp. baking powder
- 1½ tsp. salt
- 1 cup flaked coconut, toasted*
- 1 cup diced dates
- 1 cup finely chopped apples

Preheat oven to 350°. Beat egg; add milk, vanilla and oil. Sift dry ingredients together; stir in coconut. Add to egg mixture; blend well. Stir in dates and apples. Turn into greased and floured 5 x 9-inch loaf pan. Bake for 75 to 90 minutes until tester inserted into center of loaf comes out clean. Cool in pan 10 minutes. Remove and cool completely on wire rack.

Director's note: **To toast coconut, spread flaked coconut in shallow pan. Place in 375° oven for 8 to 10 minutes, stirring often for even toasting.* ***Watch closely, it burns easily.*** *Cool.*

apple raisin muffins

1 dozen

- 2 cups sifted whole wheat flour
- 4 tsp. baking powder
- ½ tsp. salt
- 1 tsp. cinnamon
- ¼ cup sugar
- 1 egg, beaten
- 1½ tsp. vanilla
- ½ cup milk
- 1 cup unsweetened applesauce
- ¼ cup corn oil
- ¾ cup raisins

Preheat oven to 425°. Sift flour, baking powder, salt, cinnamon and sugar together; mix well; set aside. Combine egg, vanilla and milk; beat with fork until well blended. Add applesauce and oil to egg mixture; mix thoroughly. Combine applesauce mixture with dry ingredients. Add raisins. Stir until blended, but do not overmix. Grease twelve 1½-inch muffin cups (or use paper liners); fill ⅔ full. Bake 25 minutes.

Director's note: *If sweeter muffins are desired, increase sugar to ½ cup.*

apricot orange bread

3 loaves

- 1 7 to 8-oz. pkg. moist-pack dried apricots
- 1 cup boiling water
- ½ cup fresh orange juice
- 2 Tbsp. butter *or* margarine, softened
- 1 cup sugar
- 2 eggs
- 2½ cups flour
- 1 tsp. baking soda
- 2 tsp. baking powder
- ¼ tsp. salt
- 1 cup blanched almonds (opt.)

Chop apricots into small pieces; place in bowl. Cover with boiling water and orange juice. Set aside to cool.

Preheat oven to 325°. Cream butter and sugar; beat in eggs 1 at a time. Sift dry ingredients together. Add to creamed mixture alternately with liquid drained from apricots. Mix in apricot pieces and almonds. Turn into 3 greased and floured 3 x 7-inch loaf pans. Bake for 40 to 45 minutes or until tester inserted into center of loaf comes out clean. Cool in pans 10 minutes. Remove and cool completely on wire rack.

banana tea bread

1 loaf

- ½ cup butter *or* margarine
- 1⅓ cups sugar
- 2 eggs
- ¼ cup sour cream
- 2 cups sifted flour
- 1½ tsp. baking powder
- ½ tsp. baking soda
- ¼ tsp. salt
- 1 cup mashed ripe banana (3 medium bananas)
- 2 Tbsp. light rum *or* milk
- 1 tsp. almond extract
- 1½ cups chopped pecans (opt.)

Preheat oven to 350°. Cream butter and sugar; beat in eggs and sour cream. Sift dry ingredients together. Blend into creamed mixture alternately with mashed banana. Add rum and almond extract; stir in pecans. Turn into greased and floured 5 x 9-inch loaf pan. Bake for 60 to 70 minutes or until tester inserted into center of loaf comes out clean. Cool in pan 15 minutes. Remove and cool completely on wire rack.

banana bread

1 loaf

What a speedy way to make delicious banana bread!

2 eggs
1/3 cup shortening
2 very ripe bananas
2/3 cup sugar
1 3/4 cups flour
3/4 tsp. baking soda
1 1/4 tsp. cream of tartar
1/4 tsp. salt

Preheat oven to 350°. Combine eggs, shortening, bananas and sugar in blender. Cover and blend 30 seconds. Sift dry ingredients together. Pour banana mixture into dry ingredients; stir until just mixed. Turn into greased and lightly floured 5 x 9-inch loaf pan. Bake for 45 minutes or until tester inserted into center of loaf comes out clean. Cool in pan 10 minutes. Remove and cool completely on wire rack.

tropical tea bread

2 loaves

1/2 cup butter, softened
2 cups sugar
2 eggs
Grated rind of 1 orange
2 cups mashed banana (about 4 large bananas)
1 cup milk
4 cups flour
2 Tbsp. baking powder
1 tsp. salt
1 tsp. cinnamon
1 cup shredded coconut, lightly toasted*
1 cup chopped macadamia nuts *or* walnuts (opt.)

Preheat oven to 325° for glass pans; 350° for metal pans. Cream butter, sugar and eggs until light and fluffy. Add orange rind, banana and milk; mix well. Stir in dry ingredients. Fold in coconut and nuts. Turn into 2 well greased and lightly floured 5 x 9-inch loaf pans. Bake for 1 to 1 1/4 hours or until tester inserted into center of loaf comes out clean. Cool in pans 10 minutes. Remove and cool completely on wire rack.

Director's note: **To toast coconut, spread in shallow pan. Bake at 375° for 8 to 10 minutes, stirring often for even toasting.* ***Watch closely, it burns easily.*** *Cool.*

ENCORE!

blueberry bread

1 loaf

3/4 cup sugar
2 tsp. baking powder
Pinch of salt
1 Tbsp. shortening (heaping)
1 egg
3/4 cup milk
2 cups flour
1 cup fresh blueberries

Preheat oven to 350°. Line sides and bottom of 5 x 9-inch loaf pan with wax paper. Combine sugar, baking powder and salt. Cut in shortening. Add egg and mix well. Add milk alternately with 1 cup of the flour. Add remaining 1 cup flour; mix well. Fold in blueberries. Turn into prepared pan. Bake for 50 to 55 minutes or until tester inserted into center of loaf comes out clean. Cool in pan 15 minutes. Lift bread from pan using paper to lift. Leave paper on bread for 1/2 hour, then remove. Cool completely on wire rack.

ENCORE!

blueberry muffins

1 1/2 dozen

1 egg
1 cup half-and-half
4 Tbsp. butter, melted
2 cups flour
1/2 tsp. salt
1 Tbsp. baking powder
1/2 cup sugar
1 1/4 cups fresh blueberries

Preheat oven to 400°. Beat egg until light; add half-and-half and butter and mix well. Into large bowl, sift flour, salt, baking powder and sugar. Make a well in flour mixture; pour in liquid all at once. Mix just enough to moisten dry ingredients (don't beat) and fold in blueberries. Pour batter into well-greased muffin tins, filling each 2/3 full. Bake for 25 minutes.

blueberry coffeecake

Serves: 15-18

- **½ cup butter**
- **1 cup sugar**
- **3 eggs**
- **1 tsp. baking powder**
- **¼ tsp. salt**
- **1 tsp. baking soda**
- **2 cups flour**
- **1 cup sour cream**
- **2 cups blueberries**

Preheat oven to 350°. Cream butter and sugar; beat in eggs. Combine dry ingredients; add to mixture alternately with sour cream. Fold in blueberries. Pour into well buttered 9 x 13-inch baking pan. Crumble Topping on batter. Bake for 30 to 40 minutes or until tester inserted into center comes out clean. Topping will partially sink into batter.

Topping

- **1 cup brown sugar**
- **¼ cup butter**
- **¼ cup flour**

Cream brown sugar and butter. Add flour; mix until crumbly.

bran muffins

3 dozen

Prepare this batter in advance and keep it in your refrigerator for up to 5 weeks. Bake what you want and store the rest.

- **1 cup boiling water**
- **2 cups all-bran**
- **1 cup 40% bran**
- **½ cup shortening**
- **1½ cups sugar**
- **2 eggs**
- **2½ cups flour**
- **2½ tsp. baking soda**
- **½ tsp. salt**
- **¾ cup raisins**
- **2 cups buttermilk**
- **½ cup chopped walnuts (opt.)**

Pour boiling water over all-bran and 40% bran; allow to cool.

Preheat oven to 400°. Cream shortening and sugar. Add eggs, 1 at a time, beating after each addition. Combine flour, baking soda and salt; stir in raisins. Add to creamed mixture alternately with buttermilk. Stir in bran mixture and nuts. Refrigerate batter at least 12 hours. To bake: without stirring, fill greased muffin tins ½ full, using a soup ladle or small cup to dip batter easily. Bake about 30 minutes.

brown bread

1 loaf

- 1 cup corn meal
- 1 cup rye flour
- 1 cup graham flour
- 2 tsp. baking soda
- 1 tsp. salt
- 3/4 cup molasses
- 1 3/4 cups sour milk* *or* buttermilk
- 1/4 cup heavy cream
- 1/4 tsp. cinnamon

Preheat oven to 350°. Combine cornmeal, rye and graham flours. Add baking soda and salt. Put molasses, sour milk, cream and cinnamon into blender and mix well. Add liquid to dry ingredients a little at a time; stir only until dry ingredients are moistened. Pour into well buttered and lightly floured 5 x 9-inch loaf pan. Bake for 1 to 1 1/2 hours or until tester inserted into center of loaf comes out clean. Cool in pan 10 minutes. Remove and cool on wire rack.

Director's note: **Add enough milk to 2 2/3 tablespoons vinegar **or** 3 tablespoons lemon juice to make 1 3/4 cups.*

beer bread

1 loaf

- 3 cups *self-rising* flour
- 3 Tbsp. sugar
- 1 12-oz. can beer
- Melted butter

Preheat oven to 350°. Combine flour, sugar and beer. Turn into well greased 5 x 9-inch loaf pan. Bake for 30 minutes. Brush top with melted butter. Bake 10 minutes more or until tester inserted into center of loaf comes out clean. Cool in pan 10 minutes. Remove and cool slightly before slicing.

cape cod corn bread

- 2 eggs
- 1 cup milk
- 1/4 cup butter, melted
- 1 cup flour
- 1 tsp. salt
- 1 Tbsp. baking powder
- 4 Tbsp. sugar
- 3/4 cup cornmeal

Preheat oven to 400°. Beat eggs until light and frothy; add milk and melted butter. Sift flour, salt, baking powder and sugar. Add cornmeal and mix well. Add dry ingredients to liquid mixture all at once. Blend by hand, using as few strokes as possible; do not beat. Turn into lightly greased 8-inch square baking pan. Bake for 22 to 25 minutes.

caraway tea bread

1 or 2 loaves

Caraway seeds lend a marvelous surprise flavor.

- **¼ cup butter, melted**
- **1 egg**
- **¾ cup sugar**
- **1⅔ cups flour**
- **3 tsp. baking powder**
- **¼ tsp. salt**
- **¾ cup milk**
- **3 tsp. caraway seeds**
- **1 tsp. vanilla**

Preheat oven to 350°. Cream butter, egg and sugar, beating well. Sift dry ingredients; add to creamed mixture alternately with milk. Add caraway seeds and vanilla. Stir to blend. Turn into 2 greased and lightly floured 2 x 3-inch loaf pans; bake for 25 minutes ***or*** turn into one 4 x 8-inch loaf pan; bake for 35 minutes. Bread is done when tester inserted into center of loaf comes out clean. Cool in pan 10 minutes. Remove and cool completely on wire rack.

cheese-nut bread

1 loaf

- **2½ cups flour**
- **2 Tbsp. sugar**
- **2 tsp. baking powder**
- **½ tsp. baking soda**
- **½ tsp. salt**
- **½ tsp. dry mustard**
- **Dash cayenne pepper**
- **¼ cup shortening**
- **1 cup shredded sharp Cheddar cheese**
- **1 cup chopped walnuts**
- **1 egg, slightly beaten**
- **1 cup buttermilk**
- **½ tsp. Worcestershire sauce**
- **Large walnut pieces (opt.)**

Preheat oven to 350°. Into large bowl, sift dry ingredients together including mustard and cayenne pepper. Cut in shortening. Using a fork, mix in cheese and chopped nuts. Combine egg, buttermilk and Worcestershire sauce. Stir into cheese mixture just until dry ingredients are moistened; dough will be stiff. Turn into greased and lightly floured 5 x 9-inch loaf pan. Press walnut pieces into top. Bake for 55 minutes or until tester inserted into center of loaf comes out clean. Cool in pans 10 minutes. Remove and cool completely on wire rack.

"Kissing don't last; cookery do!"
George Meredith

cranberry bread

1 loaf

2 cups flour
1 cup sugar
1½ tsp. baking powder
½ tsp. baking soda
½ tsp. salt
2 Tbsp. hot water
1 egg, well beaten
½ cup fresh orange juice
2 Tbsp. melted shortening
1 cup halved cranberries
Grated rind of 1 orange
½ cup chopped nuts

Preheat oven to 350°. Combine dry ingredients. Add hot water, egg, orange juice and shortening. Fold in cranberries, orange rind and nuts. Pour into well greased 5 x 9-inch loaf pan. Bake for 1 hour. Turn out onto wax paper immediately. Wrap in the wax paper, then foil, while still warm. Store in refrigerator for 24 hours before slicing.

crumb cake

Serves: 15

½ cup butter *or* **margarine**
1 cup sugar
2 eggs, separated
2 cups flour
Pinch salt
3 tsp. baking powder
1 cup milk

Preheat oven to 350°. Cream butter and sugar. Add egg yolks; mix until smooth. Combine flour, salt and baking powder; add to creamed mixture alternately with milk. Beat egg whites until stiff peaks form; fold into batter. Turn into buttered 9 x 13-inch baking pan. Sprinkle Crumb Topping over top. Bake for 30 to 40 minutes.

Crumb Topping

⅓ cup hard butter *or* **margarine**
6 Tbsp. sugar
½ cup flour
¾ tsp. cinnamon

Mix ingredients together with pastry blender or fingers until crumbs are separated and crumbly.

date nut bread

2 loaves

- 2 cups boiling water
- 1 tsp. baking soda
- 2 cups chopped dates
- 1 Tbsp. butter *or* margarine
- 2 eggs, beaten
- 1½ cups brown sugar
- 4 cups whole wheat flour
- ½ tsp. salt
- 2 tsp. cinnamon
- 3 tsp. baking powder
- 1 cup chopped nuts
- 2 tsp. vanilla

Preheat oven to 325°. Combine boiling water and baking soda; add chopped dates and butter. Combine eggs and sugar; add to date mixture. Sift flour twice; combine with other dry ingredients; add to date mixture. Add nuts and vanilla. Grease two 5 x 9-inch loaf pans; line with wax paper. Pour batter into pans. Let stand 5 minutes. Bake for 1 hour and 15 minutes. Cool in pans 10 minutes; remove and cool completely on wire rack. Wrap in foil for a day before using. Freezes well.

date and nut bread

2 loaves

- 1½ lbs. dates, cut up
- 2 cups boiling water
- 1½ cups brown sugar, packed
- ½ cup shortening
- 2 eggs, slightly beaten
- 2 tsp. baking soda
- 1 tsp. salt
- 3 cups flour
- 1 cup chopped nuts

Preheat oven to 350°. Combine dates and boiling water; let stand 5 minutes. Cream sugar, shortening, eggs, baking soda and salt; blend well. Add flour alternately with dates and water. Stir in nuts. Turn into 2 greased and floured 5 x 9-inch loaf pans. Bake for 40 to 50 minutes or until tester inserted into center of loaf comes out clean. Cool in pans 10 minutes. Remove and cool completely on wire rack.

fruit-nut bread

1 loaf

- 1 Tbsp. shortening
- 1 cup sugar
- 1 large egg
- 2 cups flour
- 2 tsp. baking powder
- ½ tsp. salt
- 1 cup milk
- 1 cup cut-up mixed candied fruits
- ½ cup chopped walnuts *or* pecans

Preheat oven to 325°. Cream shortening and sugar; add eggs; beat until fluffy. Sift dry ingredients together. Add to creamed mixture alternately with milk; blend well. Add fruit and nuts; mix well. Turn into greased and floured 5 x 9-inch loaf pan. Bake for 1 hour or until tester inserted into center of loaf comes out clean. Cool in pan 10 minutes. Remove and cool completely on wire rack.

divine coffee cake

Serves: 12-15

Luscious and moist -- and divine!

- 1 cup butter *or* margarine
- 1½ cups sugar
- 3 eggs
- 3 tsp. baking powder
- ½ tsp. salt
- 3 cups flour
- 1 tsp. baking soda
- 1 pint sour cream

Preheat oven to 350°. Cream butter and sugar; add eggs and mix well. Combine dry ingredients. Add to creamed mixture alternately with sour cream; beat until just mixed. Pour ½ of mixture into greased and lightly floured 10-inch tube pan. Sprinkle ½ of Topping over batter. Pour remaining batter into pan. Sprinkle with rest of Topping. Bake for 1 hour and 15 minutes or until tester comes out clean. Cool in pan on wire rack for ½ hour; lift center tube with cake on it out of pan. Cool completely; remove cake.

Filling and Topping

- 2 Tbsp. butter *or* margarine, melted
- ½ cup brown sugar, packed
- 2 tsp. cinnamon
- 1 6-oz. pkg. semi-sweet chocolate chips

Combine Topping ingredients.

ENCORE!

lemon bread

1 loaf

The best we've ever tasted.

- **6 Tbsp. butter** *or* **margarine**
- **1¼ cups sugar**
- **2 eggs, beaten**
- **¼ tsp. lemon flavoring**
- **1½ cups plus 1 Tbsp. flour**
- **1½ tsp. baking powder**
- **¼ tsp. salt**
- **½ cup milk**
- **Grated lemon rind**
- **4 shakes of cloves (more if desired)**
- **Juice of 1 lemon**
- **¼ cup sugar**

Preheat oven to 350°. Cream butter and the 1¼ cups sugar. Add eggs and lemon flavoring; beat thoroughly. Sift dry ingredients together; add to creamed mixture alternately with milk. Add lemon rind and cloves. Turn into greased and floured 5 x 9-inch loaf pan. Bake for 1 hour or until tester inserted into center of loaf comes out clean. Combine lemon juice and the ¼ cup sugar. Glaze bread with this mixture immediately after taking from oven. Cool in pan 15 minutes. Remove and cool completely on wire rack.

Olivia, *Twelfth Night*

monkey bread

Serves: 10-12

Good hot from the oven, but can also be eaten cold.

1 cup sugar
3 tsp. cinnamon
½ cup butter
1 cup brown sugar
3 7.5-oz. tubes buttermilk biscuits
1 cup chopped walnuts

Preheat oven to 350°. Put sugar and cinnamon into small paper bag and set aside. Melt butter and brown sugar. With scissors, cut each biscuit into quarters. Shake about a dozen pieces at a time in bag with sugar-cinnamon mixture. Into a large ungreased bundt pan, pour a little of the brown sugar and butter mixture. Sprinkle in a few nuts. Add about a dozen biscuit pieces, dropping them at random with no pattern in mind. Continue layering in this manner until pan is ⅔ full. Bake for 30 minutes.

nantucket morning glory muffins

30 large muffins

A delicious muffin from the Morning Glory Cafe in Nantucket, shared by Syracusans who are Nantucket devotees.

4 cups flour
2½ cups sugar
4 tsp. baking soda
4 tsp. cinnamon
1 tsp. salt
4 cups grated carrot
1 cup raisins
1 cup chopped pecans *or* **walnuts**
1 cup coconut
2 apples, pared and grated
6 large eggs
2 cups vegetable oil
4 tsp. vanilla

Preheat oven to 350°. Sift dry ingredients together. Stir in carrot, raisins, pecans, coconut and apple. Beat together eggs, oil and vanilla. Stir into flour mixture until blended. Spoon batter into well-greased muffin cups, filling to top; bake for 35 minutes. Let cool in tins on rack for 5 minutes.

Director's note: *This is a quantity recipe. Cut recipe in half and it will make approximately forty 2-inch muffins. Freezes well.*

"If music be the food of love, play on!"
Twelfth Night, Shakespeare

her majesty's muffins

1 dozen

A healthy taste treat -- fit for a queen.

- **½ cup plus 2 Tbsp. butter**
- **½ cup sugar**
- **2 eggs**
- **1⅔ cups flour**
- **2½ tsp. baking powder**
- **½ tsp. salt**
- **1¼ cups milk**
- **¾ cup wheat germ**
- **1 cup chopped raisins**

Preheat oven to 375°. Cream butter and sugar. Add eggs; beat until fluffy. Combine dry ingredients; add to mixture alternately with milk. Stir in wheat germ and raisins. Fill greased muffin tins ⅔ full. Bake for 15 to 20 minutes until golden brown.

orange nut bread

2 loaves

- **3 eggs, beaten**
- **1½ cups milk**
- **⅓ cup vegetable oil**
- **Grated peel of 1 large orange**
- **1½ tsp. salt**
- **3 cups flour**
- **1½ cups coarsely chopped pecans**
- **1¼ cups sugar**
- **5 tsp. baking powder**

Mix beaten eggs, milk, oil and orange peel. Combine remaining ingredients. Stir egg mixture into flour mixture until flour is just moistened. Turn batter into 2 greased and floured 4 x 8-inch loaf pans. Bake for 60 to 80 minutes or until bread pulls away from sides of pan. Cool in pans 15 minutes. Remove and cool completely on wire rack.

ENCORE!

pumpkin bread

3 loaves

- **3½ cups flour**
- **2 tsp. baking soda**
- **1½ tsp. salt**
- **1 tsp. cinnamon**
- **1 tsp. nutmeg**
- **3 cups sugar**
- **⅔ cup water**
- **4 eggs**
- **1 cup vegetable oil**
- **2 cups pumpkin**

Preheat oven to 350°. Into large bowl, sift flour, baking soda, salt, cinnamon, nutmeg and sugar. Make a well in flour mixture. Add remaining ingredients; beat together until well blended. Turn into 3 greased and floured 5 x 9-inch loaf pans. Bake for 1 hour or until tester inserted into center of loaf comes out clean. Cool in pans 10 minutes. Remove and cool completely on wire rack. Wrap in foil; keep refrigerated. Use the second day.

pineapple ralston muffins

1 dozen

Quite unusual -- delicious hot.

- **1 egg, beaten**
- **⅓ cup vegetable oil** *or* **melted shortening**
- **1 cup undrained crushed pineapple**
- **1 cup sifted flour**
- **2¼ tsp. baking powder**
- **¾ tsp. salt**
- **¼ tsp. cinnamon**
- **¾ cup Instant Ralston**
- **⅓ cup brown sugar, packed**

Preheat oven to 400°. Mix beaten egg, oil and pineapple. Sift together flour, baking powder, salt and cinnamon. Add Instant Ralston and brown sugar; blend well. Add to pineapple mixture all at once. Stir until flour is just moistened. Fill buttered muffin tins ⅔ full. Bake for 20 to 25 minutes.

Director's note: *Can be frozen after baking; reheat in aluminum foil for 20 minutes in 400° oven.*

pineapple bread

1 loaf

A light, delicately flavored bread -- delicious spread with cream cheese.

- **1 egg, room temperature**
- **½ cup butter** *or* **margarine, softened**
- **⅔ cup light molasses**
- **1 8-oz. can crushed pineapple, undrained**
- **1¾ cups flour**
- **1½ tsp. baking soda**
- **½ tsp. salt**
- **½ tsp. ginger**
- **½ tsp. cinnamon**
- **¼ tsp. cloves**

Preheat oven to 375°. Beat egg with butter. Add molasses; mix well. Heat pineapple and add to egg mixture. Stir thoroughly. Add dry ingredients and mix well. Turn into greased and floured 5 x 9-inch loaf pan. Bake for 25 minutes or until tester inserted into center of loaf comes out clean. Cool in pan 10 minutes. Remove and cool completely on wire rack.

strawberry bread

2 loaves

- 3 cups mashed fresh strawberries *or* 2 10-oz. pkgs. frozen strawberries, thawed and mashed*
- 3 cups flour
- 1 tsp. baking soda
- 1 tsp. cinnamon
- 2 cups sugar
- 1 tsp. salt
- 1¼ cups vegetable oil
- 4 eggs, well-beaten
- 1 cup chopped nuts (opt.)

Preheat oven to 350°. Drain ½ cup juice from mashed ***fresh*** strawberries; save for topping. Combine dry ingredients. Make a well in center of mixture. Add berries and remaining juice, oil and eggs. Mix by hand until thoroughly combined. Fold in nuts. Turn into 2 greased and floured 5 x 9-inch loaf pans. Bake for 50 to 60 minutes or until tester inserted into center of loaf comes out clean. Cool in pans 10 minutes. Remove and cool completely on wire rack. Drizzle Topping over bread.

Topping

- 8 oz. cream cheese, softened
- Reserved strawberry juice

Blend cream cheese and juice until smooth.

Director's note: **Use* ***all*** *the juice from* ***frozen*** *berries in the batter. For a topping, spread bread with plain cream cheese, if desired. Freezes well.*

welsh cakes

30 cakes

A breakfast or tea cake.

- ½ cup butter
- 1 cup self-rising flour
- ½ cup sugar (scant)
- 1 egg, slightly beaten
- Cinnamon *or* nutmeg
- Currants

Rub butter into flour and sugar. Make a well in mixture; pour egg into well; beat to make a stiff dough. Add spice and currants. Flour board and rolling pin. Roll dough out to less than ½-inch thickness. Cut with floured tumbler. Cook in lightly greased skillet over low heat* until delicately browned on both sides. Sprinkle with sugar while warm.

Director's note: **Skillet has to be just right, about 350°.*

zucchini date nut loaf

1 loaf

- 1¾ cups flour
- 1 tsp. baking powder
- 1 tsp. cinnamon
- ½ tsp. baking soda
- 1 tsp. allspice
- 1 tsp. nutmeg
- ½ tsp. salt
- 1 cup chopped dates
- 1 cup chopped pecans
- 2 eggs
- 1 cup sugar
- ½ cup vegetable oil
- 1 cup unpeeled shredded zucchini

Preheat oven to 350°. Sift together all dry ingredients. Spread dates and nuts on wax paper; sprinkle small amount of the flour mixture over them. In large bowl, beat eggs, sugar and oil until well blended. With wooden spoon, stir in flour mixture alternately with zucchini. Stir in dates and nuts. Turn into greased and wax paper-lined 5 x 9-inch loaf pan. Bake for 70 to 75 minutes or until tester inserted into center of loaf comes out clean. Cool in pan 10 minutes. Turn out and remove wax paper. Cool completely on wire rack.

Director's note: *This recipe doubles easily and freezes well.*

chocolate zucchini loaf

2 loaves

- 3 eggs
- ¾ cup vegetable oil
- 2 cups sugar
- 2 tsp. vanilla
- 2½ cups flour
- 1 tsp. salt
- 1½ tsp. baking soda
- 1 tsp. cinnamon
- ½ cup cocoa
- ½ cup milk
- 2 tsp. grated orange peel
- 2 cups grated zucchini
- 1 cup chopped walnuts

Preheat oven to 350°. Beat eggs; add oil, sugar and vanilla. Combine dry ingredients. Add to mixture alternately with milk. Fold in orange peel, zucchini and nuts. Turn into 2 greased and floured 5 x 9-inch loaf pans. Bake for 50 minutes or until tester inserted into center of loaf comes out clean. Cool in pans 10 minutes. Remove and cool completely on wire rack.

Set, *The Merchant of Venice*

anadama bread

2 loaves

- ½ cup yellow corn meal
- 2 cups boiling water
- 1 tsp. salt
- ½ cup margarine
- 1 pkg. active dry yeast
- ½ cup lukewarm water (105° - 115°)
- ¾ cup molasses
- 6 to 7 cups flour

Thoroughly mix cornmeal, boiling water, salt and margarine; let cool to lukewarm. Dissolve yeast in lukewarm water; add with molasses to cornmeal mixture. Stir until well mixed. Add flour, 1 cup at a time, until dough is stiff enough to handle. Turn out onto floured board; cover with clean cloth; let rest 5 minutes. Knead dough until it is smooth and elastic. Place dough in large, oiled bowl, turning to grease all sides. Cover with cloth and let rise in warm place until double in bulk, about 1 hour. Divide into 2 equal parts. Shape into loaves and place in 2 greased and floured 4 x 8-inch pans. Lightly oil tops; cover and let rise again until double in bulk, about 45 minutes. Bake in preheated 350° oven for 40 to 50 minutes. Remove bread from pans immediately; place on wire rack to cool.

trudi's aunt rosie's bagels

12-15 bagels

Contributed by Fyvush Finkel who played in GOODNIGHT GRANDPA (1981).

6 cups unbleached flour plus 6 Tbsp. for pan and kneading
2 pkgs. active dry yeast
¼ cup warm water (105° - 115°)
2 Tbsp. sugar
1 tsp. salt (opt.)
¼ cup vegetable oil
Water to moisten, start with 1 cup, add few drops at a time

Grease large cookie sheet; dust with flour. Dissolve yeast in lukewarm water. Add sugar; stir and set aside to proof. In large bowl, make a well in flour. Add yeast mixture, salt, oil and water to moisten, stirring briskly after all is added. Form into a firm ball. Knead on floured board for several minutes until smooth and elastic. Divide into 12 to 15 balls of equal size. Roll each ball into approximately 6-inch long, pretzel-like logs. Curl and pinch ends of each one together.* Leave on board while a deep frying pan, half filled with water is brought to a boil.

Cook 3 or 4 bagels at a time for about 30 seconds. Longer cooking will make a harder crust. Lift out gently with a slotted spoon or 2 forks. Return to floured board; allow to drain for a few minutes. It is important not to have them dripping wet. When all are cooked and drained,** transfer to prepared cookie sheet. Bake in preheated 350° oven for about 25 to 30 minutes or until golden brown.

Director's notes: **A suggestion: rather than rolling balls into pretzel-like logs and pinching ends to form a circle, try poking your finger through each ball to form a hole, then flattening.*
***Variations: before baking, sprinkle with chopped onion, garlic, poppy seeds or coarse salt.*
After baking, bagels can be frozen in plastic bags. Make bagels very small and use at cocktail parties.

Fyvush Finkel

"The optimist sees the doughnut But the pessimist sees the hole."
McLandburgh Wilson

roadside bean bread

2 loaves

A nifty Grandma Brown's Baked Beans recipe.

- **1¼ cups milk**
- **3 Tbsp. sugar *or* molasses**
- **3 Tbsp. butter**
- **⅔ cup Grandma Brown's Baked Beans**
- **1 tsp. salt**
- **1 pkg. active dry yeast**
- **¼ cup warm water (105° - 115°)**
- **5 cups flour**

Scald milk; pour into large mixing bowl. Add sugar, butter, beans and salt; cool to lukewarm. Sprinkle yeast on warm water; stir to dissolve. Add yeast and 3 cups of the flour to milk-bean mixture. Beat 2 minutes with mixer at medium speed or until batter is smooth. Mix in just enough remaining flour to make a soft dough. Knead on floured surface 8 to 10 minutes or until dough is smooth and satiny.

Place dough in greased bowl. Cover and let rise until double in bulk, about 30 minutes. Punch down; divide in half. Shape two loaves. Place seam-side down in well greased 5 x 9-inch loaf pans. Cover and let rise until double in bulk, about 40 to 50 minutes. Bake loaves in preheated 375° oven for 45 minutes or until bottom of loaf sounds hollow when tapped. Remove immediately.

challah bread

2 loaves

- **5 cups flour**
- **2 pkgs. active dry yeast**
- **½ to ¾ cups sugar***
- **1½ cups warm water (105° - 115°)**
- **2 oz. margarine, melted**
- **1 tsp. salt**
- **2 eggs**
- **Beaten egg yolk**

Put flour into large bowl; make well in flour. Place yeast, sugar, water, margarine, salt and eggs in well. Mix with wooden spoon until batter comes away from bowl and dough is tacky. Cover with clean cloth; let rise in warm place for 1 hour. Turn out onto floured surface, knead until dough is smooth. Return to bowl. Let rise again until double in bulk. Turn out onto floured surface and shape into loaves, braids, etc. or use for coffee cake with filling. After dough is shaped, brush with beaten egg yolk; allow to rest for ½ hour. Bake in preheated 350° oven for 25 to 30 minutes.

Director's note: **Use ½ cup sugar for coffee cake. Use ¾ cup sugar for Easter bread and add 1 teaspoon lemon extract.*

chocolate bread

4 loaves

Extra special if lightly toasted and spread with sweet butter. Nice accompaniment -- fresh fruit.

3 pkgs. active dry yeast
1 tsp. sugar
½ cup warm water (105° - 115°)
12 cups flour (approx.)
1 cup cocoa
2 Tbsp. salt
½ cup sugar
3½ cups warm water
1 egg
2 Tbsp. shortening
1 12-oz. pkg. mini-chocolate chips

Combine yeast, the 1 teaspoon sugar and the ½ cup warm water. Set aside to proof. Add remaining ingredients (except chocolate chips), using enough flour, added in several portions, to make a dough that is easily handled. Knead by hand or machine until smooth and elastic. Knead in chocolate chips. Place in greased bowl; turn to grease top. Cover with plastic wrap and let rise until double in bulk, about 1½ hours. Punch down; divide into 4 parts. Place in greased and floured 5 x 9-inch loaf pans. Let rise until double in bulk, about 1½ hours. Bake in preheated 425° oven for 15 minutes. Reduce heat to 375°; bake 15 minutes more until crusty and done. Remove from pans immediately.

dilly bread

1 loaf

This can be formed into bite-size rolls -- great for cocktail parties.

1 cup creamed cottage cheese
1 pkg. active dry yeast
¼ cup warm water (105° - 115°)
2 Tbsp. sugar
1 Tbsp. minced onion
1 Tbsp. butter
2 tsp. dill seed
1 tsp. salt
¼ tsp. baking soda
1 egg, beaten
2¼ to 2½ cups flour
Melted butter

Heat cottage cheese to lukewarm. Soften yeast in warm water. Blend thoroughly the cottage cheese, sugar, onion, butter, dill seed, salt, baking soda, egg and yeast. Add flour in 3 parts, beating well after each addition. Cover; let rise in warm place until double in bulk, about 1 hour. Stir down; turn into well-greased 1½ to 2-quart round casserole. Let rise again in warm place until light, 30 to 40 minutes. Bake in preheated 350° oven for 40 to 50 minutes. Remove from pan immediately. Brush with melted butter; sprinkle with salt.

processor french bread

2 loaves

Also makes a great pizza crust!

- **½ cup warm water (105° - 115°)**
- **2 pkgs. active dry yeast**
- **1 tsp. sugar**
- **3½ cups all-purpose** *or* **unbleached flour**
- **1 tsp. salt**
- **1 tsp. sugar**
- **1 cup warm water**
- **Extra flour for kneading**

Combine the ½ cup warm water, yeast and 1 teaspoon sugar in bowl to proof for at least 10 minutes. Place yeast mixture, flour, salt and 1 teaspoon sugar in food processor. With machine running slowly, add the 1 cup warm water. A soft ball should form in several seconds; if not, add a little more warm water. Let machine run 15 to 20 seconds, adding more flour if dough seems too soft. Transfer dough to lightly floured board; knead with additional flour for several turns.* Shape into 2 loaves; slash tops diagonally; let rise 45 minutes to 1 hour until double in bulk. Bake in preheated 450° oven with pan of water on the rack beneath for 10 minutes. Reduce heat to 400°; continue baking for 15 minutes or until golden brown.

Director's note: **To make a great pizza crust -- at this point let dough rest 10 to 15 minutes; roll out larger than pizza pan. Drape dough over pan which has been greased with olive oil. Roll up edges; put on desired toppings; bake at 400° for about 20 minutes.*

"A Jug of Wine, a Loaf of Bread -- and Thou..."
The Rubaiyat of Omar Khayyam, Edward Fitzgerald

cinnamon rolls

24 rolls

- **1 pkg. active dry yeast**
- **¼ cup warm water (105° - 115°)**
- **1 cup milk, scalded**
- **2 Tbsp. sugar**
- **2 Tbsp. shortening**
- **½ tsp. salt**
- **3½ cups sifted flour**
- **1 egg**
- **¼ cup butter *or* margarine, melted**
- **½ cup sugar**
- **2 tsp. cinnamon**

Soften yeast in warm water (110°); set aside. Combine milk, the 2 tablespoons sugar, shortening and salt; cool to lukewarm. Add 1½ cups flour; beat well ***with wooden spoon, not mixer.*** Beat in yeast and egg. Gradually add remaining flour to form soft dough, beating well. Place in greased bowl, turning once to grease surface. Cover with damp cloth; let rise until double in bulk, 1½ to 2 hours. Turn out onto lightly floured surface. Divide in half with sharp knife, separating a few inches apart. Cover again with damp cloth; let rest 10 minutes. Meanwhile, combine butter, the ½ cup sugar and cinnamon.

Roll dough out into two 8 x 16-inch rectangles. Spread cinnamon filling on dough, using ½ on each. Roll lengthwise as for jelly roll. Seal edge; cut into 1-inch slices. (Each roll cuts into about 12 slices.) Place cut side down in 2 greased 9-inch square or round pans. Cover; let rise until double in bulk, 30 to 40 minutes. Bake in preheated 375° oven for 20 to 25 minutes. Remove from pan.

Director's note: *If freezing, allow to cool for 3 hours. Wrap in foil, then Saran Wrap. Thaw at room temperature, unwrapped, for 3 hours or while still wrapped in foil, freshen in 300° oven for 20 minutes.*

haska bread

2 large braids

¾ cup milk
¾ cup sugar
½ tsp. salt
½ cup butter
2 pkgs. active dry yeast
½ cup warm water (105° - 115°)
2 eggs, beaten
5½ cups flour
¼ cup chopped citron
¼ cup raisins
¼ cup chopped almonds
Melted butter
1 egg
1 Tbsp. water
¼ cup blanched almonds

Scald milk; stir in sugar, salt and the ½ cup butter. Cool to lukewarm. In large bowl, dissolve yeast in warm water. Stir in lukewarm milk mixture, the 2 eggs, and 3 cups of the flour. Beat until smooth. Gradually stir in remainder of flour to make a soft dough. Turn out onto lightly floured board. Knead until smooth and elastic, about 10 minutes. Place in greased bowl, turning to grease top. Cover; let rise in warm place, until double in bulk, about 50 minutes.

Punch down. Turn out onto lightly floured board. Knead in citron, raisins and chopped almonds until well distributed. Divide into 3 equal pieces. Divide each in half; roll into strips 14 inches long. Braid strips on greased cookie sheet.* Brush with melted butter. Cover and let rise in warm place for 1 hour. Beat the egg and 1 tablespoon water; brush generously on top of bread; decorate with blanched almonds. Bake in preheated 375° oven for 30 to 40 minutes, until deep golden brown.

Director's note: **Braid without stretching dough, beginning in middle and working toward either end. Seal ends of strands and tuck under braid.*

Unicorn, *The Glass Menagerie*

lemon bubble ring

1 large loaf

- **5 to 6 cups flour**
- **½ cup sugar**
- **1 tsp. salt**
- **2 pkgs. active dry yeast**
- **1 cup milk**
- **½ cup water**
- **¼ cup butter** *or* **margarine**
- **2 eggs**
- **½ cup sugar**
- **Grated peel of 2 lemons**
- **¼ tsp. mace**
- **2 Tbsp. butter** *or* **margarine**

In large bowl, combine 2 cups of the flour, ½ cup sugar, salt and yeast. In saucepan over low heat, warm milk, water and the ¼ cup butter until very warm (120° to 130°, butter does not need to melt completely). Using mixer at low speed, gradually pour liquid into dry ingredients; beat until just mixed. Increase speed; add eggs and beat 2 minutes, occasionally scraping bowl. Beat in 1 to 2 cups of the remaining flour or enough to make a thick batter. Continue beating 2 minutes, occasionally scraping bowl. With spoon, stir in enough of the remaining flour (about 2 cups) to make a soft dough.

Turn onto lightly floured surface and knead until smooth and elastic, about 10 minutes. Shape dough into ball. Place in greased bowl, turning once to grease top. Cover with towel; let rise in warm place away from drafts, until double in bulk, about 1 hour. (Dough is double when 2 fingers pressed lightly into dough leave a dent.)

Punch dough down; turn onto lightly floured surface. Cut dough in half; cover with towel and let stand 15 minutes. Meanwhile combine ½ cup sugar, lemon peel and mace; set aside. Melt the 2 tablespoons butter. Cut each dough half into 16 pieces. Shape each piece into ball by tucking ends under. Place ½ of balls in greased 10-inch tube pan; brush with ½ of melted butter; sprinkle with ½ of lemon peel mixture. Repeat with remaining balls, melted butter and lemon peel mixture. Cover with towel; let rise in warm place until double, about 45 minutes.

Bake in preheated 350° oven for 35 minutes or until golden and loaf sounds hollow when lightly tapped with fingers. Cool in pan 5 minutes; remove from pan and cool on wire rack.

orange coconut coffee cake

Serves: 18

1 pkg. active dry yeast	½ cup sour cream
¼ cup warm water (105° - 115°)	8 Tbsp. butter, melted
¼ cup sugar	2¾ to 3 cups flour
1 tsp. salt	¾ cup sugar
2 eggs	1 cup coconut, toasted*
	2 Tbsp. grated orange rind

In large bowl, soften yeast in warm water. Stir in the ¼ cup sugar, salt, eggs, sour cream and 6 tablespoons of the melted butter. Gradually add flour to form a stiff dough, beating well after each addition. (For first additions of flour, use mixer on medium speed.) Cover; let rise in warm place until light and double in bulk, about 2 hours.

Turn out onto well-floured surface; knead about 15 times. Roll out ½ of dough to 12-inch circle. Brush with 1 tablespoon of the remaining melted butter. Combine the ¾ cup sugar, ¾ cup of the coconut and orange rind. Sprinkle ½ of sugar-coconut mixture on dough circle; cut into 12 wedges. Roll up, starting with wide end and rolling to point. Repeat with remaining dough. Place rolls point side down in 3 rows in well greased 9 x 13-inch pan. Cover; let rise in warm place until light and double in bulk, about 1 hour.

Bake in preheated 350° oven for 25 to 30 minutes until golden brown. Leave in pan. Pour Glaze over hot cake. Sprinkle with the remaining ¼ cup coconut.

Glaze

¾ cup sugar	2 Tbsp. orange juice
½ cup sour cream	¼ cup butter

Combine all ingredients in saucepan. Boil 3 minutes, stirring occasionally.

Director's note: **To toast coconut, spread coconut in shallow pan. Place in 375° oven for 8 to 10 minutes, stirring often for even toasting.* ***Watch closely, it burns easily.*** *Cool.*

aunt lena's $1,000 orange rolls

18 rolls

A winner in the Better Homes and Gardens magazine contest when $1,000 was $1,000!

1 cup milk
¼ cup butter
½ cup sugar
1 tsp. salt
1 pkg. active dry yeast
¼ cup warm water (105° - 115°)
3 eggs, well beaten
4 cups flour
Grated rind of 1 large orange
1 cup sugar
½ cup butter, softened

Scald milk; stir in the ¼ cup butter, the ½ cup sugar and salt; cool to lukewarm. In large warm bowl, dissolve yeast in warm water. Stir in lukewarm milk mixture and eggs. Gradually add flour; beat until smooth. Turn out onto lightly floured board; knead until smooth and elastic, about 5 minutes. Place in greased bowl; turn to grease top. Cover and let rise in warm place until double in bulk, about 45 minutes.

Punch down. Roll dough flat as for jelly roll. Combine orange rind, the 1 cup sugar and the ½ cup butter. Spread on dough. Roll up from the long side. Slice about ½ inch thick. Place in greased muffin tins. Let rise again. Bake in preheated 375° oven about 18 minutes. Don't overbake; they burn easily.

puffy pillows

18 large rolls

1 pkg. active dry yeast
¼ cup warm water (105° - 115°)
2 cups milk
4 Tbsp. shortening
2 Tbsp. sugar
1 tsp. salt
4 cups flour
1 egg, beaten

Dissolve yeast in warm water. Bring milk to simmer; remove from heat. Add shortening, sugar and salt. Let cool to warm. In large bowl, combine flour, milk mixture and yeast. Stir well. Add egg and stir again. Leave a wooden spoon in the mixture while it is rising.* Punch the dough down every 15 minutes for 1 hour. Place large spoonfuls of dough on greased cookie sheet. Let rise until double in bulk.* Bake in preheated 400° oven for 15 minutes.

Director's note: **Do not cover dough during rising; it is too sticky.*

crusty rolls

18 rolls

- **1 pkg. active dry yeast**
- **¼ cup warm water (105° - 115°)**
- **¾ cup boiling water**
- **1 Tbsp. sugar**
- **2 Tbsp. shortening**
- **1½ tsp. salt**
- **3¼ to 3½ cups flour**
- **2 egg whites, slightly beaten**

Soften yeast in warm water; set aside. Combine boiling water, sugar, shortening and salt; stir until shortening melts. Cool to lukewarm. Add 1 cup of the flour; beat well. Stir in egg whites and yeast mixture. Add enough of remaining flour (between 2¼ to 2½ cups) to make a soft dough. Turn out onto floured surface; knead until smooth and elastic, about 10 minutes. Place in lightly greased bowl.Turn dough once to grease surface. Cover; let rise in warm place until double in bulk, about 1 hour. Punch down; cover and let rest 10 minutes. Shape into 18 round rolls. Place about 2½ inches apart on greased baking sheet. Cover; let rise until double in bulk, about 1 hour. Place large shallow pan on bottom oven rack; fill with boiling water. On rack above water, bake rolls in preheated 450° oven for 10 to 12 minutes.

hap's yeast dinner rolls

3 dozen

Even though this recipe takes time, the rolls are well worth it.

- **1 pkg. active dry yeast**
- **1 cup warm water (105° - 115°)**
- **½ cup butter, melted**
- **1 tsp. salt**
- **½ cup sugar**
- **3 eggs, well beaten**
- **4½ cups flour**
- **Extra melted butter**

Sprinkle yeast over warm water; let stand 5 minutes. Add butter, salt, sugar and eggs, in that order. Add 3 cups of the flour; beat vigorously. Mix in remaining flour; place dough in greased bowl, turning once to grease surface of dough. Cover and refrigerate several hours.

Divide dough into 3 parts; roll each part into a circle on floured board. Spread melted butter on circle, then cut into 12 pie-shaped pieces. Roll pieces by beginning at broad end of triangle. If smaller rolls are desired, make smaller circles of dough and cut smaller wedges. Let rolls rise in warm place, about 3 hours or double in size. Bake in preheated 375° oven for 10 to 15 minutes.

refrigerator ideal rolls

2 dozen

Contributed by James and Gerardine Clark. Jim is the Managing Director of Syracuse Stage. Geri played in A STREETCAR NAMED DESIRE (1977), A CHRISTMAS CAROL (1981) and DEATH OF A SALESMAN (1983).

- **1 pkg. active dry yeast**
- **1 cup warm water (105° - 115°)**
- **1 tsp. salt**
- **3 eggs**
- **1/3 cup sugar**
- **1/3 cup melted shortening**
- **4 cups flour**
- **Melted shortening**
- **Melted butter**

Stir yeast into warm water. Add salt, eggs, sugar, melted shortening and 2 cups of the flour. Beat 4 minutes with mixer. With spoon, add the remaining 2 cups flour. Brush top of dough with melted shortening; let stand 1 hour. Refrigerate overnight. Two hours before baking, roll out dough; cut with biscuit cutter. With pastry brush, pat top of each with melted butter. Fold over in the shape of Parker House rolls. Place on greased cookie sheet. Let rise for 1 to 1 1/2 hours. Bake in preheated 400° oven for 9 to 10 minutes.

Director's note: *Dough can be prepared a day or two in advance and refrigerated until ready to bake.*

Gerardine Clark
James A. Clark

herb spread (low cholesterol)

Serves: 8

- **1/2 cup corn oil margarine, softened**
- **1/4 cup finely chopped parsley**
- **2 tsp. lemon juice**
- **1 tsp. dried basil**
- **1 tsp. dried marjoram**
- **1 clove garlic, minced**

Blend ingredients well.

Director's note: *To serve on Italian bread, spread mixture between slices, wrap in foil and bake at 375° for 20 minutes or until hot.*

Improvisation

Eggs/Cheese

*A good luncheon dish

Photo on p. 113:
Betrayal, 1981 - Richard Greene (Jerry), Edmond Genest (Robert)

carlton house oven omelet

Serves: 12-14

Great for company brunch.

- **¼ cup butter**
- **18 eggs**
- **1 cup sour cream**
- **1 cup milk**
- **2 tsp. salt**
- **¼ tsp. white pepper**
- **¼ cup chopped scallions (opt.)**

Preheat oven to 325°. In oven, melt butter in 9 x 13-inch baking dish.* Tilt dish to coat bottom with butter. In large mixing bowl, beat eggs, sour cream, milk, salt and pepper until blended. Stir in onion. Pour into baking dish. Bake until eggs are set but still moist, about 35 minutes.

Director's note: **Recipe divides in half easily using 8-inch square dish.*

Suggested wine: New York or California Champagne

crab-sauced brunch eggs

Serves: 4-6

- **1 6-oz. pkg. frozen King crab, thawed and drained**
- **6 hard-boiled eggs**
- **⅛ tsp. salt**
- **1 tsp. prepared mustard**
- **2 Tbsp. mayonnaise**
- **½ cup finely chopped celery**
- **2 Tbsp. chopped scallions**
- **⅛ tsp. salt**
- **6 Tbsp. mayonnaise**
- **3 English muffins, halved and toasted**
- **1 10¾-oz. can cream of celery soup**
- **⅓ cup milk**
- **1 Tbsp. chopped parsley**

Halve eggs; remove yolks. Mash yolks with ⅛ teaspoon salt, mustard and the 2 tablespoons mayonnaise. Fill egg white halves with yolk mixture. Combine celery, scallions, ⅛ teaspoon salt and the 6 tablespoons mayonnaise. Spread over toasted muffins. Place 2 egg halves on each muffin half. Bake at 350° for 5 to 7 minutes or until heated through. Combine soup, milk and parsley. Drain and slice crabmeat; add to soup mixture. Heat through; serve over warm eggs and muffins.

Suggested wine:
Sparkling German Riesling
Sparkling Spanish Semi-Secco

eggs birmingham

Contributed by Eli Wallach, who played in TWICE AROUND THE PARK (1982). Mr. Wallach attributes the following recipe to Tennessee Williams, who mentions it in his one act play, "The Unsatisfactory Supper."

"Cut a hole in a piece of whole wheat toast. Drop an egg into the hole. Cover and steam."

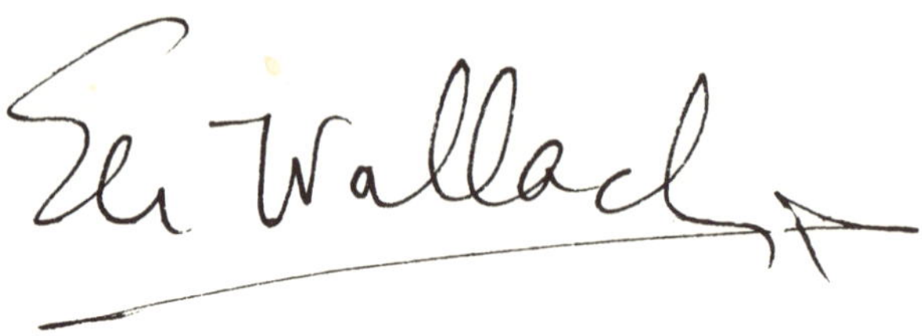

sausage apple ring

Serves: 8-10

Great for brunch. Serve scrambled eggs in the center.

2	**lbs. bulk sausage**	**½**	**cup milk**
1½	**cups cracker crumbs**	**¼**	**cup minced onion**
2	**eggs, slightly beaten**	**1**	**cup finely chopped apple**

Mix all ingredients with a fork. Either shape with hands into a ring or press into a 6-cup ring mold. Turn out onto a baking pan with sides. Bake at 350° for 1 hour. Put on paper towels to soak up excess grease.

Director's note: *Freezes well after baking; reheat in foil with few drops of water.*

Suggested wines:

Alsatian Gewurztraminer
California Sauvignon Blanc

"The critical period in matrimony is breakfast time."
Sir Alan Patrick Herbert

breakfast-brunch egg casserole

Serves: 6-8

2 cups garlic and onion croutons
1 cup grated Cheddar cheese
4 eggs
2 cups milk
½ tsp. salt
Dash pepper
⅛ tsp. onion powder
½ tsp. dry mustard
4 slices bacon, cooked, drained and crumbled

Combine croutons and cheese. Place in bottom of 8-inch square, greased, glass baking dish. Combine eggs, milk, salt, pepper, onion powder and dry mustard. Pour over crouton mixture. Bake at 325° for 45 to 55 minutes, or until set. Sprinkle with crumbled bacon. Serve hot.

Suggested wines:
French Champagne
California Sparkling Wine

boston common brunch

Serves: 8-12

8 slices day-old bread
2 cups fresh mushrooms, sliced
1 small onion, chopped
4 Tbsp. butter
2 cups diced ham
4 cups grated Cheddar *or* **Swiss cheese**
2 Tbsp. flour
2 tsp. dry mustard
8 eggs
3 cups milk
1 tsp. salt
¼ tsp. nutmeg

Remove crusts and cube bread into bite-size pieces. Spread in bottom of greased 9 x 13-inch baking dish. Saute mushrooms and onion in butter. Spoon over bread. Arrange ham on top. Combine cheese, flour and dry mustard; sprinkle over ham. Beat eggs; add milk, salt and nutmeg. Pour over everything. Tightly cover dish with foil; refrigerate at least 4 hours, preferably overnight. Bake in center of preheated 350° oven for 50 to 55 minutes or until set.

Suggested wines:
Dry White California Table Wine (Chablis)
California Grenache Rose

scranton brunch

Serves: 8

New York State Cheddar Cheese is among the best in the world. Colosse Cheese from Colosse, New York, makes all cheese dishes extra special.

4 chicken bouillon cubes
1 cup boiling water
16 slices French *or* Italian bread, buttered
1 lb. sharp Cheddar cheese, grated
8 eggs, beaten
1 cup white wine
1 tsp. nutmeg

Dissolve bouillon cubes in boiling water; let cool. Layer ½ the bread in greased casserole. Top with ½ the cheese. Repeat layers. Combine beaten eggs with wine, cooled bouillon and nutmeg. Pour over bread. Refrigerate at least 24 hours. Bake at 350° for 1 hour. Serve immediately.

Suggested wines:
Pennsylvania Seyval Blanc
New York State Dry Cayuga

clam quiche

Serves: 6-8

A change of taste in quiche.

1 15-oz. can Snow's New England Clam Chowder
½ cup chopped onion
½ cup sour cream
2 Tbsp. parsley flakes
4 eggs, beaten
Salt and pepper to taste
1 9-inch unbaked pie shell
3 slices American cheese

Preheat oven to 325°. Mix chowder, onion, sour cream, parsley, eggs, salt and pepper until thoroughly blended. Pour ⅔ of mixture into pie shell. Place cheese slices on mixture; pour remaining filling on top of cheese. Bake for 1 hour or until quiche puffs up and is lightly brown.

Suggested wines:
German Riesling (Kabinett)
California Johannisberg Riesling

"Put all your eggs in the one basket and -- WATCH THAT BASKET."
Mark Twain

ENCORE!

quiche lorraine

Crust

1⅓ cups flour
Pinch salt
3 oz. cream cheese, softened
½ cup margarine, softened

Preheat oven to 375°. Sift flour and salt; cut in margarine and cream cheese. Mixture will crumble, but eventually will form a ball. Set aside for 30 minutes. Roll out between wax paper and line 10-inch pie plate. Pour Filling into pastry; sprinkle with nutmeg. Bake for 35 to 40 minutes, until puffy and set.

Filling

8 thin slices cooked ham
8 oz. Swiss cheese, thinly sliced
2 cups sour cream
3 eggs plus 1 egg yolk
2 Tbsp. minced scallions including tops
Nutmeg

Cut ham and cheese into 1-inch pieces. Cover pastry, alternating ham and cheese. Combine remaining ingredients except nutmeg; mix well.

Suggested wines:

New York or California Johannisberg Riesling
French Anjou Rose

Cleante, *Tartuffe*

quiche

Serves: 6-8

- **1 lb. Monterey Jack cheese, grated**
- **1 lb. cottage cheese**
- **½ cup margarine, melted**
- **½ cup flour**
- **1 tsp. baking powder**
- **¼ cup finely chopped onion**
- **1 dozen eggs, beaten**
- **2 4-oz. cans green chilies, chopped**

Preheat oven to 400°. Mix all ingredients together; pour into greased 10 x 14-inch baking pan. Cover with foil; bake for 15 minutes. Reduce heat to 350°; remove foil; bake 30 minutes more. Turn oven off and leave quiche in oven until cool. Cut into 1-inch squares for appetizer or larger pieces for a meal.

Director's notes: *Reheat in heavy duty foil in low oven. In hot weather, serve at room temperature or cold.*

Suggested wines:

California Grenache Rose
California Fume Blanc

spinach-jarlsberg quiche

Serves: 6

- **4 oz. Jarlsberg cheese, shredded**
- **½ of 10-oz. pkg. frozen spinach, thawed and squeezed dry**
- **1 10-inch unbaked pie shell**
- **1 cup heavy cream**
- **1 cup milk**
- **3 eggs**
- **¼ cup minced onion**
- **¼ cup unsifted flour**
- **¾ tsp. salt**
- **¼ tsp. pepper**
- **¼ tsp. nutmeg**

Preheat oven to 400°. Sprinkle cheese and spinach over bottom of pie shell. In large bowl, combine cream, milk, eggs, onion, flour, salt, pepper and nutmeg; mix well. Pour egg mixture over cheese and spinach. Bake for 35 to 40 minutes.

Suggested wines:

New York Johannisberg Riesling
Austrian Pinot Blanc

"Being kissed by a man who didn't wax his moustache was like eating an egg without salt."
Rudyard Kipling

crustless ham and vegetable pie

Serves: 6

A tomato salad and warm crusty bread make this a complete supper.

¼ lb. fresh mushrooms, sliced
1 small green pepper, diced
1 small zucchini, diced
3 Tbsp. butter
1 cup diced ham
1 cup grated Mozzarella cheese
1 lb. Ricotta cheese
3 eggs
1 cup chopped spinach
Salt and pepper to taste
1 tsp. dill weed
2 Tbsp. olive oil

Preheat oven to 350°. Saute mushrooms, green pepper and zucchini in butter until crisp-tender. Add ham; cool. Combine cheeses and eggs. Add to ham mixture. Add spinach, salt, pepper, dill weed and olive oil. Pour into lightly oiled 9 x 11-inch baking dish. Bake about 45 minutes until set.

Suggested wines:
French Macon Villages
French Beaujolais

spinach or broccoli bars

Delicious as a main dish or appetizer.

4 Tbsp. butter
3 eggs
1 cup flour
1 cup milk
1 tsp. salt
1 tsp. baking powder
1 lb. grated Cheddar cheese
1 10-oz. pkg. frozen chopped spinach *or* frozen chopped broccoli, thawed and drained
1 small onion, chopped
½ cup chopped mushrooms (opt.)

Melt butter in 9 x 13-inch baking pan. Mix remaining ingredients together and spoon into pan. Bake at 350° for 35 minutes. Cool slightly before cutting. Can be served hot or at room temperature.

Suggested wines:
New York State Dry Cayuga
New York State Chardonnay

ringtum ditty

Serves: 6

- **1 10¾-oz. cream of tomato soup**
- **½ cup water**
- **2 medium onions, sliced**
- **1 lb. American cheese, sliced**
- **1 tsp. paprika**
- **½ tsp. salt**
- **1 tsp. dry mustard**
- **½ tsp. pepper**
- **1 tsp. Worcestershire sauce**
- **3 eggs, separated**
- **Toast**

Mix soup and water in top of double boiler. Add onions; simmer over direct heat 10 minutes. Place over boiling water; add cheese and cook, stirring, until cheese is melted. Add seasonings which have been mixed with beaten egg yolks. Beat egg whites until stiff but not dry. Fold into cheese mixture, stirring until blended. Serve on toast.

Suggested wines:

Italian Soave
French White Bordeaux

bonny's shrimp casserole

Serves: 6-8

- **½ lb. shrimp**
- **½ lb. Cheddar cheese, grated**
- **6 slices white bread**
- **½ cup butter, melted**
- **1¾ cups milk**
- **3 eggs**
- **½ tsp. dry mustard**
- **Salt and pepper to taste**

Remove crusts and cube bread. In 9-inch square greased pan, layer ½ the shrimp, cheese and bread. Drizzle butter over mixture. Layer remaining shrimp, cheese and bread. Mix milk, eggs, mustard, salt and pepper; pour over mixture. Cover pan with foil; refrigerate overnight. Bake, covered, at 350° for 50 minutes.

Suggested wines:

German Mosel Spatlese
California French Colombard

"Many's the long night I've dreamed of cheese -- toasted, mostly."
Treasure Island, Robert Louis Stevenson

Central Action

Beef

Veal

Pork

Ham

Lamb

Photo on p. 123:
Twice Around the Park, 1982 - Anne Jackson (Margaret; Edie), Eli Wallach (Gus; Leon)

baked eye-of-round with rosemary

Serves: 8-10

Terrific for cocktail party suppers as well as dinner.

Eye of Round beef roast
Seasoned salt
Garlic salt
Black pepper
1 tsp. crushed rosemary
1 tsp. shortening

If convenient, season meat 2 days before cooking; otherwise, season the night before cooking.* Rub entire surface of meat liberally with mixture of seasonings. Wrap tightly in aluminum foil and refrigerate. One hour before cooking, remove from refrigerator and remove foil to bring meat to room temperature. Brown meat on all sides in the teaspoon shortening (just enough to grease skillet). Place in shallow baking pan. Bake at 325° to desired doneness; rare, 15 minutes per pound; medium, 20 minutes per pound; well done, 22 minutes per pound. Thinly sliced, a 5-pound roast will serve 8 to 10. For cocktail suppers for 20, prepare two 5-pound roasts.

Director's note: **Meat can be seasoned just before cooking, but is better if done some time ahead.*

Suggested wines:
California Cabernet Sauvignon
Spanish Rioja

steak diane

Serves: 2

2 rib eye steaks
1 Tbsp. butter
Salt and pepper to taste
2 Tbsp. cognac
1 Tbsp. dry sherry wine
2 Tbsp. butter
Juice of ½ lemon
½ tsp. hot English mustard
2 tsp. chopped parsley
2 tsp. Worcestershire sauce
1 Tbsp. chopped chives

Saute steaks in the 1 tablespoon butter over medium high heat to desired doneness, adding salt and pepper as they cook. Reduce heat; add cognac and sherry. Flame. When flame dies, remove steaks and keep warm in oven. Add remaining ingredients to pan juices. Heat to bubbling; pour over steaks. Serve immediately.

Suggested wines:
Red Bordeaux
California Merlot

fabulous beef

Serves: 6

The name says it all!

- **1 4-lb. eye roast of beef**
- **Garlic cloves, cut in halves**
- **2 tsp. seasoned tenderizer**
- **1 Tbsp. vegetable oil**
- **1 cup Port wine**

Slit surface of meat in many places and insert garlic in slits. Sprinkle tenderizer over all. Poke holes in roast, using sharp kitchen fork. Pour oil over roast. Bake in roasting pan, uncovered, at 190° for 4 hours. During the last ½ hour of cooking, pour on wine. This makes a clear gravy. The meat is rare.

Director's note: *To reheat leftovers, wrap in foil and reheat at 200° for 45 minutes.*

Suggested wine: California Cabernet Sauvignon or Zinfandel

fillet of beef vermouth

- **4 fillets of beef, 1-inch thick**
- **2 Tbsp. butter**
- **½ cup sliced green olives**
- **¾ tsp. salt**
- **¼ tsp. freshly ground black pepper**
- **¼ cup dry vermouth**
- **¼ cup heavy cream**

Remove any fat from meat. Melt butter in frying pan. Add fillets and olives. Cook over high heat for 2 minutes on each side. Shake pan a few times. Add salt, pepper, vermouth and cream. Cook over low heat for 4 minutes or to desired degree of doneness. Arrange fillets on a hot serving platter; pour sauce over. Serve at once.

Director's note: *If a thicker sauce is desired, after removing meat to heated platter, cook sauce a few more minutes to thicken.*

Suggested wines:
French Red Bordeaux
California Merlot

"Oh, tough as a steak was Yukon Jake
Hard-boiled as a picnic egg."
Edward E. Paramore, Jr.

pot roast "center stage"

Serves: 4-6

The noodles are a not-to-be-missed treat!

- 1 2 to 3-lb. pot roast
- 1 large onion, sliced
- Red wine
- 4 Tbsp. vegetable oil
- 4 to 6 Tbsp. water
- 4 Tbsp. flour
- 2 beef bouillon cubes
- ½ cup hot water
- ½ tsp. crushed garlic
- ½ tsp. rosemary
- ½ tsp. thyme
- Salt and pepper
- 4 large carrots, scraped

Marinate meat and onion overnight in red wine. Remove meat from marinade. Drain onion rings; reserve wine. In Dutch oven, saute onion in oil until soft; remove and set aside. Brown meat in oil; remove. Combine the 4 tablespoons water and flour; add to oil and stir until dark brown. Dissolve bouillon cubes in the ½ cup hot water. Add with reserved wine to pot. Add garlic and seasonings. Return beef to pot and add carrots. Simmer, tightly covered, for 3 hours. Serve with Sour Cream Noodles.

Sour Cream Noodles

- 1 8-oz. pkg. noodles
- 1 cup sour cream
- ¾ cup grated Parmesan cheese

Cook noodles according to package directions. Drain; rinse with cold water. Mix with sour cream. Add ½ cup of the cheese; place in buttered casserole. Sprinkle remaining cheese on top. Bake at 225° for 1 hour.

Suggested wines:

French Rhone Red
California Cabernet Sauvignon

"break-a-leg" beef

Serves: 8

Break-a-leg in theater parlance is good-luck; to us this is good-eating!

- **1 4-lb. beef rump pot roast**
- **2 Tbsp. flour**
- **2 Tbsp. vegetable oil**
- **2 medium onions, sliced**
- **1 12-oz. can beer**
- **1 cup water**
- **1 clove garlic, crushed**
- **1 Tbsp. parsley flakes**
- **¼ cup brown sugar, firmly packed**
- **1 bay leaf**
- **¼ tsp. cinnamon**
- **2 tsp. salt**
- **¼ tsp. pepper**
- **1 11-oz. pkg. mixed dried fruit**
- **3 Tbsp. flour**

Dredge meat with the 2 tablespoons flour. Heat oil in 4 to 5-quart Dutch oven; lightly brown meat on all sides. Reduce heat; remove meat from kettle. Add onion and cook, stirring occasionally, until soft but not brown. Add beer, water, garlic, parsley, brown sugar, bay leaf, cinnamon, salt and pepper. Bring to boil over high heat, scraping in the brown particles that cling to the bottom and sides of pan. Return meat to the Dutch oven. Cover tightly; braise in a 300° oven for about 2 hours. Remove from oven and add the dried fruit; return for 1 more hour or until meat is tender.

Remove meat and fruit and keep warm. Pour gravy into a bowl. Skim 4 tablespoons of fat and return to Dutch oven. Skim remaining fat and discard. Add the 3 tablespoons flour to fat in Dutch oven; blend until smooth. Gradually add gravy; cook over low heat until thickened, stirring constantly. Arrange meat and fruit on a platter; spoon a little gravy over top. Pass extra gravy separately.

Suggested wines:

French "Cru" Beaujolais
California Zinfandel

"One can become a cook, but one is born a roaster of meat."
Anthelme Brillat-Savarin

sirloin with sauce provencale

Serves: 6-8

Sirloin steak to serve 6 to 8
4 tomatoes, peeled, seeded, cut into 6 wedges each
½ tsp. sugar
2 Tbsp. butter *or* margarine
¼ cup chopped scallions
½ cup dry sherry
½ cup butter *or* margarine
3 cloves garlic, minced
2 Tbsp. snipped parsley

Sprinkle tomato wedges with sugar; set aside. Melt the 2 tablespoons butter in frying pan. Add scallions; just heat through. Add sherry; cook and stir until liquid is slightly reduced. Add tomatoes; heat through (do not allow tomatoes to lose their shape). Add the ½ cup butter, garlic and parsley. Heat, stirring gently, just until butter melts. Season to taste with salt and pepper. Serve over broiled steak.

Suggested wine: Italian Amarone

Set, *Sleuth*

beef roulades

Serves: 6

Nifty for entertaining!

- 3 lbs. sirloin, cut into ½-inch thick slices (about 5)
- Salt and pepper
- ½ cup chopped onion
- ½ cup chopped green pepper
- ¼ cup butter *or* margarine
- 1 lb. sausage meat
- ½ cup fine dry bread crumbs
- ¼ cup flour
- ⅓ cup vegetable oil
- 1½ cups sliced carrots
- ½ cup sliced onion
- 1 16-oz. can whole tomatoes in tomato puree
- 1 beef bouillon cube
- 1 cup boiling water
- 2 Tbsp. flour

Trim excess fat from meat; cut each piece into 3 portions. Pound meat on both sides with mallet to 1/16-inch thickness. Sprinkle meat lightly on both sides with salt and pepper. Cook chopped onion and green pepper in melted butter until tender, stirring occasionally; set aside.

In bowl or food processor, mix sausage, cooked vegetable mixture and bread crumbs. Spoon about 3 tablespoons stuffing onto each slice of meat. Roll up; secure with toothpicks. Roll meat rolls in the ¼ cup flour. Heat oil in large frying pan; add meat and cook until lightly browned on all sides. Reduce heat; remove meat from frying pan; add carrots and sliced onion. Cook vegetables, stirring occasionally until crisp-tender. Return meat to pan; add tomatoes. Dissolve bouillon cube in boiling water; add to tomatoes. Cover frying pan; cook 60 to 70 minutes over low heat until meat is tender.

Remove from heat. Place meat rolls in warm serving dish. Pour meat gravy into 1-quart measuring cup. Skim off 3 tablespoons fat; return it to frying pan. Skim off remaining fat and discard. Blend the 2 tablespoons flour into fat in pan. Gradually add gravy in measuring cup; cook over low heat until thickened, stirring constantly. Serve gravy over meat rolls.

Suggested wines:

California Zinfandel
French Gamay

"A tale without love is like beef without mustard: an insipid dish."
Anatole France

beef stroganoff (salt-free)

Serves: 4

1 lb. top round steak
Juice of ½ lemon
4 Tbsp. butter (approx.)
½ cup chopped onion
½ cup sliced mushrooms
1 Tbsp. flour
1 pint sour cream
Cooked noodles or rice

Cut steak into narrow strips; marinate in lemon juice at least 20 minutes. In large frying pan, melt 1 tablespoon of the butter. Saute onion until lightly browned; remove. In same pan, saute mushrooms, adding butter if needed; remove. In same pan, saute meat, turning to cook quickly and evenly. Sprinkle with flour. Return onion and mushrooms to pan. Remove from heat.* Add sour cream quickly, stirring with a whisk. Re-heat if necessary over very low heat. Serve over buttered noodles or rice.

Director's note: **Stroganoff can be prepared to this point in advance and refrigerated. To serve: reheat slowly until heated through. Remove from heat. Add sour cream as above.*

Suggested wines:
California Pinot Noir
French Red Burgundy

pepper steak with red wine

Serves: 6

2 lbs. round steak
2 Tbsp. olive oil
½ tsp. minced garlic
1 Tbsp. butter
½ cup sliced fresh mushrooms *or* 1 large can mushrooms, drained
3 to 4 green peppers, slivered
3 large onions, thinly sliced
1 tsp. salt
1 tsp. black pepper
½ tsp. minced garlic
¾ cup red wine

Cut meat into narrow strips; brown in olive oil. Add ½ teaspoon garlic. Remove meat from oil; set aside. Add butter; saute mushrooms, green pepper and onion. Add salt, pepper and ½ teaspoon garlic; mix well. Stir in wine; return meat to mixture. Cook, covered, for 1½ hours. Serve with rice.

Suggested wines:
French Chateauneuf du Pape
Australian Cabernet Sauvignon

ragout

Serves: 4-6

2 lbs. sirloin, trimmed and cut into ¼-inch strips
2 Tbsp. butter
3 Tbsp. flour
½ cup white wine
¾ cup diced green pepper
½ cup diced onion
1½ cups sliced mushrooms
1 Tbsp. butter
1 4-oz. jar pimiento, drained and sliced
½ tsp. salt
Dash bottled hot pepper sauce
Dash Worcestershire sauce

Saute sirloin in the 2 tablespoons butter just until brown; remove and set aside. Pour drippings into measuring cup; skim 2 tablespoons off top and place in saucepan. Add flour and blend well. Cook and stir until bubbly, about 1 minute. Remove from heat. Add water to juices remaining in measuring cup to make 1 cup; add to flour mixture and blend. Cook, stirring constantly, until thickened, about 5 minutes. Stir in wine; set aside. In same frying pan saute green pepper, onion and mushrooms in the 1 tablespoon butter until tender. Add beef, gravy, pimiento, salt, hot pepper sauce and Worcestershire sauce. Bring to a boil, then simmer 30 minutes. Add more water at any time if a thinner gravy is desired. Serve with buttered noodles or rice.

Suggested wines:
Spanish Rioja
California Red Table Wine

"He hath eaten me out of house and home."
Henry IV, Shakespeare

hungarian goulash

Serves: 4

- 1 lb. beef, cubed
- ½ to 1 cup minced onion
- ½ tsp. dry mustard
- 1 tsp. paprika
- 2 Tbsp. brown sugar
- 1¼ tsp. salt
- 3 Tbsp. Worcestershire sauce
- ½ tsp. cider vinegar
- 6 Tbsp. catsup
- 1 cup water
- 3 Tbsp. flour
- ½ cup water
- 1 6-oz. pkg. noodles

Brown meat on all sides; add onion. Combine mustard, paprika, brown sugar and salt. Blend in Worcestershire, vinegar and catsup. Add to meat with the 1 cup water. Stir and cover. Cook over low heat 2½ hours until meat is tender. Blend flour with the ½ cup water; add to meat mixture. Stir until thickened. Cook noodles according to package directions. Serve goulash over noodles.

Suggested wines:

California Red Table Wine
Bulgarian Red Wine

ENCORE!

lazy weekend beef casserole

Serves: 4-5

An excellent and easy dish for entertaining. It improves with long, slow cooking.

- 1½ lbs. stew beef, cubed
- 1 10½-oz. can consomme
- 1 medium onion, chopped
- 1 tsp. salt
- ½ tsp. pepper
- ½ cup red wine
- ¼ cup bread crumbs
- ¼ cup flour
- Green pepper, diced (opt.)
- Mushrooms (opt.)

Place beef, consomme, onion, salt, pepper and wine in Dutch oven. Mix well. Mix bread crumbs and flour together. Stir into casserole. Cover and bake at 300° for 3 hours.

Director's note: *When doubling recipe, only double meat and wine. When tripling recipe, triple meat only, doubling all other ingredients. Progressions for large groups should be made in this manner.*

Suggested wines:

California Cabernet
French Red Bordeaux

stefado - greek beef stew

Serves: 4

An interesting variation of an old standby.

1 lb. stew beef
Vegetable oil
3 to 4 large onions, sliced
½ 6-oz. can tomato paste
⅓ cup red wine
2 Tbsp. wine vinegar
1 Tbsp. brown sugar
2 cloves garlic
1 inch of stick cinnamon
¾ cup water
3 Tbsp. raisins
1 bay leaf
10 whole cloves
¼ tsp. ground cumin

Put small amount of oil in heavy pan; add beef. Cook and stir until meat loses red color, but do not brown. Add onion; saute until golden. Combine tomato paste with remaining ingredients; add to pan with beef and onion. Mix well and bring to a boil. Lower heat to simmer; cook, covered, for 2 hours. You may need to add more water. Serve over hot noodles.

Suggested wines:
Chilean Cabernet Sauvignon
Italian Barbera d'Alba

sweet-sour stew

Serves: 4-5

Something the whole family will enjoy.

2 lbs. beef *or* lamb stew meat, cut into 1-inch cubes
¼ cup flour
1 tsp. salt
Dash pepper
¼ cup vegetable oil
1 cup water
½ cup catsup
¼ cup brown sugar
¼ cup vinegar
1 Tbsp. Worcestershire sauce
1 tsp. salt
1 cup chopped onion
3 carrots, cut up

Combine flour, 1 teaspoon salt, and pepper; dredge meat with mixture. Brown meat on all sides in hot oil. Combine water, catsup, brown sugar, vinegar, Worcestershire sauce and 1 teaspoon salt. Stir into browned meat; add onion. Cover and cook over low heat for 45 minutes, stirring once or twice. Add carrots; cook 45 minutes more or until meat and carrots are tender.

Suggested wines:
California Merlot
French Gamay

beef barbecue

Serves: 6-8

Great on hamburger buns.

3 lbs. lean stew beef
2 cups water
1 large onion, chopped
2 Tbsp. butter
1 cup catsup
2 Tbsp. vinegar
2 Tbsp. brown sugar
4 Tbsp. lemon juice
3 Tbsp. Worcestershire sauce
1 tsp. mustard
1 tsp. salt
Dash red pepper

Cook beef in water slowly for 3 to 4 hours. Shred meat; set aside. Brown onion in butter. Add remaining ingredients and cook 20 minutes. Add sauce to meat; cover and refrigerate overnight. Reheat slowly.

Director's note: *Must stand overnight to taste best. May be frozen after cooking.*

Suggested wines:
Spanish Rioja
Italian Sicilian Red

short ribs burgundy

Serves: 4-6

4 lbs. of 3-inch *lean* short ribs
1 cup mashed tomatoes
1 cup consomme
½ cup Burgundy wine
¼ cup finely chopped onion
2 Tbsp. horseradish
1 tsp. salt
1 tsp. pepper
¼ tsp. ginger
2 bay leaves
Flour (opt.)

Brown and drain short ribs. Place in covered casserole along with remaining ingredients. Cover and bake at 350° for 2½ hours or until meat is tender. Remove meat from sauce. Thicken sauce with flour if desired. Serve ribs on heated platter; pass sauce separately.

Suggested wine: French "Cru" Beaujolais

"I am a great eater of beef, and I believe that does harm to my wit."
Twelfth Night, Shakespeare

7-layer casserole

Serves: 4

A family favorite.

1 lb. lean ground beef
3 large carrots, chunked
3 stalks celery, chopped
1 large potato, thinly sliced
1 medium onion, thinly sliced
1 4-oz. can mushrooms, drained
1 green pepper, chopped
Salt and pepper to taste
¼ tsp. basil
¼ tsp. tarragon
1 10¾-oz. can cream of tomato soup

In a 9 x 13-inch baking dish, layer ingredients in order listed. Cover with foil. Bake at 350° for 1½ hours.

Director's note: *Can be prepared ahead and refrigerated until baking.*

Suggested wines:
California Red Table Wine
French Cotes du Rhone

The Ghost of Christmas Present, *A Christmas Carol*

"2nd man" meatloaf

Serves: 6-8

1½ lbs. lean ground beef
½ lb. bulk pork sausage
¾ cup milk
1 cup herb-seasoned stuffing mix
2 Tbsp. finely chopped onion
½ cup sliced green olives
2 eggs, slightly beaten
1 tsp. salt
Dash pepper

Pour milk over stuffing mix; set aside until milk is absorbed. Combine remaining ingredients. Add stuffing mixture; mix thoroughly. Place in 5 x 9-inch loaf pan. Bake at 350° about 1½ hours.

Suggested wines:
Italian Inferno
Rumanian Cabernet Sauvignon

ENCORE!

two-ton casserole

Serves: 6

1 lb. ground beef
1 onion, minced
3 Tbsp. vegetable oil
3 8-oz. cans tomato sauce
1 cup Burgundy wine
¼ tsp. oregano
Pinch of rosemary, basil and marjoram
1 Tbsp. sugar
½ tsp. salt
¼ tsp. pepper
½ lb. thin spaghetti, broken in 2-inch lengths
1 cup (¼ lb.) grated Cheddar cheese

In large skillet, saute beef and onion in oil until brown. Add tomato sauce, wine, oregano, rosemary, basil, marjoram, sugar, salt and pepper. Simmer, covered, stirring occasionally for 1 hour. Meanwhile, cook spaghetti and drain. Add to sauce with ½ cup of the cheese. Place in 3-quart baking dish; refrigerate. About 1½ hours before serving, sprinkle casserole with remaining cheese. Cover and bake at 325° for 45 minutes. Uncover and bake 30 minutes more.

Director's note: *Can be made 2 days in advance and refrigerated until baking time. Freezes well after baking.*

Suggested wines:
Italian Barbera
California Zinfandel

ENCORE!

trittini

Serves: 6-8

- 2 lbs. ground beef
- ½ cup minced onion
- 2 6-oz. cans tomato paste
- 2 8-oz. cans tomato sauce
- ¾ lb. mushrooms
- 2 tsp. dried basil
- 2 tsp. sugar
- 2 tsp. parsley flakes
- ¼ tsp. pepper
- 1 tsp. oregano
- 2 10-oz. pkgs. frozen spinach, thawed
- 1 lb. cottage cheese
- 6 oz. Mozzarella cheese

Brown ground beef and onion together. Add tomato paste, tomato sauce, mushrooms, basil, sugar, parsley flakes, pepper and oregano. Simmer 15 minutes. Meanwhile combine spinach and cottage cheese. Divide meat mixture into 5 equal portions. Divide spinach and cottage cheese mixture the same way. In a greased 9 x 13-inch baking pan, place 3 layers of spinach cheese mixture and 2 layers of meat mixture, alternating layers. Crumble ½ of Mozzarella cheese over top. Alternate remaining mixtures layering 3 layers of meat and 2 layers of spinach cheese. Sprinkle remaining Mozzarella cheese on top. Bake at 350° for 30 minutes or until bubbly.

Director's note: *Can be prepared in advance and refrigerated until ready to bake.*

Suggested wines:

Chianti Classico
Zinfandel

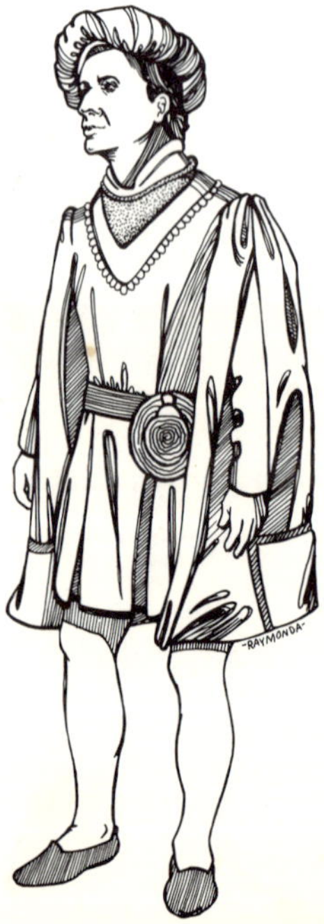

Bassanio, *The Merchant of Venice*

cincinnati chili

Serves: 4-6

Contributed by a member's daughter-in-law who lives in Cincinnati. Supposedly this authentic Cincinnati Chili is served several ways, the most popular being a "Four Way", that is, on spaghetti with grated cheese and onion.

2 lbs. lean ground beef
1 quart water
2 medium onions, minced
2 8-oz. cans tomato sauce
5 whole allspice
¼ tsp. ground red pepper
1 tsp. cumin
4 Tbsp. chili powder
1 tsp. cinnamon
½ oz. unsweetened baking chocolate
4 cloves garlic
2 Tbsp. vinegar
1 large bay leaf
5 whole cloves
2 tsp. Worcestershire sauce
1½ tsp. salt

Add ground beef to water in 4-quart kettle. Stir until beef separates to a fine texture. Boil gently for 30 minutes. Add remaining ingredients; stir to blend. Return to a boil; reduce heat and simmer, uncovered, about 3 hours (during the last hour, kettle may be covered when chili reaches desired consistency). Refrigerate overnight. Before reheating, remove any fat from surface of chili.

To serve:

1. as is, in a bowl
2. with accoutrements: beans (cooked separately), chopped onions, grated cheese, sour cream
3. over spaghetti with any or all accoutrements
4. on a hot dog with any or all accoutrements (try using cornbread instead of hot dog buns)

Suggested wine: Italian Barolo or Barbaresco

diane's chili

Serves: 6

In Fayetteville, New York, the "Resolution Run" on New Year's Day has become a tradition where over 200 people, some in costume, travel a route through Fayetteville and Manlius and resolve "to start off on the right foot by burning off their excess alcohol from New Year's Eve." With "champagne stops" along the way, perhaps more is consumed than burned off, but the tradition, started by Jerry and Diane Smith, continues undaunted with the runners ending at Hullar's Restaurant in Fayetteville for Diane's chili.

1 lb. ground beef
1 Tbsp. vegetable oil
1 large onion, diced
1 green pepper, diced
1 or 2 1-lb. cans red kidney beans, drained
1 large can tomato puree with tomatoes
1 8-oz. can tomato sauce
3 Tbsp. hot chili powder
1 to 1½ tsp. salt
1 bay leaf
Paprika to taste
Cayenne pepper to taste
3 to 4 Tbsp. ground cumin (opt.)
1 to 2 Tbsp. cumin seed (opt.)

Brown meat in oil. Add onion and pepper; saute until soft. Add beans, tomato puree, tomato sauce, chili powder, salt, bay leaf, paprika, cayenne pepper, cumin and cumin seed. Cover and simmer for 1½ hours. Serve hot. Freezes well.

Suggested wine: Italian Barolo *or* Barbaresco

"Double, double toil and trouble; Fire burn and cauldron bubble."
Macbeth, Shakespeare

summer stock pizza

Serves: 4

Crust

- **4 oz. Cheddar cheese, grated**
- **4 oz. Mozzarella cheese, grated**
- **4 cups grated zucchini**
- **2 eggs**
- **2 Tbsp. Bisquick**
- **¼ tsp. salt**

Combine crust ingredients. Press into 10 x 15-inch greased baking dish, bringing dough up the sides about ¼-inch to form a rim. Bake at 400° for 15 minutes. Spoon beef and tomato Topping over crust. Sprinkle cheeses on top. Bake at 400° for 20 minutes.

Toppings

- **1 medium onion**
- **1 clove garlic, minced**
- **1 lb. ground beef**
- **2 Tbsp. vegetable oil**
- **1 cup tomato sauce**
- **Salt, pepper to taste**
- **1 tsp. oregano**
- **2 oz. Mozzarella cheese, grated**
- **2 oz. Cheddar cheese, grated**

Saute onion, garlic and beef in oil for 10 minutes. Drain. Add tomato sauce, salt, pepper and oregano. Mix well.

Suggested wines:

Spanish Rioja
Italian Valpolicella

razz-a-ma-tazz hash

Serves: 4

- **1 15-oz. can corned beef hash**
- **2 Tbsp. chopped onion**
- **1 clove garlic, minced**
- **Dash freshly ground pepper**
- **2 eggs, beaten**
- **½ cup sour cream**
- **¼ cup Burgundy**
- **1 cup soft bread crumbs**
- **1 Tbsp. butter *or* margarine, melted**
- **Dash paprika**

Combine hash, onion, garlic, pepper, eggs, sour cream and Burgundy; mix well. Spoon into an 8-inch pie plate. Combine bread crumbs, butter and paprika; sprinkle over hash mixture. Bake at 350° for 25 to 30 minutes. Slice into wedges and serve hot.

Suggested wines:

Chicken Cabernet Sauvignon
California Red Table Wine

ENCORE!

pizza fondue

Great for Sunday supper, after skiing, football games, etc.

- **½ lb. ground beef**
- **1 onion, chopped**
- **2 Tbsp. butter *or* margarine**
- **1½ tsp. fennel seeds**
- **1½ tsp. oregano**
- **¼ tsp. garlic powder**
- **1 Tbsp. cornstarch**
- **2 10½-oz. cans pizza sauce**
- **10 oz. Cheddar cheese, grated**
- **1 cup grated Mozzarella cheese**
- **French *or* Italian bread**

Brown beef and onion in margarine. Stir seasonings and cornstarch into pizza sauce; add to meat. Stir well. When sauce thickens and boils, add both cheeses. Heat and stir until cheeses melt. Transfer to fondue pot. Serve with cubes of French or Italian bread to be dipped into sauce with extra long forks.

Suggested wines:

Italian Valpolicella
Spanish Rioja

She Stoops to Conquer

veal au currante

Serves: 8

- 2 lbs. veal, thinly sliced
- 1 cup flour
- ¼ tsp. salt
- ½ tsp. paprika
- ½ tsp. sage
- ⅓ cup butter
- ⅓ cup vegetable oil
- 3 Tbsp. catsup
- 1 10½-oz. can consomme
- ½ cup currant jelly
- ¼ cup dry sherry
- Pinch of garlic salt and cayenne pepper
- 1 to 2 cups sliced mushrooms

Wipe veal dry. Combine flour, salt, paprika and sage. Dredge veal in flour mixture; brown quickly in hot butter and oil. Place in 9 x 13-inch baking dish. In same pan with butter and oil, combine catsup, consomme, currant jelly, sherry, garlic salt and cayenne. Stir and bring to a boil; pour over veal. Add mushrooms to casserole. Cover with foil and bake at 325° for 60 minutes.

Director's note: *This dish can be prepared, refrigerated and baked when desired.*

Suggested wines:
French Sancerre
California Sauvignon Blanc

veal marsala

Serves: 6-8

- 1½ to 2 lbs. veal scaloppine
- Flour
- 4 Tbsp. butter
- 4 Tbsp. olive oil
- 2 cloves garlic, sliced
- 1 cup Marsala wine
- 1 lb. mushrooms, sliced
- ½ tsp. oregano
- ½ cup tomato sauce
- 2 tsp. Worcestershire sauce
- 1 tsp. sugar

Dredge veal lightly with flour. Heat butter and oil in frying pan; saute garlic; remove. Brown veal quickly on both sides in same pan; transfer to hot platter and keep warm. Add wine to pan; simmer 5 minutes. Add remaining ingredients. Cook, stirring occasionally, until mushrooms are tender. Pour sauce over veal; serve immediately.

Director's note: *Add a little water or additional wine if desired.*

Suggested wines:
Italian Spanna
Italian Vino Nobile di Montepulciano

dick's pork roast

Contributed by attorney Richard Scolaro, who demonstrates his culinary skills at the Country Kitchen in Fayetteville, New York.

- **1 3½-lb. pork tenderloin**
- **5 Tbsp. peanut oil**
- **Juice of ½ lemon**
- **3 sprigs parsley**
- **1 bay leaf**
- **1 sprig dried savory** *or* **sage**
- **Pinch of oregano**
- **1 tsp. dry mustard**
- **3 cups white wine**
- **3 cups brown stock** *or* **veal stock**
- **Salt and pepper to taste**
- **5 cloves garlic, minced**
- **5 shallots, minced**
- **1 cup mixed raisins and walnuts, minced (opt.)**
- **¼ cup demiglaze**
- **½ cup Madeira wine**
- **½ pint heavy cream**

Combine oil, lemon juice, parsley, bay leaf, savory, oregano and dry mustard. Rub mixture into tenderloin, covering all sides. Place meat in roasting pan just large enough to hold it; add wine and stock. Refrigerate for 4 hours, turning meat occasionally. (Follow optional direction in Director's note at this point.)

Preheat oven to 350°. Add garlic and shallots to roasting pan. Cover pan and roast until meat thermometer reaches 135° (about 1½ to 2 hours). Remove cover and continue cooking until meat thermometer reaches 145°. Remove meat to warm platter; pour liquid in pan into saucepan. Return meat to roasting pan; cook until thermometer reaches 155°. Meanwhile, gently boil cooking liquid until reduced to 2 cups. When meat is ready, remove to platter and keep warm. Add demi-glaze to cooking juices. Strain. Return to heat; add Madeira and cream. Simmer about 2 minutes. Sauce may be thickened with roux, if desired. Season to taste.

Director's note: *After marinating meat, with sharpening steel pierce meat lengthwise through center. Force mixture of walnuts and raisins into both ends until tightly packed. Return meat to roasting pan with marinade; continue as above.*

Suggested wines:

French Pouilly Fume
French Sancerre

"Good wine is a good familiar creature if it be well used."
Othello, Shakespeare

indonesian pork roast

Serves: 8

Fabulous flavor! Fruit salad and rice are perfect with this.

1 4-lb. loin pork roast
1 cup chicken broth
½ cup soy sauce
¼ cup sugar
1 clove garlic, crushed

Remove as much fat from loin as possible. Brown in heavy Dutch oven. Reduce heat. Mix broth, soy sauce, sugar and garlic. Pour mixture over meat. Cover and simmer roast on top of stove for 3 hours (longer, if desired). Turn roast over during cooking to insure that flavor permeates meat. Serve meat on platter; pass sauce separately.

Suggested wines:
New York State Chardonnay
French St. Veran

smothered pork chops

Serves: 4-6

Grand old family recipe -- excellent with rice.

4 to 6 pork chops
½ cup apple jelly
½ cup soy sauce
¼ cup catsup
1 clove garlic, minced
2 lbs. sauerkraut
1 Tbsp. cornstarch
1 Tbsp. hot water

Place chops in large shallow baking dish. Combine jelly, soy sauce, catsup and garlic. Pour over chops. Spread sauerkraut over all. Bake at 325° for 90 minutes. To make gravy, combine cornstarch and water. Stir into pan juices. Cook over low heat; stir until thick.

Suggested wine: New York State Chardonnay

"prompter side" pork chops

Enough for 50 chops

- **Pork chops**
- **Worcestershire sauce**
- **6 Tbsp. salt**
- **6 Tbsp. sugar**
- **1 Tbsp. dry lemon gelatin**
- **2 Tbsp. MSG**
- **2½ Tbsp. black pepper**
- **1 Tbsp. paprika**

Coat chops lightly with Worcestershire sauce. Mix other ingredients together. Coat chops with mixture.* Grill approximately 15 minutes on each side or until done.

Director's note: **Mixture may be stored in airtight container in refrigerator indefinitely.*

Suggested wines:

French Beaujolais
California Gamay

kapoosta

Serves: 6

Serve hot with dark rye bread, coffee or beer.

- **2 lbs. fresh pork ribs**
- **2 Tbsp. vegetable oil**
- **1 large onion, chopped**
- **1 medium head cabbage, shredded**
- **1 2-lb. bag sauerkraut**
- **Freshly ground pepper to taste**
- **2 Tbsp. brown sugar**
- **1 tsp. Gravy Magic (opt.)**

Separate ribs between each bone. Brown pork in large pan with oil and onion. Add remaining ingredients. Cover and simmer until meat falls from bone. Stir now and then.

Director's note: *Can be frozen after cooking.*

Suggested wines:

California Sauvignon Blanc
German Beer or Ale

**"'Tis not the meat, but 'tis the appetite
Makes eating a delight."**
Sir John Suckling

mother's barbecued spareribs

Serves: 4

- 2 lbs. pork spareribs*
- ½ cup light molasses
- ½ cup catsup
- ½ cup chopped onion
- 1 clove garlic, minced
- 4 strips of orange peel, diced
- 2 Tbsp. orange juice
- 3 whole cloves
- 1 tsp. vinegar
- 1 Tbsp. vegetable oil
- ½ tsp. prepared mustard
- ¼ tsp. salt
- ¼ tsp. pepper
- 1 Tbsp. Bovril (opt.)
- ½ tsp. Worcestershire sauce
- ¼ tsp. Tabasco
- 1 Tbsp. margarine

In 325° oven, bake spareribs, one-layer deep, in shallow pan covered with foil for ½ hour. Pour fat off ribs, recover and bake another ½ hour. Make barbecue sauce by combining remaining ingredients; boil 5 minutes. Pour fat off ribs again; pour sauce over ribs. Increase temperature to 400°. Roast uncovered, basting often, for 45 minutes or until tender and glazed.

Director's note: **Beef can be used and will cook faster because of less fat.*

Suggested wines:

French Hermitage (red)
California Petite Sirah

ham-actor style

Serves: 16

Great for a late night buffet after the theater.

- Cold baked ham slices
- 1 tsp. dry mustard
- 1 tsp. paprika
- ½ tsp. ginger
- Dash of salt
- 1 Tbsp. water
- Grated rind of 2 oranges
- 2 Tbsp. orange juice
- 1 Tbsp. lemon juice
- ¼ cup currant *or* apple jelly
- 2 Tbsp. port wine
- ½ orange, sliced and quartered

In saucepan, combine dry mustard, paprika, ginger, salt, water, orange rind and juices. Let stand 30 minutes. Add jelly to mixture; heat and stir until jelly is dissolved. Cool and strain. Add wine and orange slices. Arrange thin, cold, ham slices on platter; serve with sauce.

Suggested wines:

French Vin Rose
California Sparkling Blanc de Noir

baked ham with spicy sauce

Serves: 8-10

1 6-lb. boneless fully-cooked ham *or* **5-lb. canned ham**
1 cup orange *or* **pineapple juice**
3/4 cup light brown sugar, packed
2 tsp. dry mustard
1/4 tsp. cloves
1/8 tsp. nutmeg
1/2 tsp. ginger
1 Tbsp. rum *or* **2 tsp. rum extract**
Whole cloves
1/2 cup raisins, plumped in boiling water
1 Tbsp. lemon juice
1 Tbsp. cornstarch
1 Tbsp. water
1/2 Tbsp. rum *or* **1 tsp. rum extract**

Mix juice, sugar, mustard, cloves, nutmeg and ginger; bring to a boil. Simmer, stirring, until sugar is dissolved. Add 1 tablespoon rum. Pierce ham several times with fork; cover with marinade. Let stand 4 hours, basting occasionally with marinade. Remove ham; place in baking pan. Bake at 325° for 1 hour, basting occasionally. Remove from oven and score with knife. Stud with cloves. Increase temperature to 425°; bake 30 minutes longer, basting ***frequently***. Remove ham. Add drained raisins and lemon juice to pan drippings. Blend cornstarch and the 1 tablespoon water; stir into mixture. Cook stirring, until thickened. Add 1/2 tablespoon rum. Serve sauce with ham.

Suggested wine: Alsatian Gewurztraminer

gourmet ham

1 12-lb. boneless ham
Whole cloves
1 15-oz. can crushed *or* **chunk pineapple**
1 lb. brown sugar
1 small jar yellow mustard
1/2 cup gingerale

Remove net from ham and wipe clean. Score in crisscross pattern forming diamond shapes. Stud with whole cloves at points of each diamond. Place ham in open baking pan. Mix pineapple with brown sugar and mustard; pour over ham. Add gingerale to pan. Bake at 350° approximately 2 1/2 hours. Baste every half-hour to build up sugar mixture on ham.

Suggested wine: French or California Blanc de Noir

grenadine ham glaze

¾ cup grenadine syrup
1 cup cider vinegar
½ Tbsp. prepared mustard

Heat grenadine and vinegar; stir in mustard. Keep glaze hot while glazing ham. Baste every 5 or 10 minutes during last 30 minutes of baking.

ham and cheese casserole

Serves: 4

A favorite of all ages.

1½ cups diced cooked ham
½ cup diced onion
¼ cup diced green pepper
½ cup diced celery
2 Tbsp. butter *or* margarine
1 cup milk
8 oz. cream cheese, softened
½ tsp. salt
1 tsp. garlic salt
½ cup grated Parmesan cheese
4 oz. noodles, cooked and drained

Saute onion, green pepper and celery in butter until crisp-tender; set aside. In large bowl, blend milk and cream cheese. Add salt, garlic salt, ½ the Parmesan cheese, the ham, and sauteed vegetables. Place noodles in 2-quart baking dish; pour cheese mixture over top. Stir well; sprinkle remaining Parmesan cheese on top. Bake at 350° for 30 minutes.

Suggested wines:
California Gamay Rose
French Beaujolais

daven haven loaf

Serves: 6

1½ lbs. smoked ham
½ lb. veal
⅓ cup bread crumbs
⅓ cup tapioca
¼ tsp. pepper
2 eggs
1 cup milk

Have meats ground together. Mix meats with remaining ingredients thoroughly. Place in greased 5 x 9-inch loaf pan. Pour some of Topping over loaf. Baste with remainder of Topping during cooking. Bake at 350° for 1½ to 2 hours. Serve with Horseradish Sauce.

Topping

1½ cups brown sugar
1 Tbsp. dry mustard
½ cup vinegar
½ cup cold water

Mix ingredients thoroughly.

Horseradish Sauce

½ cup cream, whipped
3 Tbsp. *drained* **horseradish**
¼ tsp. salt
1 Tbsp. mayonnaise

Mix ingredients thoroughly.

Suggested wines:
French Beaujolais Villages
California Gamay Beaujolais

a "two-hander"

Serves: 12

2 to 3 doz. German-style frankfurters
½ cup chopped onion
2 Tbsp. butter *or* **margarine**
¼ cup horseradish
1½ cups tomato juice
2 to 3 Tbsp. sugar
3 28-oz. cans sauerkraut

Saute onion in butter until transparent; add horseradish, tomato juice, sugar and ***drained*** sauerkraut. Place mixture in casserole. Brown frankfurters in frying pan or oven; place on sauerkraut. Bake at 350° for 45 minutes or until bubbly.

Suggested wines:
Becks Beer
New Amsterdam Amber

gigot a la moutarde

To dress up the serving platter, try artichoke hearts sauteed in garlic butter and tiny roasted potatoes, scooped out of raw, peeled potatoes with a melon-baller.

1 6-lb. leg of lamb
½ cup dark French mustard
2 Tbsp. soy sauce
1 clove garlic, mashed
1 tsp. rosemary
¼ tsp. ginger
2 Tbsp. olive oil

Combine mustard, soy sauce, garlic, rosemary and ginger; beat in olive oil very slowly. Sauce will be a cream-like consistency. Paint lamb with mixture several hours before roasting. Baste during roasting.

Suggested wines:
Red Bordeaux
California Cabernet Sauvignon

marinated lamb

Serves: 6

3 lbs. lamb, cubed
½ cup pineapple juice
Juice of 1 lemon
¼ cup vegetable oil
½ tsp. salt
½ tsp. pepper
¼ tsp. sage
¼ tsp. dry mustard
⅛ tsp. oregano
1 onion, chopped
1 clove garlic, minced

Combine lamb with all remaining ingredients. Refrigerate overnight, stirring several times. Drain marinade. Broil lamb to desired degree of doneness.

Director's note: *After draining marinade, lamb cubes may be placed on skewers with small onions, green pepper chunks, tomato wedges, etc. for shish kabob.*

Suggested wines:
California Cabernet Sauvignon
French Red Bordeaux

shashlik russe

Serves: 4

Easy enough for the busiest people -- special enough for the company president.

2 lbs. boneless lamb, cut into 2-inch cubes
1 cup vegetable oil
1 tsp. salt
½ tsp. pepper
2 tsp. lemon juice
1 tsp. dill weed
1 small clove garlic, minced
1 bay leaf
Tops of 3 stalks of celery, chopped
3 tomatoes*, quartered
2 onions*, cut into wedges *or* **can of small whole onions**
2 green peppers*, cut into squares

Place lamb cubes in bowl or shallow dish. Combine in a jar, oil, salt, pepper, lemon juice, dill weed, garlic, bay leaf and celery. Shake thoroughly; pour over lamb. Cover and refrigerate for 6 to 8 hours or overnight, stirring occasionally. To cook, use 4 skewers and thread lamb, tomato, onion and green pepper on each one. Use 4 or 5 cubes of lamb on each skewer. Grill over medium coals 12 to 16 minutes, turning once. If grilling in oven, place skewers on rack in shallow baking pan 4 inches from broiler. Broil 10 minutes, turning once. Brush with additional marinade, if desired. Serve with rice.

Director's note: **Any vegetable can be used, i.e. mushrooms, zucchini, carrots, etc.*

Suggested wine: California Zinfandel

"Some hae meat and canna eat,
And some wad eat that want it;
But we hae meat, and we can eat,
And sae the Lord be thankit."
The Selkirk Grace, Robert Burns

In the Wings

Chicken

*A good luncheon dish

Cornish Hen

Duck

Sauces

Photo on p. 153:
Death of a Salesman, 1983 - John Carpenter (Willy Loman)

almond chicken

Serves: 4

A quick and delicious Chinese dish.

- 2 chicken breasts, split, skinned and boned
- 1 Tbsp. cornstarch
- 2 Tbsp. dry sherry
- 2 Tbsp. peanut oil
- ½ cup slivered almonds
- 1 Tbsp. peanut oil
- 1 medium onion, sliced
- ¼ cup soy sauce
- 1 tsp. sugar
- 1 tsp. sesame oil
- Cooked rice

Cube chicken breasts. Marinate in cornstarch and sherry at least 1 hour. Heat the 2 tablespoons peanut oil in frying pan or wok and saute almonds; remove. Stirfry chicken in same oil for 2 minutes until lightly browned; remove. Add the 1 tablespoon peanut oil; saute onion. Return chicken and almonds to pan. Add soy sauce, sugar and sesame oil. Heat thoroughly. Serve immediately with rice.

Suggested wines:
New York Johannisberg Riesling
California French Colombard

Mrs. Hardcastle,
She Stoops to Conquer

chicken dijon

Serves: 4

Good "left-overs", if there are any.

- 3 whole chicken breasts, split, skinned and boned
- 2 Tbsp. butter
- 2 cups dry white wine
- ¼ tsp. dried tarragon
- Pinch of thyme
- 1 small bay leaf
- ½ tsp. salt
- ¼ tsp. pepper
- 2 egg yolks, beaten
- 1 cup sour cream
- 2 Tbsp. Dijon mustard
- Pinch of cayenne pepper

Brown chicken well on both sides in butter. Add wine, tarragon, thyme, bay leaf, salt and pepper; bring to a boil. Cover and simmer for 45 minutes until chicken is tender. Remove chicken to heated serving dish and keep warm. Discard bay leaf. While stirring briskly, gradually add a little sauce to beaten egg yolks. Return to pan. Add sour cream, mustard, and cayenne pepper. Heat slowly, stirring constantly; ***do not boil.*** Pour over chicken.

Suggested wines:

California Dry Chenin Blanc
California Sauvignon Blanc

chicken and artichokes

Serves: 10-12

- 6 whole chicken breasts, split, skinned and boned
- Paprika, salt and pepper
- ½ cup butter
- 2 15-oz. cans artichoke hearts, drained
- 1 lb. fresh mushrooms
- ½ cup butter
- ¼ tsp. tarragon
- 6 Tbsp. flour
- 1 cup dry sherry
- 3 cups chicken broth

Sprinkle chicken breasts with paprika, salt and pepper. Saute in ½ cup butter. Transfer to large, shallow baking dish; add artichokes on top. Saute mushrooms for 5 minutes in ½ cup butter and tarragon. Sprinkle with flour; stir in sherry and chicken broth. Simmer for 5 minutes. Pour sauce over chicken and artichokes. Cover and bake at 350° for 45 minutes.

Suggested wines:

California Fume Blanc
French Pouilly Fume

chicken oriental

Serves: 15-20

An easy and delicious way to feed a crowd!

- **15 whole chicken breasts, split, skinned and boned**
- **2 8-oz. bottles red Russian salad dressing**
- **2 env. onion soup mix**
- **6 Tbsp. apricot preserves**
- **1 cup boiling water**

Place chicken in large, flat baking dish. Combine all other ingredients and mix well. Pour over chicken; cover with aluminum foil. Bake at 350° for 1 hour. Uncover and bake for 30 minutes more to brown.

Suggested wine: California or New York State Chardonnay

chicken paprikash

Serves: 4-6

Excellent company dish!

- **4 whole chicken breasts, split, skinned and boned**
- **4 Tbsp. butter**
- **1 Tbsp. paprika**
- **¼ cup flour**
- **1 tsp. salt**
- **2 Tbsp. shortening**
- **1 medium onion, minced**
- **¾ cup finely diced celery**
- **⅔ cup water**
- **2 Tbsp. flour**
- **½ cup sour cream**

Brown chicken in 2 tablespoons of the butter. Cream remaining 2 tablespoon butter, paprika, the ¼ cup flour and salt to make a paste. Spread over chicken. Cover; cook over low heat 30 minutes. Melt shortening in another pan; saute onion. Add celery and water.* Cover and cook 8 to 10 minutes. Pour mixture over chicken; cover and cook 15 minutes more. Stir the 2 tablespoons flour into sour cream; combine with juice in pan. Cover and cook 5 to 6 minutes longer.

Director's note: **A chicken bouillon cube may be added to water when cooking celery if desired.*

Suggested wines:

French White Rhone
California Chardonnay

"A hen is only an egg's way of making another egg."
Samuel Butler

country style chicken kiev

Serves: 3-4

- **2 whole chicken breasts, split, skinned and boned**
- **½ cup bread crumbs**
- **2 Tbsp. Parmesan cheese**
- **1 tsp. basil**
- **1 tsp. oregano**
- **½ tsp. garlic salt**
- **¼ tsp. salt**
- **⅔ cup butter, melted**
- **¼ cup white wine**
- **¼ cup chopped fresh parsley**
- **¼ cup chopped scallions**

Combine bread crumbs, cheese, basil, oregano, garlic salt and salt. Dip chicken in melted butter. Roll in crumb mixture. Place in 9-inch square baking dish. Bake at 375° for 30 to 40 minutes. To the leftover butter, add wine, parsley and onion. Pour over baked chicken and bake 10 minutes more.

Suggested wine: French or California Sauvignon Blanc

chicken astor

Serves: 4-6

- **3 whole chicken breasts, split, skinned and boned**
- **¼ cup mayonnaise**
- **½ cup fine bread crumbs**
- **5 Tbsp. butter *or* margarine**
- **½ cup chopped onion**
- **2 Tbsp. butter *or* margarine**
- **3 Tbsp. flour**
- **1½ cups water**
- **3 Tbsp. lemon juice**
- **3 chicken bouillon cubes**
- **¼ cup chopped parsley**
- **½ cup mayonnaise**
- **Paprika**

Coat chicken with the ¼ cup mayonnaise; roll in bread crumbs. Slowly brown chicken in the 5 tablespoons butter until tender; keep warm. In saucepan, saute onion in the 2 tablespoons butter. Stir in flour until well blended. Gradually stir in water. Add lemon juice, bouillon cubes and parsley. Cook and stir until mixture comes to a boil. Cool a little; add the ½ cup mayonnaise. Heat gently, stirring constantly; do not boil. Before serving, spoon sauce over chicken; dust with paprika.

Director's note: *Can be prepared a few hours in advance. Place in baking dish and reheat at 350° for 30 minutes.*

Suggested wine: California Johannisberg Riesling

"I drink to the general joy of the whole table."
Macbeth, Shakespeare

easy vip chicken

Serves: 8

A slice of tomato and a green vegetable and dinner's ready!

4 whole chicken breasts, split, skinned and boned
¼ cup vegetable oil
1 egg
1 12 to 16-oz. container cottage cheese
1 small can mushrooms, drained
Salt, pepper, onion, garlic to taste
Brown rice
1 lb. Muenster cheese, sliced

Mix oil, egg, cottage cheese, mushrooms and seasonings. Lightly oil bottom of baking pan; sprinkle with layer of uncooked brown rice. Arrange chicken breasts in single layer over rice; pour cottage cheese mixture over all. Arrange Muenster slices overlapping to edges of pan. Bake at 450° for 10 minutes; reduce temperature to 350° and bake for 1 to 1¼ hours until golden brown. Cut into squares containing chicken breasts.

Director's note: *Keeps well in warm oven for about ½ hour.*

Suggested wines:
New York State Dry Ravat
Austrian Pinot Blanc

ENCORE!

chicken breasts in lemon sauce

Serves: 4-6

3 chicken breasts, split, skinned and boned
Salt and pepper
½ cup butter *or* margarine
2 Tbsp. sherry *or* vermouth
2 tsp. grated lemon peel
2 Tbsp. lemon juice
1 cup cream
6 thin pats of butter
Grated Parmesan cheese

Pound chicken to flatten; salt and pepper. Saute 10 minutes in hot butter, turning chicken once to brown on all sides. Remove to oven-proof platter. Add wine, lemon peel and juice to frying pan. Cook 1 minute, stirring constantly. Salt and pepper sauce to taste. Stir in cream slowly. Pour sauce over chicken. Place pat of butter on each piece of chicken; sprinkle with cheese. Place under broiler to brown. Serve immediately.

Suggested wines:
French Mersault
New York State Chardonnay

chicken cheese rolls

Serves: 6

Dressed up...and different! A nice luncheon dish.

3 large whole chicken breasts, split, skinned and boned
8 oz. herbed cream cheese
1 Tbsp. butter
6 slices bacon

Place chicken breasts between wax paper; pound to ½ inch thickness. Spread each with about 3 tablespoons cheese;* dot with butter. Fold ends over filling. Wrap 1 slice bacon around each roll. Place seam side down in shallow baking pan. Bake on top rack of oven at 400° for 40 minutes, or until juices run clear when chicken is pierced. Broil 5 minutes until bacon crisps.

Director's note: **Hint: freeze cream cheese in ¾ inch thick strips; place 1 on each chicken breast for easy wrapping.*

Suggested wines:
California Sauvignon Blanc
French St. Veran

peach glazed chicken

Serves: 4

2 whole chicken breasts, split, skinned and boned
4 Tbsp. butter *or* margarine
¼ tsp. mace
¼ tsp. sweet basil
¼ tsp. nutmeg
1 tsp. salt
1 Tbsp. brown sugar
1 cup Peach Puree*
2 Tbsp. frozen orange juice concentrate, thawed
2 Tbsp. lemon juice

Melt butter and add spices, salt and brown sugar. Heat only until well blended. Mix peach puree, orange juice and lemon juice; add to spice mixture. Heat again only enough to blend mixture to a smooth sauce. If cooking chicken on a grill, cook 1 side for 10 minutes; turn and cook other side for 8 minutes. If cooking chicken in oven, place in shallow baking dish; cook for 20 minutes at 350°. After pre-cooking, drain off any fat. Baste chicken on all sides with peach glaze. Continue to cook for about 20 minutes, or until tender, turning frequently and basting often with the glaze.

Peach Puree* Use firm peaches. Wash, halve and remove pits; blend in blender until smooth or mash peeled, pitted and cut-up peaches with a potato masher or fork. Canned, well drained peaches can be substituted.

Suggested wine: Idaho Johannisberg Riesling

pecan-breaded chicken breasts with mustard sauce

Serves: 4

Magnificent!

2 whole chicken breasts, split, skinned and boned
Salt and freshly ground pepper
6 Tbsp. butter
2 Tbsp. Dijon mustard *or* **similar strong mustard**
5 to 6 oz. finely ground pecans
4 Tbsp. butter
2 Tbsp. safflower oil *or* **mild vegetable oil**
⅔ cup sour cream
1 Tbsp. Dijon mustard
1 tsp. salt
¼ tsp. pepper

Between 2 pieces of wax paper, lightly flatten chicken breasts with mallet. Season chicken with salt and pepper. Melt the 6 tablespoons butter in small saucepan over medium heat. Remove from heat; whisk in the 2 tablespoons mustard. Spread ground pecans in shallow dish. Dip each piece of chicken into butter mixture, then roll in ground pecans to coat heavily. Put them on by hand, if necessary. Turn oven on to low (200°). Melt the 4 tablespoons butter in large frying pan; stir in oil. Saute as many pieces of chicken at a time as possible without crowding them, about 3 minutes on each side. Remove to baking dish; keep warm in oven. Continue cooking chicken in frying pan until all pieces are done. Discard butter and oil. Spoon any pecans remaining in pan onto chicken unless they are too burned. If so, discard them also. Deglaze frying pan with sour cream, scraping up all the browned particles. Whisk the 1 tablespoon mustard, 1 teaspoon salt and ¼ teaspoon pepper into sour cream. Remove from heat. Place a dollup of sour cream sauce in middle of each ***warmed*** dinner plate. Place a piece of chicken over it. Only a small portion of sauce should accompany each piece of chicken so as not to overpower it.

Suggested wine: Oregon Sauvignon Blanc

"Tis an ill cook that cannot lick his own fingers."
Romeo and Juliet, Shakespeare

chicken tarragon

Serves: 4-6

Hot, buttered noodles garnished with parsley are perfect with this.

3 whole chicken breasts, split, skinned and boned
4 Tbsp. butter
2 Tbsp. brandy
½ cup sliced mushrooms
2 Tbsp. minced onion
¼ tsp. minced garlic
2 Tbsp. flour
1 tsp. catsup
⅛ tsp. salt
Dash cayenne pepper
1 cup chicken broth
½ cup light cream
1 tsp. tarragon
6 large mushrooms
2 tsp. tarragon vinegar

In frying pan, brown chicken in butter, about 4 minutes per side. Heat brandy; ignite and pour over chicken. Remove chicken and set aside. Add the ½ cup mushrooms, onion and garlic. Simmer 5 minutes. Stir in flour, catsup, salt and cayenne. Gradually stir in chicken broth and ⅓ of the cream. Bring to a boil, stirring constantly. Return chicken to frying pan; add tarragon and large mushrooms. Simmer, covered, 25 to 30 minutes until chicken is tender. Remove chicken to heated platter. Stir in remaining cream and tarragon vinegar. Pour sauce over chicken.

Suggested wines:
French St. Veran
California Chardonnay

Set, *Twelfth Night*

poulet farci du fromage et epinards (chicken stuffed with cheese and spinach)

Serves: 2

- 2 chicken halves (split broilers)
- 1 10-oz. pkg. frozen chopped spinach, thawed and squeezed dry
- 1 cup cottage cheese
- 1 egg
- ¼ cup Parmesan cheese
- Salt and pepper
- ½ tsp. garlic powder
- Vegetable oil
- Oregano, thyme, rosemary

With your fingers, raise the skin off the entire piece of chicken to form a pocket (do not remove skin). Mix spinach, cottage cheese, egg, Parmesan cheese, salt, pepper and garlic powder. Stuff mixture into pocket under skin. Brush top of skin with oil; sprinkle with oregano, thyme, rosemary, salt and pepper. Bake at 350° for 1½ hours.

Suggested wines:
Italian Verdicchio
Italian Chardonnay

"house-to-half" chicken

Serves: 4

Great with candied yams and fresh broccoli.

- 1 3-lb. frying chicken
- Salt and freshly ground pepper
- 4 Tbsp. butter *or* margarine
- 2 cloves garlic, minced
- 2 large apples, pared and sliced
- 1 cup dry white wine

Cut chicken into serving pieces; wash and pat dry. Season with salt and pepper. Melt butter in large frying pan; add garlic and chicken. Brown lightly on all sides. Place in 1-quart casserole; place apple slices on top. Pour wine over all. Cover tightly; bake at 350° for 1¼ hours.

Director's note: *Can be prepared in advance, even the day before serving, and refrigerated.*

Suggested wines:
French Macon
New York State Chardonnay

alabama chicken

Serves: 8-10

2 lbs. chicken breasts, cooked and cut-up
1 cup chopped green pepper
1 cup chopped celery
1 cup chopped onion
½ cup butter *or* margarine
½ lb. pasteurized process cheese, cut-up
1 cup sliced green olives
½ cup sliced ripe olives
1 8-oz. can mushrooms, drained
1 10¾-oz. can cream of chicken soup
1 4½-oz. pkg. green noodles, cooked
Cracker crumbs

Saute green pepper, celery and onion in butter. Add cheese, green and ripe olives, mushrooms, soup, cooked noodles and chicken. Place in 3-quart casserole. Top with cracker crumbs. Bake at 300° for 45 minutes.

Suggested wines:
California Fume Blanc
French Sancerre

"saturday night supper" chicken

Serves: 8-10

Holds well for a buffet supper.

4 to 5 lbs. chicken pieces
½ cup bread crumbs
¼ cup grated Parmesan cheese
½ tsp. oregano
Generous dash garlic powder and pepper
2 10¾-oz. cans cream of mushroom soup *or* chicken soup *or* 1 of each
1 cup milk
¼ cup grated Parmesan cheese
Paprika

Mix bread crumbs, ¼ cup Parmesan cheese, oregano, garlic powder and pepper together. Roll chicken in crumb mixture. Place skin side down in buttered baking dish. Bake at 400° for 20 minutes. Turn and bake for 20 minutes more. Mix 2 cans of soup with milk; pour over chicken. Sprinkle with ¼ cup Parmesan cheese and paprika. Bake 20 minutes more until golden and bubbly.

Suggested wines:
California Chardonnay
California Sauvignon Blanc

moghul chicken curry

Serves: 4

Contributed by Yolande Bavan who played in THE COMEDY OF ERRORS (1980).

- **1 3-lb. chicken**
- **8 oz. curd** *or* **plain yogurt**
- **3 large cloves garlic**
- **1 or 2 red chilies** *or* **3 tsp. dried red Mexican chilies**
- **1 inch piece of ginger** *or* **1 tsp. ground ginger**
- **1 Tbsp. water**
- **Salt**
- **1 heaping Tbsp. butter**
- **1 large onion, chopped**
- **6 black peppercorns**
- **4 whole cloves**
- **½ tsp. ground cardamom**
- **1 cup water**
- **2 tsp. lemon juice**

Skin chicken and cut into 12 pieces. Whip the curd. Grind garlic, chilies, ginger and water into a thin paste. Add to whipped curd; salt to taste. Put chicken pieces into mixture; mix well. Cover and refrigerate for 3 hours.

Heat butter to smoking hot in deep pan. Add onion, peppercorns, cloves and cardamom. Stir fry until onions are golden. Add chicken mixture; stir for 5 minutes. Add water. Cover tightly; simmer 1 hour or until chicken is done. Add lemon juice just before serving.

Director's note: *Sauce may be thickened with cornstarch and served over rice.*

Suggested wine: Italian Gewurztraminer

deviled chicken

Serves: 4

- **1 chicken, cut into serving pieces**
- **4 Tbsp. butter** *or* **margarine**
- **½ cup honey**
- **¼ cup prepared mustard**
- **1 tsp. salt**
- **1 tsp. curry powder**
- **Cooked rice**

Wash chicken and pat dry. Melt butter in shallow baking pan. Stir in remaining ingredients. Roll chicken pieces in mixture to coat both sides. Arrange meaty side up in single layer in same pan.* Bake at 375° for 1 hour or until chicken is tender and glazed. Serve on a bed of rice. Spoon sauce over chicken and rice.

Director's note: **May be refrigerated at this point and baked later.*

Suggested wine: California Sauvignon Blanc

terry's honey chicken

Serves: 4

Contributed by Terry Schreiber who directed WHO'S AFRAID OF VIRGINIA WOOLF? (1980), A DOLL'S HOUSE (1981), BETRAYAL (1981), and K-2 (1982).

1 large chicken, cut into serving pieces
1 small jar honey
Italian seasoning

Preheat oven to 550° or broil. Place chicken pieces in broiler pan, skin side down. Cover with honey; sprinkle with Italian seasoning. Put under broiler on lowest rack to prevent burning. Cook for approximately 20 minutes or until brown. Turn; baste with more honey and seasoning. Cook for approximately 20 minutes more or until brown (after the first 10 minutes on the second side, baste again with the honey). Serve immediately.

Suggested wines:
Italian Riesling
Italian Gewurztraminer

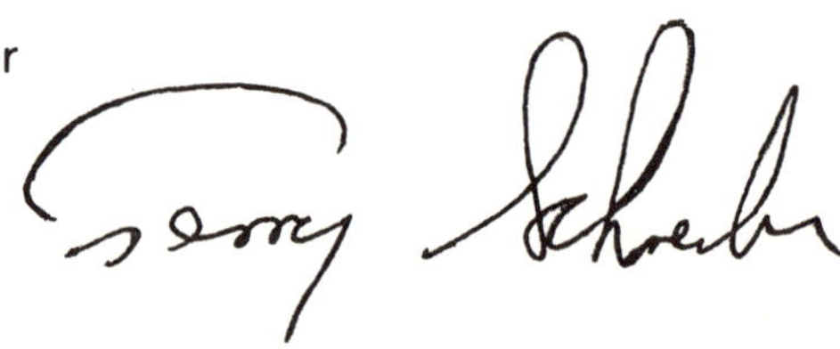

starring role chicken

Serves: 6

Chicken pieces of your choice to serve 6; skinned and boned
6 Tbsp. butter *or* margarine
½ cup chopped onion
8 slices bacon, finely diced
2 Tbsp. flour
1 Tbsp. curry powder
1 cup condensed beef broth
¼ cup orange marmalade
2 Tbsp. catsup
2 Tbsp. lemon juice

Melt butter; dip pieces of chicken into butter to coat well. Place in baking dish. In separate pan, brown onion and bacon. Add flour, stirring to a smooth paste. Add remaining ingredients; simmer 15 minutes. Spread ½ of sauce on chicken. Bake at 400° for 20 minutes. Spoon remaining sauce over chicken; bake 20 minutes more.

Suggested wines:
California Sauvignon Blanc
French Sancerre

erika's chicken and sausage

Serves: 6-8

Contributed by Erika Petersen who played in A DOLL'S HOUSE (1981) and THE MERCHANT OF VENICE (1982).

- **1½ lbs. sweet *or* hot Italian sausage links**
- **1 3-lb. chicken, cut into serving pieces**
- **Salt, freshly ground pepper**
- **3 Tbsp. olive oil**
- **1 cup chopped celery**
- **1 cup chopped onion**
- **½ lb. mushrooms, sliced**
- **8 flat fillets of anchovies**
- **½ cup imported black olives, preferably in brine and from Italy or Greece**
- **1 Tbsp. drained capers**
- **¼ cup dry white wine**
- **¼ cup tomato sauce**

Cut sausage links into 3-inch pieces. Place in heavy frying pan; cook, turning, until browned all over. Remove; drain and place in casserole with tight lid. Discard fat. Sprinkle chicken pieces with salt and pepper to taste. In another frying pan, heat olive oil and brown chicken pieces lightly on all sides. Add to sausage. Meanwhile, place celery in saucepan. Add water to cover; salt to taste. Bring to a boil; simmer about 5 minutes until crisp-tender. Drain, reserving both celery and liquid. To fat remaining in skillet after chicken is cooked, add onion and mushrooms. Cook, stirring until onion and mushrooms are soft. Add anchovies, olives, capers, drained celery, wine and tomato sauce; simmer 10 minutes. Add this mixture to chicken and sausage; salt and pepper to taste. Cover tightly; simmer on top of stove about 30 minutes or until chicken is tender. As dish cooks, if it becomes too dry, add a little of reserved celery liquid or a bit more tomato sauce.

Suggested wine: California Chardonnay

chicken with wild rice and herbs

Serves: 4-6

An easy dish after a day of meetings.

- **Chicken for 4 to 6 servings, pieces of your choice**
- **1 6-oz. box Uncle Ben's long grain and wild rice**
- **1 env. onion soup mix**
- **2 cups boiling water**
- **½ cup white wine *or* dry vermouth**

Mix rice, soup mix, water and wine in 9 x 13-inch baking dish. Top with chicken pieces. Cover with aluminum foil. Bake at 350° for 1 hour. Remove cover; bake ½ hour more until chicken is brown.

Suggested wine: Alsatian Gewurztraminer

Method for cooking chicken breasts for use in casseroles:

Melt butter in large frying pan. Place boned chicken breasts in pan; press down flat. Cut sheets of wax paper to fit pan. Butter paper generously on 1 side; place buttered side down on chicken. Saute over medium heat; turn chicken; replace paper and saute other side. Cooking time depends on thickness of chicken. Do not overcook as chicken will be cooked for 1 hour in most casseroles. Chicken can be prepared in advance and combined in casserole later.

country captain chicken

Serves: 4-6

4 whole chicken breasts, split, skinned and boned
$\frac{1}{4}$ to $\frac{1}{2}$ cup flour
Salt and pepper
$\frac{1}{4}$ cup vegetable oil
1 large garlic clove
2 medium onions, thinly sliced
1 small green pepper, chopped
$\frac{1}{2}$ cup chopped celery
1 Tbsp. curry powder
1 tsp. salt
1 28-oz. can tomatoes
$\frac{1}{2}$ cup dark seedless raisins *or* currants
2 tsp. butter *or* margarine
$\frac{1}{2}$ cup blanched whole almonds
3 cups cooked rice

Coat chicken with flour, salt and pepper. In large skillet, brown chicken on all sides in hot oil; remove. Saute garlic, onion, green pepper, celery, curry powder and salt until vegetables are tender, about 10 minutes, stirring occasionally. Stir in tomatoes with their liquid and raisins. Add chicken; heat to boiling. Reduce heat to low; cover and simmer 30 to 35 minutes until chicken is tender. Meanwhile, in small skillet, brown almonds in hot butter, stirring occasionally. To serve, arrange chicken on warm platter; remove garlic from sauce. Spoon sauce over chicken. Sprinkle with almonds. Serve with rice.

Suggested wines:
California Sauvignon Blanc
French Pouilly Fume

"All human history attests
That happiness for man -- the hungry sinner!
Since Eve ate apples, much depends on dinner."
George Noel Gordon, Lord Byron

julie nixon eisenhower's chicken divan

Serves: 6-7

- 2 whole cooked chicken breasts, sliced
- 2 Tbsp. butter, melted
- 2 cups cooked rice
- ½ lb. fresh *or* frozen cooked broccoli
- 1 cup mayonnaise
- 2 10¾-oz. cans cream of chicken soup
- 1 Tbsp. lemon juice
- ½ to 1 tsp. curry powder
- 1 cup shredded Cheddar cheese
- ½ cup bread crumbs

In 3-quart casserole, spread melted butter. Layer rice, broccoli and chicken slices. Combine mayonnaise, soup, lemon juice and curry powder. Pour over chicken. Top with shredded cheese and bread crumbs. Bake at 350° for 25 minutes.

Director's note: *Can be prepared in advance and refrigerated or frozen.*

Suggested wines: California Chardonnay
French Pouilly Fuisse

cashew chicken

Serves: 6 ***or*** 30 appetizers

Fussy, but worth it.

- 2 whole chicken breasts, boned and thinly sliced*
- ¼ cup cornstarch
- 2 tsp. salt
- ¼ tsp. MSG (opt.)
- 1 tsp. sugar
- 1½ Tbsp. dry sherry
- 2 egg whites
- 1¼ cups finely grated cashews
- 2 cups vegetable *or* peanut oil

Combine cornstarch, salt, MSG, sugar and sherry. Beat egg whites lightly; gradually stir in sherry mixture. Place cashews on wax paper. Dip chicken into egg mixture; roll in cashews. Place on another piece of wax paper. Heat oil in electric frying pan to 375°. Drop chicken, a few pieces at a time, into hot oil. Fry, turning to brown on all sides, about 2 minutes. Remove and drain on paper towels. Serve hot as appetizer or main dish.

Director's notes: **Freeze 1 hour for easy slicing. Chicken can be prepared in advance and reheated in foil in oven.*

Suggested wines: California Pinot Blanc
French St. Veran

orange chicken in the wok

Serves: 4

This is "fast food" at its best!

- 2 whole chicken breasts, skinned and boned
- 2 Tbsp. rum
- 1 Tbsp. soy sauce
- 4 scallions, chopped
- 1 tsp. minced ginger root
- 1 clove garlic
- 1/4 tsp. red pepper flakes
- 1 Tbsp. cornstarch
- 1/2 tsp. sugar
- 1/2 tsp. salt
- 3/4 cup orange juice
- 1 orange
- 3 Tbsp. vegetable oil
- 1/3 cup cashews
- Cooked white rice

Cut chicken into thin strips. Combine with rum, soy sauce, scallions, ginger root, garlic and red pepper flakes; set aside. Combine cornstarch with sugar, salt and orange juice; set aside. Cut peel from orange; cut orange into 1-inch squares. In large frying pan or wok, heat oil until very hot. Stir fry orange peel until it begins to brown at edges. Remove from pan and discard. Add chicken and rum mixture to orange-flavored oil; toss until chicken loses its pink color. Add orange juice mixture; cook until thickened. Stir in orange squares and cashews. Serve immediately over white rice.

Suggested wines:

California Chenin Blanc
French Vouvray

Mona Kent, *Dames at Sea*

chicken tetrazzini

Serves: 6-8

- 2 chicken bouillon cubes
- 2 cups hot water
- 1 8-oz. pkg. thin spaghetti
- 2 Tbsp. butter
- 2 Tbsp. flour
- ½ tsp. salt
- ½ tsp. pepper
- ⅛ tsp. cayenne pepper
- 1 cup milk
- 1 cup sour cream
- 1 cup cottage cheese
- 2 cups diced, cooked chicken
- 1 4-oz. can sliced mushrooms
- 2 Tbsp. minced onion
- 4 Tbsp. minced parsley
- ½ cup grated cheese

Dissolve bouillon cubes in hot water. Cook spaghetti in bouillon until done. Set aside and keep warm. Melt butter; blend with flour and seasonings. Add remaining ingredients, except cheese, 1 at a time, blending each in well. Cook over low heat, stirring often, until mixture has boiled about 5 minutes. Stir in spaghetti and remove mixture to large baking dish. Sprinkle cheese on top. Bake at 350° for 30 to 45 minutes or until golden brown and bubbling hot.

Suggested wines:

Italian Gavi
California Fume Blanc

baked chicken casserole

Serves: 8

For a busy day -- make this the night before.

- 4 cups cut-up cooked chicken
- ¾ cup mayonnaise
- ¾ cup cream of chicken soup
- 2 cups chopped celery
- 4 hard-boiled eggs, sliced
- 1 tsp. salt
- 1 tsp. minced onion
- 2 Tbsp. lemon juice
- 2 Tbsp. chopped pimiento
- 1 cup crushed potato chips
- ⅔ cup finely shredded sharp Cheddar cheese
- ⅓ cup chopped almonds (opt.)

Combine chicken, mayonnaise, soup, celery, eggs, salt, onion, lemon juice and pimiento. Place in shallow 2½-quart baking dish. Combine potato chips with cheese and almonds; sprinkle on top. Chill overnight or at least 4 hours. Bake at 400° for 25 minutes or until hot and bubbly.

Suggested wines:

Italian Veronese White
California French Colombard

stage struck chicken casserole

Serves: 6

An easy and delicious "do-ahead" to serve at those luncheon meetings.

- **4 cups cut-up cooked chicken**
- **8 to 10 bread slices**
- **4 eggs, beaten**
- **2 cups milk**
- **½ lb. fresh mushrooms, sliced**
- **¼ cup butter *or* margarine**
- **1 8-oz. can sliced water chestnuts, drained**
- **1 2-oz. jar pimiento, drained and diced**
- **1 10¾-oz. can cream of mushroom soup**
- **1 10¾-oz. can cream of celery soup**
- **½ cup mayonnaise**
- **½ cup grated sharp Cheddar cheese**
- **2 cups packaged bread stuffing cubes**
- **4 Tbsp. butter, melted**

Remove crusts and cube bread slices. Cover bottom of shallow, buttered 3-quart casserole with cubed bread. Combine beaten eggs and milk; pour ½ of mixture over bread cubes. Top with chicken. Saute mushrooms in the ¼ cup butter for 5 minutes; spoon over chicken. Add water chestnuts and pimientos. Combine soups and mayonnaise; spoon over top. Sprinkle with cheese. Pour remaining egg and milk mixture over all. Cover with foil; ***refrigerate overnight.*** Bake, covered, at 350° for 30 minutes. Uncover and sprinkle bread stuffing cubes on top. Pour the 4 tablespoons melted butter over cubes. Bake, uncovered, for 30 minutes more.

Director's note: *3 to 4 whole chicken breasts will yield 4 cups chicken.*

Suggested wines:

French White Bordeaux
California Dry Chenin Blanc

marinade for chicken

Serves: 4-6

- **2 tsp. lime juice**
- **¼ cup vegetable oil**
- **2 Tbsp. vinegar**
- **1 Tbsp. Worcestershire sauce**
- **⅛ tsp. Tabasco**
- **1 tsp. salt**
- **1 Tbsp. sugar**
- **½ tsp. garlic salt**
- **½ tsp. paprika**

Combine all ingredients; blend well. Pour over chicken. Marinate at least 2 hours, turning once. Drain, reserving marinade; use to baste chicken during cooking.

anne jackson's barbecue sauce for chicken

Serves: 4

Contributed by Anne Jackson who played in TWICE AROUND THE PARK (1982).

- **1 16-oz. bottle barbecue sauce**
- **1 8-oz. can tomato sauce**
- **1 26-oz. jar Aunt Millie's meatless spaghetti sauce**
- **1 Tbsp. lemon juice**
- **Onion flakes**
- **2 cloves garlic**
- **1 tsp. Italian seasoning**

Combine ingredients thoroughly. Marinate chicken in sauce for a few hours. Bake at 350° for 1 hour or broil for 10 to 12 minutes.

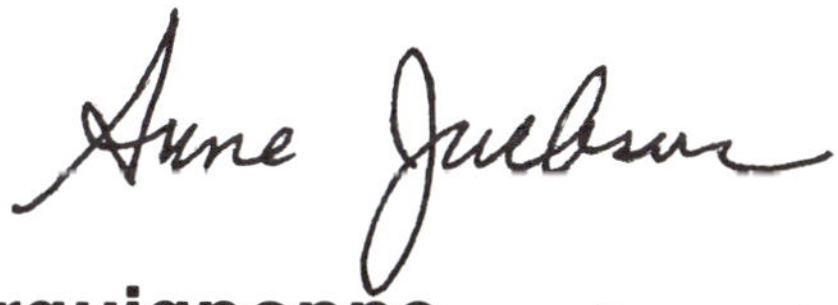

rock cornish hen bourguignonne

Serves: 4

- **4 Cornish hens**
- **1 tsp. salt**
- **¼ tsp. cloves**
- **¼ tsp. nutmeg**
- **¼ tsp. pepper**
- **¼ tsp. thyme**
- **4 slices bacon, cut in half**
- **1¼ cups dry red wine**
- **½ tsp. instant chicken bouillon**
- **½ cup boiling water**
- **2 Tbsp. finely chopped onion**
- **2 Tbsp. snipped parsley**
- **3 to 4 cups cooked brown *or* white rice**
- **⅓ cup currant jelly**

Mix salt, cloves, nutmeg, pepper and thyme; rub outside and cavities of birds with mixture. Place breast side up in shallow roasting pan. Crisscross bacon over breasts. Mix wine, bouillon, water, onion and parsley. Pour into pan. Roast, uncovered, at 350° for 1 hour. Increase temperature to 400°; roast about 10 minutes or until drumstick feels soft when pressed with thumb and finger. Remove hens to warm platter. Remove bacon; cut into small pieces. Stir bacon into rice. Strain hot juices from pan into saucepan; stir in currant jelly. Heat, stirring constantly until jelly is melted. Skim off fat. Arrange rice around hens; spoon sauce over hens.

Suggested wines:

French Rhone Valley Red
French Red Burgundy

fesenjan

A really different taste. Plain boiled rice is the traditional accompaniment to this dish.

4 to 5 lb. duck, quartered and trimmed of fat
2 medium onions, peeled and sliced ¼-inch thick
½ tsp. turmeric
¼ cup olive oil
4 cups water
2 tsp. salt
3½ cups shelled walnuts, pulverized in a blender
Freshly ground black pepper
¼ cup apricot nectar
⅓ cup fresh lemon juice
¼ cup sugar

Saute onions and turmeric in olive oil for 8 to 10 minutes or until onions are richly brown. Transfer onions to a 5 to 6-quart Dutch oven, setting the frying pan aside. Add water, salt, walnuts and pepper; stir until thoroughly blended. Bring to a boil; reduce heat and simmer, partially covered, for 20 minutes.

Meanwhile, reheat frying pan and brown the duck lightly, turning pieces so they brown evenly without burning. Add more oil if necessary. Transfer duck to simmering walnut mixture, coating pieces evenly. Bring to a boil. Reduce heat to low; cover tightly and simmer for 1½ hours or until duck is almost tender. Remove as much fat as possible from the surface of the sauce. Combine apricot nectar, lemon juice and sugar; add to sauce. Simmer for 30 minutes more; taste for seasoning.

To serve, arrange the duck on a platter; pour a little sauce over it. Serve the rest of sauce separately.

Suggested wines:
French Cotes du Rhone
California Cabernet/Merlot

"If all be true that I do think,
There are five reasons we should drink:
Good wine -- a friend -- or being dry --
Or lest we should be by and by --
Or any other reason why."
Henry Aldrich

Scene Stealers

Fish

Seafood

*A good luncheon dish

Photo on p. 175:
The Impromptu of Outremont, 1983 - Delphi Lawrence (Fernande), Mary Jay (Lucille), LeClanche du Rand (Yvette)

"first act" fish

Serves: 6

6 rainbow trout
2 Tbsp. lemon juice
Salt and pepper
1 cup dry white wine
¼ cup sliced scallions
2 Tbsp. chopped fresh parsley
2 Tbsp. fine dry bread crumbs
¼ cup melted butter *or* margarine
Dill, preferably fresh
6 thinly sliced lemons

Preheat oven to 400°. Wash and dry trout. Brush inside of trout with some of lemon juice; sprinkle with salt and pepper. Arrange trout in shallow baking dish or broiler pan; brush with remaining lemon juice; sprinkle with salt and pepper. Pour wine into dish. Sprinkle fish evenly with scallions and parsley. Sprinkle with bread crumbs lightly; spoon melted butter over each. Bake, uncovered, 25 minutes or until fish can be easily flaked with a fork. Place trout on serving platter; garnish with dill and lemon slices.

Suggested wines: Italian Chardonnay
New York State Johannisberg Riesling

sea bass with ginger sauce

Serves: 2

Contributed by Sylvia Harman who played in GOODNIGHT GRANDPA (1981).

2 whole sea bass,* each weighing about 1 lb.
2 Tbsp. chopped *or* sliced fresh peeled ginger
4 Tbsp. peanut oil
4 Tbsp. soy sauce
4 scallions, chopped
4 tsp. chopped fresh coriander *or* 1 tsp. dried coriander (opt.)

Place fish in boiling water to cover. When water returns to a boil, lower heat immediately. Poach gently, using the Canadian method of cooking fish, which is 10 minutes to the inch of thickness. Prepare sauce as follows. Fry ginger in hot oil about 2 to 3 minutes. Have all other ingredients ready. Place fish carefully on a platter when done and douse with hot ginger and oil mixture. Immediately add soy sauce on top and garnish with scallions and coriander. Serve immediately.

Director's note: **Any firm-fleshed fish can be substituted for sea bass. Plain or fried rice is a nice accompaniment.*

Suggested wine: French Muscadet

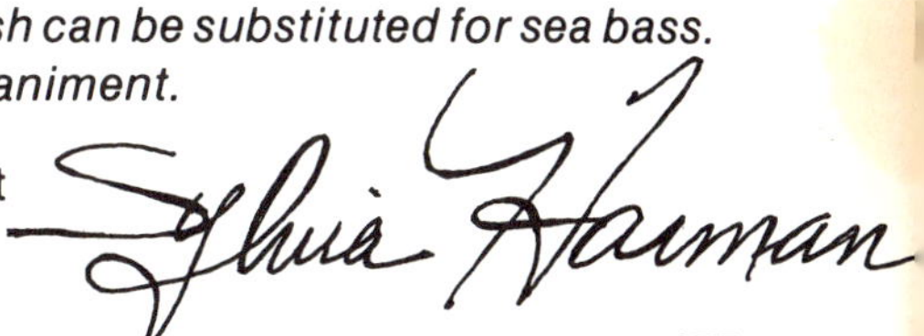

salmon steaks with sour cream

Serves: 4

- 4 salmon steaks
- 2 Tbsp. lemon juice
- 2 tsp. instant minced onion
- ½ tsp. salt
- Dash pepper
- ¼ cup sour cream
- 1 tsp. grated lemon peel
- ½ tsp. dried dill weed

Place salmon steaks in lightly greased baking dish. Combine lemon juice and onion; sprinkle over salmon. Season with salt and pepper. Bake, uncovered, at 400° for 15 to 20 minutes or until fish flakes easily. Remove from oven; spread sour cream over salmon. Sprinkle with lemon peel and dill weed. Return to oven; bake 3 minutes longer. Serve with lemon wedges, if desired.

Suggested wines:
French White Rully
California Chardonnay

marinated salmon

Serves: 4

Scrumptious flavor and low in calories.

- 4 salmon steaks *or* whole, fresh salmon
- ½ cup dry vermouth
- ½ cup vegetable oil
- 2 Tbsp. fresh lemon juice
- ¾ tsp. salt
- ⅛ tsp. pepper
- ½ tsp. thyme
- ½ tsp. marjoram
- ¼ tsp. sage
- 1 Tbsp. minced parsley

Combine all ingredients except salmon. Marinate salmon in mixture for 2 to 3 hours. Broil or grill salmon, basting frequently, for 6 to 8 minutes on each side or until fish flakes with fork.

Suggested wines:
California Chardonnay
French White Burgundy

"Fish and guests in three days are stale."
Euphues, John Lyly

stuffed salmon loaf

Serves: 6

- 1 15½-oz. can salmon
- 1 cup soft bread crumbs
- 3 eggs, beaten
- 1 Tbsp. lemon juice
- ¼ cup finely chopped onion
- ½ tsp. salt
- 1½ cups sliced fresh mushrooms
- 4 Tbsp. butter *or* margarine
- 1 cup packed fresh spinach leaves, sliced into thin strips

Drain salmon, reserving liquid; flake. Combine salmon with bread crumbs, eggs, lemon juice, onion and salt. Pat half of mixture into greased loaf pan. Saute mushrooms in butter about 1 minute; add spinach and stir just until wilted. Spread mushroom mixture evenly over salmon mixture in pan, leaving a 1-inch border around edge of pan. Top with remaining salmon mixture. Bake at 350° for 40 minutes or until set and top is golden brown. Serve with lemon sauce.

Lemon Sauce

- Milk
- 1 Tbsp. butter *or* margarine
- 1 Tbsp. flour
- ⅛ tsp. salt
- Dash pepper
- 1 egg yolk
- 1 to 2 Tbsp. lemon juice

Add enough milk to reserved salmon liquid to make ⅔ cup. Melt butter; blend in flour, salt and pepper. Gradually blend in milk mixture; cook until thickened. Beat egg yolk; quickly stir in small amount of thickened sauce. Return to pan. Cook over low heat until thickened. Blend in lemon juice.

Suggested wines:

California Chardonnay
French White Burgundy

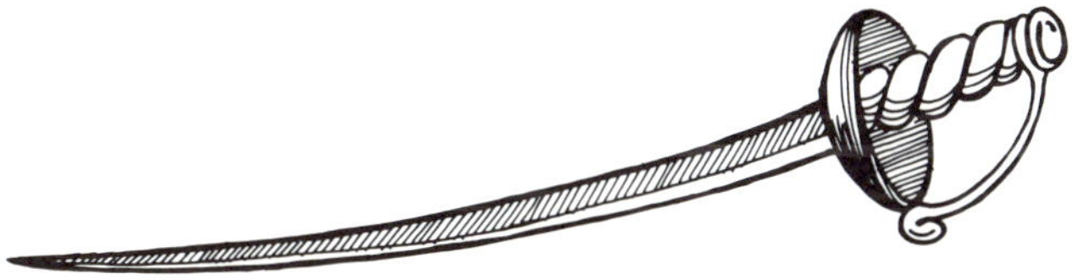

quenelles and veloute sauce

A favorite of Dr. Phillip Ikins, who tells us that quenelles are a 19th century delicacy that was originally available exclusively among royalty. The quenelle is also a rather romantic ancestor of the familiar Passover favorite, gefilte fish. The development of the food processor and microwave oven have made the preparation of this dish -- which can also be served as an appetizer -- relatively quick and simple.

- **½ lb. salmon** *or* **pike, chopped**
- **½ tsp. sea salt**
- **White pepper**
- **⅛ tsp. freshly ground nutmeg**
- **1 egg, separated**
- **1 cup creme fraiche, chilled**
- **Fish stock**

Combine chopped salmon, sea salt, pepper and nutmeg in food processor. Process until fine. Remove and knead a bit. Return to processor; process again. Add egg white. When mixture forms a ball, pour creme fraiche down the tube. Chill forcemeat for 1 hour.

Butter bottom of large frying pan. Have iced water on hand to chill 2 dessert teaspoons. Form small footballs of the forcemeat with spoons; place in frying pan. When pan is full of quenelles, add boiling fish stock until they float. Cook about 4 minutes; gently turn over and cook 4 minutes more. Remove quenelles; reserve stock. Set aside at room temperature while preparing Veloute Sauce. Serve sauce over quenelles.

Veloute Sauce

- **3 Tbsp. butter**
- **3 Tbsp. granular flour**
- **2 cups reserved stock**

Combine butter and flour in glass pan; cover with saran wrap. Place in microwave on high for 3 minutes. Bring to a boil the strained fish stock. Add to the roux. Return to microwave for 3 minutes more. Remove; quickly blend in reserved egg yolk.

Suggested wine: French Muscadet

"A meal without wine is like a day without sunshine."
Anthelme Brillat-Savarin

fillet of sole in cider sauce

Serves: 4

1½ to 2 lbs. fillet of sole
¼ cup butter
2 medium onions, chopped
2 Tbsp. cream
1¼ cups chicken broth
½ to ¾ cups cider *or* apple juice
½ tsp. salt
Dash pepper
¼ tsp. grated lemon peel
1½ Tbsp. butter
2 Tbsp. flour
6 Tbsp. heavy cream
Nutmeg
1 tsp. prepared mustard
Drops of lemon juice
4 Tbsp. fine bread crumbs
1 Tbsp. butter

In small saucepan, heat the ¼ cup butter. Add onion; cook until soft. Puree the mixture. Add the 2 tablespoons cream. Force through a sieve; set aside. Place fillets, folded in half, or whole fish in a baking pan. Combine broth, cider, salt, pepper and lemon peel. Bring to simmer. Simmer 10 minutes; strain onto fish. Cover fish with a buttered piece of wax paper, cut to fit the pan. Place on top of stove; bring the liquid to a simmer. Place in preheated 400° oven and poach for 5 to 10 minutes. Whole fish will require a longer time.

Melt the 1½ tablespoons butter in saucepan; blend in flour. Strain poaching liquid from fish into saucepan, stirring constantly until smooth. Add reserved pureed onions, the 6 tablespoons cream, nutmeg, mustard and lemon juice. Bring to a boil; stir and simmer a few minutes. If desired, transfer fish to oven-proof serving dish. Pour sauce over fish. Mix bread crumbs and the 1 tablespoon butter; sprinkle on top. Place under broiler for 2 minutes until golden. Garnish with parsley.

Suggested wine: German Riesling Mosel Kabinett

fillet of sole florentine

Serves: 4

- 4 fillets of sole
- 1 10-oz. pkg. frozen chopped spinach, thawed, squeezed dry
- Salt and pepper
- ½ tsp. mace
- 3 Tbsp. chopped parsley
- ½ cup grated Swiss cheese

Season spinach with salt, pepper and mace. Spread in 8 x 12-inch baking dish. Skin the sole; sprinkle with chopped parsley. Roll up fillets; place on top of spinach.* Pour Sauce over fish; sprinkle with grated cheese. Bake at 350° for approximately 25 minutes.

Sauce

- 4 Tbsp. flour
- 3 Tbsp. butter, melted
- ⅔ cup light cream
- ⅓ cup dry white wine
- Salt and pepper

Stir flour into melted butter; cook over low heat for 1 minute. Add cream; cook and stir until sauce thickens. Add wine; salt and pepper to taste. Cook until mixture comes to a boil.

Director's note: **Sole may be prepared to this point, covered and refrigerated. Finish preparation with sauce when ready to bake.*

Suggested wines: New York State Aurora
Australian Riesling

saratoga sole

Serves: 4

- 2 lbs. fillet of sole
- 1 tsp. salt
- ¼ tsp. pepper
- 8 oz. sharp Cheddar cheese, grated
- ½ cup chopped onion
- 1 egg, beaten
- 2 Tbsp. water
- 3 slices bread, crumbed
- ¾ cup melted butter
- Fresh parsley and lemon wedges

Sprinkle each fillet with salt, pepper, cheese and onion. Roll jelly-roll style and secure with toothpicks. Combine egg and water. Dip each fillet into egg wash. Coat with bread crumbs. Place in well buttered baking dish. Pour melted butter over top. Bake at 400° for 25 to 30 minutes. Place under broiler until bread crumbs brown, 1 to 2 minutes. Serve with parsley and lemon wedges.

Suggested wines: California Dry Chenin Blanc
Austrian Grunveltliner

bourbon street trout

Serves: 4

8 trout fillets
5 Tbsp. butter
1 cup coarsely chopped artichokes
1¼ cups sliced mushrooms
½ tsp. salt
⅛ tsp. pepper
½ cup Brown Sauce
2 Tbsp. lemon juice
½ cup butter, melted

Melt the 5 tablespoons butter in large frying pan; add trout, artichokes and mushrooms. Sprinkle with salt and pepper. Cook 7 to 8 minutes over medium heat until fish flakes easily with a fork. Remove fish and vegetables and keep warm in low oven. Combine the ½ cup Brown Sauce, lemon juice and the ½ cup melted butter. Mix with wire whisk and cook over low heat until heated through. To serve, ladle sauce over each fillet.

Brown Sauce

1½ Tbsp. butter
1½ Tbsp. flour
2 cups chicken broth

Melt butter; blend in flour. Stir in broth. Bring to a boil and cook 3 to 5 minutes. Simmer, uncovered, 30 minutes, stirring occasionally, until sauce is reduced to approximately 1⅓ cups. Extra sauce should be stored in refrigerator.

Suggested wine: German Riesling Kabinett

brown trout with mint

Serves: 2-3

1 2-lb. brown trout, skinned and cut into 4 pieces
1 large onion, sliced
4 Tbsp. butter
2 Tbsp. vegetable oil
¼ to ½ cup vinegar
10 sprigs fresh mint
Dash salt (opt.)

Saute onion in butter and oil until soft; move aside in pan and place trout in center. Cook, uncovered, on both sides about 5 minutes. Cover and cook another 5 minutes. Mince fresh mint over fish and onions. Add vinegar. Heat and stir until nicely seasoned, about 3 minutes. Place fish on heated platter; arrange onion on top and around it.

"Ruling a big country is like cooking a small fish."
Lao Tzu (6th century B.C.)

drunken trout

Serves: 4

4 small trout, cleaned but whole
4 Tbsp. butter
¼ lb. mushrooms, finely chopped
3 Tbsp. butter
2 cups cooked rice
1 Tbsp. chopped parsley
¼ tsp. thyme
½ tsp. salt
Pepper to taste
½ cup heavy cream
3 Tbsp. Scotch whiskey

Saute trout in the 4 tablespoons butter until lightly browned. Make 4 sheets of aluminum foil or parchment paper, each large enough to hold 1 trout and stuffing. Grease sheets and place 1 trout on each; set pan aside. Meanwhile, in separate pan, saute mushrooms in the 3 tablespoons butter; stir in rice, parsley, thyme, salt and pepper. Divide equally; place in trout and on top. Pour cream and Scotch into frying pan where trout browned; scrape up pan juices. Bring to a boil and pour equally over each trout and rice mixture. Seal foil over each trout. Bake at 400° for about 15 minutes.

Suggested wines:
French Macon Villages
New York State Cayuga (Dry)

"spotlight" scrod

Serves: 4

1¼ to 1½ lbs. scrod fillets
¼ cup butter *or* margarine, melted
½ tsp. Worcestershire sauce (opt.)
Juice of 1 lemon
½ cup dry bread crumbs
3 Tbsp. chopped fresh parsley
½ to 1 tsp. salt
½ tsp. paprika

Preheat broiler pan. Mix butter, Worcestershire sauce and lemon juice in small saucepan. Combine the remaining dry ingredients in shallow dish. Roll fillets first in butter mixture, then dry ingredients. Lay fillets on preheated pan, skin side down. Broil 2 to 3 inches from heat, about 5 minutes for ½-inch thick fillets, 8 to 10 minutes for 1-inch thick fillets. Serve on heated platter with fresh lemon wedges.

Suggested wines:
New York State Chardonnay
French Macon

seafood "ile-de-france"

Serves: 4-6

When you want to splurge for a special occasion!

2 to 3 cups lobster meat
2 to 3 cups crabmeat

Sauce Amerique*

2 Tbsp. chopped onion
1 clove garlic, crushed
1 Tbsp. olive oil
1 2-lb. 3-oz. can tomatoes
1½ tsp. dried tarragon
1½ tsp. dried chervil
⅛ cup Pernod (opt.)

Saute onion and garlic in oil until golden. Stir in tomatoes and remaining ingredients. Simmer, uncovered, until reduced to 1½ cups sauce. Puree mixture and strain. Combine with Cream Sauce. Add seafood. Blend well and warm through. Serve over rice.

Cream Sauce

3 Tbsp. butter
3 Tbsp. flour
¾ tsp. salt
Dash pepper
Nutmeg
1 cup milk
½ cup heavy cream

Melt butter; add flour, blending until smooth. Add remaining ingredients; stir and cook slowly over low heat until sauce thickens and is smooth and creamy.

Director's note: **Sauce Amerique can be prepared ahead and refrigerated. Reheat slowly when ready to combine with Cream Sauce.*

Suggested wines:

French White Burgundy
California Chardonnay

shrimp creole

Serves: 4-5

Contributed by Ellen Barry, who played in TALLY'S FOLLY (1982).

- **2 lbs. fresh** *or* **frozen shrimp, peeled**
- **2 Tbsp. lemon juice**
- **1 Tbsp. Worcestershire sauce**
- **1 tsp. salt**
- **3 Tbsp. butter**
- **½ cup chopped onion**
- **½ cup chopped green pepper**
- **½ cup chopped celery**
- **1 clove garlic, minced**
- **2 Tbsp. flour**
- **½ tsp. salt**
- **1 tsp. sugar**
- **¼ tsp. pepper**
- **¼ tsp. chili powder**
- **1 20-oz. can tomatoes**
- **1 8-oz. can tomato sauce**
- **1 3 to 4-oz. can mushrooms and liquid (opt.)**

Boil shrimp until ***just pink*** (as soon as water foams, about 5 minutes). Drain and sprinkle with lemon juice, Worcestershire sauce and salt; set aside. Melt butter in large frying pan. Add chopped onion, green pepper, celery and garlic. Saute over low heat until tender. Blend in flour, salt, sugar, pepper and chili powder. Add tomatoes, tomato sauce, mushrooms and liquid; mix thoroughly. Cover and simmer over low heat for about 45 minutes. Add shrimp; heat through. Serve with rice.

Director's notes: *Can be prepared in advance and rewarmed. Can be frozen after cooking.*

Suggested wines:
California Sauvignon Blanc
California Dry Chenin Blanc

Ellen Barry

seafood casserole

Serves: 6-8

Delicious for dinner party, buffet or luncheon.

- **2 6 or 7-oz. pkgs. King Crab**
- **1 10¾-oz. can cream of shrimp soup**
- **2 8-oz. cans sliced mushrooms and juice**
- **1 cup heavy cream**
- **1 cup uncooked rice**
- **1 jigger Sherry**
- **Garlic powder to taste**

Mix all ingredients together; turn into 7 x 12-inch shallow baking dish. Bake at 350° for 45 minutes.

Director's note: *Can be prepared ahead, refrigerated and baked just before serving.*

Suggested wines: French White Burgundy, California Chardonnay

ENCORE!

crabmeat asparagus pie

Serves: 6

What a terrific way to delight luncheon guests!

- **1 7-oz. pkg. frozen crabmeat**
- **1 10-oz. pkg. frozen asparagus**
- **1½ cups flour**
- **2 tsp. baking powder**
- **Dash salt**
- **½ cup butter, softened**
- **¼ cup milk**
- **1 Tbsp. chopped chives**
- **3 hard-boiled eggs**
- **½ cup diced celery**
- **2 Tbsp. minced scallions**
- **1 cup grated Cheddar cheese**
- **1 cup mayonnaise**

Drain and cut crabmeat into bite-size pieces. Cook and drain asparagus. Combine flour, baking powder and salt. Cut in butter until crumbly. Stir in milk and chives until dough forms a ball. Pat into 9-inch pie plate to form a shell. Fold crabmeat, chopped eggs, celery, scallions and cheese into mayonnaise. Place cooked asparagus on bottom of shell; fill with crabmeat mixture. Bake in preheated 350° oven for 30 minutes or until bubbling lightly.

Suggested wines:

California Chardonnay
French White Burgundy

"follow-spot" seafood

Serves: 10-12

A delectable casserole for any occasion.

- **2 6-oz. cans shrimp, rinsed and drained**
- **1 12-oz. can tuna fish, drained**
- **3 cups cooked rice**
- **1 10¾-oz. can cream of mushroom soup**
- **1 14-oz. can sweetened condensed milk**
- **1 cup mayonnaise**
- **1 green pepper, chopped**
- **1 cup chopped celery**
- **½ cup chopped onion**
- **1 tsp. lemon juice**
- **Slivered almonds** *or* **potato chips**

Combine rice with all ingredients except almonds. Turn into 3-quart baking dish. Top with almonds. Bake at 350° for 30 minutes or until hot and bubbly.

Suggested wines:

French Muscadet
Italian Frascati

crab and spinach casserole

Serves: 8

- 2 7-oz. cans crabmeat, drained and flaked
- ½ to 1 lb. spinach, cooked and drained
- 4 Tbsp. butter
- ¼ cup chopped onion
- 2 10¾-oz. cans cream of mushroom soup
- 1 6-oz. can diced mushrooms, plus liquid
- 1 cup sour cream
- ½ cup grated Parmesan cheese
- ½ tsp. dry mustard
- ½ tsp. MSG
- 2 Tbsp. sherry
- Dash Angostura bitters
- 1 Tbsp. chopped parsley *or* chives

Melt butter; saute onion until tender. Add soup, mushrooms, sour cream, cheese and seasonings. Cook until smooth. Stir in crabmeat, sherry, Angostura bitters and parsley. Place spinach in 2-quart baking dish. Spoon crabmeat mixture over top. Bake at 350° for 20 minutes or until bubbly.

Director's note: *May be prepared in advance. Reheat, covered, in 325° oven for 30 minutes or until heated through.*

Suggested wines: California Chenin Blanc, New York State Ravat

shrimp dream

Serves: 4-6

Contributed by Toby Johnson, chef at the Syracuse Corinthian Club. A wonderful treat for a luncheon.

- 1 6 to 7-oz. can shrimp, rinsed and chopped
- 6 oz. cream cheese, softened
- 4 Tbsp. mayonnaise
- 2 tsp. Worcestershire sauce
- 1 Tbsp. minced onion
- ½ cup diced celery
- 4 English muffins, split and toasted
- Paprika

Blend cream cheese with mayonnaise. Add Worcestershire sauce, onion and celery. Fold in shrimp. Spread on toasted muffins. Sprinkle with paprika. Place under broiler.

Director's note: *For variation, place slice of Cheddar cheese on each, then broil.*

Suggested wines:

California Johannisberg Riesling
German Rhinegau Riesling Kabinett

Asides

Vegetables

Photo on p. 189:
A Doll's House, 1981 - Erika Petersen (Nora), Kenneth Gray (Torvald)

asparagus parmesan

Serves: 4-6

2½ lbs. fresh asparagus
4 Tbsp. butter
3 Tbsp. chopped scallions
¼ tsp. curry powder
½ tsp. salt
⅓ cup flour
1⅔ cups milk
⅓ cup dry white wine
⅓ cup grated Parmesan cheese

Cut asparagus into 2-inch long pieces. Cook until crisp-tender; drain. Melt butter; add scallions, curry powder and salt. Cook 4 minutes. Stir in flour; gradually add milk. Cook and stir until mixture boils and thickens. Stir in wine and asparagus; place in shallow baking dish. Sprinkle with cheese. Bake at 350° for 45 minutes.

artichokes au gratin

Serves: 6-8

3 9-oz. pkgs. frozen artichoke hearts
4 Tbsp. butter
4 Tbsp. flour
1½ cups milk
Dash Tabasco
½ cup grated Swiss *or* **Gruyere cheese**
½ cup heavy cream
Salt and pepper
2 Tbsp. butter
½ cup Parmesan cheese

Cook artichokes according to package directions; drain and place in shallow, 2-quart or 8-inch square baking dish. Melt the 4 tablespoons butter in saucepan; stir in flour. Cook over low heat for 2 to 3 minutes. Heat milk to just below boiling; add to roux all at once, stirring vigorously. Simmer 5 minutes. Add Tabasco, Swiss cheese, cream and seasonings. Stir until cheese is melted.* Pour over artichoke hearts. Melt the 2 tablespoons butter; pour over top; sprinkle with Parmesan cheese. Bake at 400° for 10 to 12 minutes or until bubbly.

Director's note: **Can be made to this point in advance and refrigerated. Do not combine artichoke hearts and sauce until ready to complete casserole and bake.*

ann's beans

Serves: 10-14

Great for picnics.

- 1 cup chopped onion
- 1 cup chopped green pepper
- 1 cup chopped celery
- 1 cup catsup
- 3 Tbsp. vinegar
- Dash garlic powder (opt.)
- 1 Tbsp. prepared mustard
- 1 tsp. salt (opt.)
- 1¼ cups brown sugar
- 1 1-lb. can pork and beans, drained
- 1 1-lb. can kidney beans, drained
- 1 10-oz. pkg. frozen Lima beans, cooked and drained
- Bacon, uncooked

Combine all ingredients except bacon. Place in 9 x 13-inch baking pan. Top with pieces of uncooked bacon. Bake, uncovered, at 350° for 45 to 60 minutes.

Director's note: *Freezes after cooking.*

baked beans with red wine

Serves: 6-8

Super for a cold winter night!

- 2 medium onions, diced
- 2 Tbsp. butter
- 1 thick slice ham, chopped
- 1 cup canned consomme
- 1 cup red wine
- ½ tsp. salt
- ¼ tsp. cayenne pepper
- 2 8-oz. cans kidney beans
- 6 to 8 slices bacon, cut into 1-inch squares
- ½ cup grated Cheddar cheese

Preheat oven to 350°. Saute onion in butter, but ***do not*** brown. Add ham, consomme and wine. Simmer until sauce begins to thicken; add salt and cayenne pepper. Simmer for 10 minutes. Add beans; blend well. Pour into 2-quart baking dish. Top with bacon; bake for 20 minutes. Remove from oven; sprinkle with cheese; bake 10 minutes more.

"In vino veritas."
"In wine is truth."
Proverb quoted by Plato

bourbon baked beans

Serves: 8

- **4 20-oz. cans baked beans**
- **1 Tbsp. molasses**
- **¼ tsp. dry mustard**
- **½ cup chili sauce**
- **½ cup bourbon**
- **⅓ cup strong coffee**
- **1 8-oz. can crushed pineapple**
- **½ cup brown sugar**
- **Crisp bacon**

Blend everything but pineapple, brown sugar and bacon. Let stand 3 hours. Bake at 325° for 30 minutes. Add pineapple and brown sugar; bake 30 minutes more. Place bacon on top before serving.

casserole "revue"

Serves: 6-8

- **1 lb. green beans, fresh *or* frozen**
- **4 green peppers, sliced into strips**
- **2 Tbsp. vegetable oil**
- **½ lb. mushrooms, sliced**
- **4 medium onions, sliced**
- **2 cloves garlic, minced**
- **1 tsp. fresh dill weed (opt.)**
- **1 15-oz. can stewed tomatoes**
- **Salt and pepper to taste**
- **3 Tbsp. vegetable oil**

Cook beans in lightly salted water until crisp-tender; drain. Saute green peppers in the 2 tablespoons oil until slightly soft. Add mushrooms and onions, cook until soft. Put beans in lightly oiled, 2-quart baking dish. Add pepper, onion and mushroom mixture. Sprinkle with minced garlic and dill. Cover with stewed tomatoes. Drizzle the 3 tablespoons oil over the top. Bake at 325° for 30 to 40 minutes or until bubbly.

panned broccoli with garlic

Serves: 4

- **1 large bunch broccoli**
- **4 Tbsp. butter, *not* margarine**
- **4 large cloves garlic, peeled and sliced**

Wash broccoli; leave it moist. Cut broccoli into florets. Peel thick stalk; slice thinly. Melt butter in large frying pan; clarify, if desired. Over low heat, saute garlic until just golden. Add broccoli; spread out as much as possible. Cover; saute over very low heat. Stir occasionally to coat with butter mixture, about 20 minutes or until crisp-tender. Remove garlic. Serve broccoli immediately.

broccoli with almonds

Serves: 6

- **2 10-oz. pkgs. frozen broccoli**
- **2 Tbsp. butter**
- **2 Tbsp. flour**
- **2 cups milk**
- **¾ cup grated Cheddar cheese**
- **½ tsp. salt**
- **¼ tsp. pepper**
- **½ cup chopped almonds**
- **4 slices bacon, cooked and crumbled**
- **½ cup buttered bread crumbs**

Cook broccoli until tender; drain. Place in buttered, 2-quart baking dish. Melt butter in saucepan; stir in flour until smooth. Heat milk; add to flour mixture, beating constantly over medium heat until thick. Add cheese, salt, pepper and almonds. Pour over broccoli. Sprinkle bacon and bread crumbs on top. Bake at 350° for 20 minutes.

walnut broccoli

Serves: 8-10

- **3 10½-oz. pkgs. frozen chopped broccoli**
- **½ cup butter *or* margarine**
- **¼ cup flour**
- **2 tsp. instant chicken bouillon**
- **2 cups milk**
- **⅔ cup water**
- **6 Tbsp. butter *or* margarine**
- **⅔ of a 7-oz. pkg. fine bread stuffing mix**
- **⅔ cup chopped walnuts**

Cook broccoli until crisp-tender. Drain and place in shallow, greased 9 x 13-inch baking dish. Melt the ½ cup butter; blend in flour and bouillon. Simmer, stirring for 3 to 4 minutes. Blend in milk; cook, stirring until thickened. Pour over broccoli. Heat water and the 6 tablespoons butter together; pour over stuffing; toss to coat thoroughly. Stir in nuts. Top broccoli with this mixture; bake in preheated 400° oven for 20 minutes or until thoroughly heated through and stuffing begins to brown.

brussels sprouts

Serves: 6

- 4 cups Brussels sprouts
- 1 stalk celery, chopped
- 4 Tbsp. butter, melted
- Salt and pepper
- ½ cup grated Gruyere cheese
- ¼ cup grated Parmesan cheese
- 2 Tbsp. butter, melted

Preheat oven to 350°. Steam sprouts and celery until crisp-tender. Meanwhile, coat bottom of 1½-quart baking dish with the 4 tablespoons melted butter; sprinkle with salt and pepper. Heat in oven for 5 minutes. Increase temperature to 425°. Combine cheeses. Layer sprouts and celery with cheeses in dish, ending with cheese. Drizzle the 2 tablespoons melted butter over top. Bake 10 minutes or until cheese is melted and vegetables begin to bubble.

brussels sprouts and wild rice

Serves: 4

- 1 cup wild rice
- Boiling water
- 2½ cups water
- 1 tsp. salt
- ¼ cup butter
- 3 shallots, finely chopped
- 1 clove garlic, minced
- 1 pint fresh Brussels sprouts*
- Salt and pepper

Simmer rice in boiling water to cover for 2 minutes; drain. Cover rice again with boiling water and repeat procedure twice. Bring the 2½ cups water and salt to a boil; add drained rice and cook for about 30 minutes or until tender. (If necessary, keep rice warm in 300° oven.) Meanwhile, melt butter; saute shallots and garlic for 2 minutes. Cook Brussels sprouts until tender; drain and chop coarsely. Toss gently with cooked rice, shallots and garlic. Season with salt and pepper.

Director's note: *Can be prepared in advance. Reheat, covered, in slow oven. *Frozen sprouts can be substituted for fresh.*

"Training is everything. The peach was once a bitter almond; cauliflower is nothing but cabbage with a college education."
Mark Twain

c.e.d.d. (cheap, easy, delicious & different)

Serves: 4-6

Contributed by Arthur Storch, Producing Director at Syracuse Stage.

- 1 medium head of cabbage
- 1 to 2 Tbsp. butter
- 1 clove garlic, minced
- Heavy cream
- White pepper
- Cinnamon, allspice (opt.)
- Salt (opt.)

Shred cabbage into ½-inch pieces. Saute lightly in butter with garlic until slightly limp. Add a dash or two of heavy cream and pepper. Add cinnamon, allspice and salt, if desired. Serve immediately.

bavarian cabbage

Serves: 4-6

This may make a cabbage lover out of you.

- ½ large head of cabbage, finely sliced
- ½ cup chopped onion
- ½ cup chicken broth
- Dash salt
- 1 tsp. black pepper
- ¼ tsp. caraway seed *or* to taste

In covered saucepan, combine all ingredients. Cover and simmer for 35 to 45 minutes, stirring occasionally.

ENCORE!

old-fashioned german red cabbage

Serves: 6

- 2 Tbsp. bacon fat
- ¼ to ½ cup chopped onion
- 1 apple, pared and sliced
- 1 Tbsp. sugar
- 1 Tbsp. vinegar
- 1 tsp. salt
- ½ tsp. pepper
- ½ cup water
- 1 medium head red cabbage, shredded

Place bacon fat in kettle; add onion and brown. Add remaining ingredients. Simmer about 2 hours until tender. Serve hot or cold.

brandied carrots

Serves: 4

24 small carrots
2 Tbsp. Triple Sec
1/4 cup brandy
1/4 cup honey
Juice of 1 lemon
Parsley

Cook carrots until crisp-tender. Arrange in buttered, shallow casserole. Mix remaining ingredients and pour over carrots. Bake at 350° for 15 minutes. Serve with parsley garnish.

cheddar carrots

Serves: 6

4 cups sliced cooked carrots
1 1/2 cups croutons
1 1/4 cups shredded sharp Cheddar cheese
2 eggs, beaten
1/4 cup half-and-half
1/4 cup butter *or* margarine, melted
1 tsp. Worcestershire sauce
1 tsp. salt

Place carrots in buttered 1 1/2-quart casserole. Stir in croutons and cheese. Combine remaining ingredients; pour over carrot mixture.* Bake, uncovered, at 400° for 20 minutes, or until brown.

Director's note: **May be refrigerated at this point; baking time will be a bit longer.*

pineapple carrots

Serves: 8

Very delicate flavor.

2 lbs. carrots, sliced
1 tsp. salt
2 cups boiling water
1/2 cup sugar
4 tsp. cornstarch
1 6-oz. can pineapple juice
2 Tbsp. butter *or* margarine
2 Tbsp. chopped fresh mint leaves

In saucepan, combine carrots, salt and water. Cover; simmer 20 minutes or until tender; drain. Combine sugar, cornstarch and pineapple juice. Cook over medium heat, stirring constantly, until sauce thickens and boils for 3 minutes. Add butter and stir until melted. Stir in carrots and mint.

piquant carrots

Serves: 6-8

2 1-lb. cans small *whole* carrots *or* 4 cups fresh*
1 Tbsp. cornstarch
1 Tbsp. orange-flavored instant breakfast drink
¼ tsp. salt
Several dashes nutmeg
2 Tbsp. butter *or* margarine
Chopped parsley

Drain carrots, reserving liquid. If necessary, add water to liquid to make ¾ cup. In saucepan, blend cornstarch with instant drink, salt and nutmeg; stir in reserved liquid. Bring to a boil, stirring constantly. Reduce heat; cook, stirring until mixture thickens. Add butter and carrots; heat through. Sprinkle with parsley.

Director's note: **If using fresh carrots, cook in small amount of water until crisp-tender - proceed with recipe.*

cauliflower au gratin

Serves: 4-6

2 Tbsp. butter
2 Tbsp. flour
½ tsp. salt
⅛ tsp. dry mustard
Dash white pepper
1 cup milk
2 cups grated sharp cheese
1 medium head cauliflower, cooked
Paprika

Melt butter in saucepan; stir in flour; allow to bubble 1 minute. Mix in seasonings; gradually add milk. Cook, stirring until sauce thickens. Stir in cheese; continue cooking until cheese melts and mixture is thickened to medium sauce. Place cooked cauliflower in 1½-quart baking dish. Cover with cheese sauce; sprinkle with paprika. Bake at 350° for 15 minutes.

curried cauliflower

Serves: 4-6

1 large head cauliflower
½ tsp. salt
1 10¾-oz. can cream of chicken soup
4 oz. shredded Cheddar cheese
⅓ cup mayonnaise
1 tsp. curry powder
¼ cup dried bread crumbs
2 Tbsp. butter, melted

Break cauliflower into florets. Cook in boiling, salted water for 10 minutes. Drain well. In 2-quart baking dish, stir together soup, cheese, mayonnaise and curry. Add cauliflower; mix well. Toss bread crumbs in melted butter; sprinkle on top. Bake at 350° for 30 minutes, or until bubbly.

eggplant casserole

Serves: 6-8

2 medium eggplants
2 eggs (more if needed)
2 Tbsp. parsley flakes
1 tsp. garlic salt
½ tsp. pepper
Grated Parmesan cheese
Vegetable oil
Tomato sauce*
1 to 1½ cups shredded Mozzarella cheese

Peel and slice 2 medium eggplants about ½-inch thick. Beat two eggs; add parsley flakes, garlic salt, pepper and 1 tablespoon Parmesan cheese. Dip eggplant into egg mixture. Fry in enough oil to cover bottom of frying pan, about ⅛-inch thick. Brown on both sides. (Add more eggs if there is not enough mixture.) Remove eggplant; place on paper towels to absorb grease after frying. Line 6 x 9-inch baking dish with about ¼ inch tomato sauce. Make layers of eggplant, sauce and about 2 tablespoons Parmesan cheese. Repeat. Sprinkle Mozzarella cheese on top. Cover and bake at 350° for 30 minutes or until cheese has melted and casserole has heated through.

Tomato Sauce*

1 28-oz. can tomato puree
¼ can of water
1 tsp. salt
½ tsp. pepper
2 tsp. parsley flakes
1 tsp. sweet basil

Combine ingredients in saucepan. Cook over low heat at least ½ hour while frying eggplant. Stir occasionally.

Ivar, *A Doll's House*

broiled herbed eggplant

Serves: 4

1 medium eggplant
¼ cup olive oil
⅛ tsp. basil
⅛ tsp. thyme
⅛ tsp. oregano
1 tsp. salt
½ tsp. minced garlic
2 Tbsp. butter
¼ cup minced fresh parsley
¼ cup bread crumbs, fresh *or* dried
Dash black pepper

Wipe eggplant and cut into 8 round 1-inch slices. In small saucepan or frying pan, mix oil, basil, thyme, oregano, salt and garlic. Brush mixture on 1 side of eggplant slices. Place slices on cookie sheet; bake at 375° for 15 minutes. Turn slices; brush with herb mixture; bake 15 minutes more. Melt butter in oil-herb pan; stir in parsley and bread crumbs. Spoon over top of each slice. Sprinkle with pepper. Broil until brown, 2 or 3 minutes.

stuffed rolled eggplant

Serves: 6-8

1 medium eggplant
Bread crumbs
½ lb. Ricotta cheese
2 eggs
Salt and pepper to taste
1 8-oz. can tomato sauce

Preheat oven to 350°. Slice eggplant ⅛ to ¼-inch thick. Dip into bread crumbs. Place on cookie sheet; bake 3 to 5 minutes.* Mix Ricotta, eggs, salt and pepper. Place 1 tablespoonful of cheese filling on each slice of eggplant; roll up. Pour enough sauce in baking dish to cover bottom. Place rolled eggplant on sauce; cover with more sauce. Bake for ½ hour.

Director's note: **Eggplant slices can be frozen at this point. Thaw completely before finishing preparation. Finished dish can be frozen, also.*

hominy casserole

Serves: 6-8

2 1-lb. cans white hominy
½ cup chopped onion
3 mild green chilies, chopped
Dot of butter
1 cup grated Cheddar *or* Monterey Jack cheese
½ cup bread crumbs

Combine hominy, onion and green chilies. Place in 1½-quart casserole. Dot with butter. Sprinkle with grated cheese. Top with bread crumbs. Bake at 350° for ½ hour. Serve hot.

baked mushrooms

Serves: 4-6

- **12 oz. fresh mushrooms**
- **2 tsp. lemon juice**
- **1 Tbsp. minced onion**
- **2 Tbsp. butter**
- **¼ tsp. salt**
- **⅛ tsp. pepper**
- **1 Tbsp. flour**
- **2 Tbsp. grated Parmesan cheese**
- **1 cup heavy cream**
- **2 egg yolks, lightly beaten**
- **2 Tbsp. fine white bread crumbs**
- **1 Tbsp. butter**

Wash mushrooms and slice. Sprinkle with lemon juice to prevent discoloration. Simmer in tightly covered saucepan with minced onion, the 2 tablespoons butter, salt and pepper. Stir in flour and Parmesan cheese; cook about 3 minutes. Place mixture in 4-cup casserole. Mix cream and egg yolks together; pour over mushrooms. Sprinkle with bread crumbs; dot with the 1 tablespoon butter. Bake at 350° about 30 minutes.

elegant mushroom casserole

Serves: 4-5

- **¾ lb. mushrooms**
- **4 scallions, sliced**
- **2 Tbsp. butter *or* margarine**
- **2 tsp. lemon juice**
- **Salt and pepper**
- **1 9-oz. pkg. frozen artichoke hearts, cooked and drained**
- **2 Tbsp. butter *or* margarine**
- **2 Tbsp. flour**
- **1 cup canned chicken broth**
- **½ tsp. salt**
- **⅛ tsp. nutmeg**
- **½ cup cream**
- **1 Tbsp. sherry**
- **⅓ cup fresh bread crumbs**
- **⅓ cup grated Parmesan cheese**

Wash, dry and halve or quarter mushrooms. Saute mushrooms and scallions in 2 tablespoons butter until golden. Sprinkle with lemon juice, salt and pepper. Place in 1½-quart casserole with artichoke hearts. Melt 2 tablespoons butter in saucepan; blend in flour. Blend in chicken broth; stir over medium heat until mixture bubbles and thickens. Season with the ½ teaspoon salt, dash pepper and nutmeg. Add cream and sherry; pour over mushrooms. Mix bread crumbs and cheese; spread over top. Bake at 400° about 15 minutes.

mushroom supreme

Serves: 6-8

A delicious buffet casserole.

1 lb. whole mushrooms
2 Tbsp. butter
2 beef bouillon cubes
½ cup hot water
¼ cup butter
2 Tbsp. flour
½ cup cream
⅛ tsp. salt
Dash pepper
½ cup bread crumbs
½ to 1 cup grated Parmesan cheese

Saute mushrooms in the 2 tablespoons butter. Dissolve beef cubes in hot water. In saucepan, melt the ¼ cup butter; blend with flour. Add cream, salt, pepper and beef broth. Place mushrooms and gravy in buttered 5-cup casserole.* Mix bread crumbs and cheese together; sprinkle on mushrooms. Bake at 350° for 30 minutes.

Director's note: **Can be prepared to this point and refrigerated. Top with crumbs and cheese just before baking.*

gorgeous onions!

Serves: 6-8

4 cups sliced sweet white *or* Spanish onion
5 Tbsp. butter
2 eggs
1 cup cream
Salt and pepper
⅔ cup grated Parmesan cheese

Saute onions and butter until transparent. Place in shallow, 6-cup baking dish. Beat eggs until light. Mix in cream, salt and pepper. Pour over onions. Sprinkle Parmesan cheese on top. Bake at 425° for 15 to 20 minutes until lightly browned.

julienne vegetables

Serves: 6

A great combination of flavors.

2 medium potatoes, peeled
3 large carrots, peeled
1 bunch fresh broccoli
4 Tbsp. butter
Salt and pepper
2 Tbsp. chopped parsley

Slice potatoes, carrots and broccoli stems into julienne strips and steam separately until crisp-tender. (Save broccoli tops for another use.) Run under cold water; drain. When ready to serve, melt butter until foamy. Saute vegetables 3 to 4 minutes, turning and stirring to coat well with butter. Season with salt and pepper. Sprinkle with parsley.

potatoes au gratin

Serves: 4

- **4 large potatoes, thinly sliced**
- **½ cup butter, melted**
- **Salt and pepper**
- **½ cup grated Parmesan cheese**
- **½ cup grated Gruyere cheese**
- **¼ cup heavy cream**

Place layer of potatoes in buttered, 1½-quart baking dish. Pour some melted butter over potatoes. Sprinkle with salt, pepper and some of cheeses. Continue layers of potatoes, melted butter, salt, pepper and cheeses until all ingredients are used. Pour cream over the top; cover dish with foil. Bake at 375° for 1 hour. Remove foil 10 minutes before serving to brown top.

jefferson potatoes

Serves: 8

- **4 cups sliced potatoes**
- **6 Tbsp. butter**
- **6 Tbsp. flour**
- **1 cup milk**
- **½ cup cream**
- **1 10¾-oz. can chicken broth**
- **Salt and pepper**

Cook potatoes a few minutes until ***partially*** cooked; drain. Place in 2-quart baking dish. Melt butter in saucepan; add flour and mix well. Add milk, cream and chicken broth. Cook, stirring until thickened. Add salt and pepper to taste; pour over potatoes, making sure all layers are covered. Bake, uncovered, at 350° for 45 minutes until golden brown.

potato porcupines

Serves: 4-6

Kids go wild over these.

- **3 medium potatoes**
- **1 egg**
- **1 heaping Tbsp. flour**
- **1 tsp. salt**
- **½ cup shortening**

Wash, peel and shred raw potatoes; drain on paper towels. Combine egg, flour and salt; blend well. Immediately add shredded potatoes to egg mixture; stir until evenly mixed. In hot shortening, place tablespoonfuls of potatoes to fry until golden brown on both sides. Keep cooked porcupines warm until all are cooked; serve hot.

potatoes chantilly

Serves: 4-5

4 medium Idaho potatoes
½ cup heavy cream
3 Tbsp. butter
Salt and pepper
Chopped parsley
½ cup grated Cheddar cheese

Pare and cut potatoes as for French fries. Place in center of large sheet of aluminum foil. Pour cream over; dot with butter; sprinkle with salt, pepper, parsley and cheese. Fold foil over, making tight package. Place package in shallow baking pan.* Bake at 425° for 40 minutes. You can serve from foil or place in serving dish.

Director's note: **Can be refrigerated at this point for a few hours; do not prepare the night before.*

potato-cheese-mushroom bake

Serves: 4

2 potatoes, thinly sliced
¼ lb. mushrooms, sliced
4 oz. Swiss cheese, grated
1 clove garlic, minced
Dash salt, pepper
Dash cinnamon, cloves
3 Tbsp. butter, melted
Parmesan *or* Romano cheese
Paprika, oregano

Preheat oven to 350°. Oil bottom of 9-inch pie plate. Layer ½ of potatoes, mushrooms, cheese and garlic. Sprinkle on ½ of seasonings and spices; pour on ½ of melted butter. Layer remaining potatoes, mushrooms, cheese and garlic. Sprinkle on remaining spices. Pour remaining melted butter over top. Sprinkle with cheese, paprika and a pinch of oregano. Bake for 20 to 30 minutes.

elegant potatoes

Serves: 10-12

- ½ cup snipped parsley
- 2 cups chopped onion
- ¼ cup butter
- 2½ lbs. potatoes, cooked and pared
- 4 hard-boiled eggs, sliced
- 4 medium tomatoes, cut into small pieces
- 2 cups sour cream
- 3 Tbsp. flour
- 1½ cups grated Cheddar cheese
- Salt and pepper
- ⅛ tsp. paprika
- ¾ cup butter
- 1 cup bread crumbs

Saute parsley and onion in the ¼ cup butter. Slice cooked potatoes ¼-inch thick. Place ½ of sliced potatoes in greased 3-quart casserole.* Cover with onion mixture and eggs. Add tomatoes. Blend sour cream, flour, cheese, salt, pepper and paprika. Spread ½ of sour cream mixture over tomatoes. Melt the ¾ cup butter; drizzle ½ of it over sour cream. Cover with remaining potatoes. Spread remainder of sour cream mixture. Sprinkle with bread crumbs that have been mixed with 1 tablespoon of the melted butter. Pour remaining melted butter over top. Sprinkle with extra paprika. Bake at 350° for ½ hour or until bubbly and top is brown.

Director's note: **Two 1½-quart casserole dishes can be used.*

Taylor, *K-2*

salt potatoes

Contributed by Hinerwadel's Grove, noted for clambakes and salt potatoes. According to legend, workers at Will and Baumer Candle Company dipped their potatoes into the nearby salt wells, and salt potatoes were born. They are a sensational taste treat that can be enjoyed summer or winter -- indoors or out.

Basic Brine

3 quarts water
1 lb. salt
4 lbs. potatoes (1 inch to 2¼ inches maximum)

Bring water and salt to a boil. Add 4 pounds potatoes and cook 20 minutes or until done. Serve hot with butter or margarine; eat with skins on.

southern hash browns

Serves: 10-12

1 2-lb. bag frozen hash brown potatoes, thawed
1 cup sour cream
⅓ cup chopped onion
1½ cups grated sharp Cheddar cheese
¼ cup butter, melted
1 10¾-oz. can cream of chicken soup
½ soup can milk
2 Tbsp. butter, melted
1 cup crushed cornflakes

Mix all ingredients together except the 2 tablespoons melted butter and cornflakes. Turn into 2½ to 3-quart casserole. Mix the 2 tablespoons melted butter and cornflakes together; sprinkle on top. Bake at 350° for 1½ hours or until done.

sweet potato casserole

Serves: 6-8

6 large sweet potatoes
½ cup butter, softened
½ cup light cream
½ cup Madeira wine
½ tsp. cinnamon
½ tsp. salt
½ tsp. nutmeg
1 Tbsp. grated orange rind
Butter, chopped pecans *or* walnuts

Preheat oven to 375°. Bake sweet potatoes for 40 minutes or until tender. Reduce temperature to 350°. Mash potatoes, adding butter, cream and wine. Add cinnamon, salt, nutmeg and orange rind; taste for seasoning. Place in buttered, 2-quart baking dish. Dot with butter; sprinkle with nuts. Bake for 25 minutes.

tidewater sweet potato bake

Serves: 8-10

Wonderful for the holidays.

- 2 1-lb. cans sweet potatoes *or* yams
- 1 tsp. salt
- ¼ tsp. pepper
- ½ cup butter *or* margarine, melted
- ½ cup light brown sugar, firmly packed
- ½ tsp. nutmeg
- 2 medium cooking apples, pared and thinly sliced

Mash potatoes. Season with salt, pepper and 4 tablespoons of the melted butter; set aside. Combine remaining butter with brown sugar and nutmeg in 8-cup baking dish. Arrange apple slices on mixture. Top with sweet potato mixture. Bake at 350° for 45 minutes or until heated through.

spinach timbales

Serves: 6

Contributed by Fred and Betty O'Hara, well known culinary experts.

- 4 cups (1 pkg.) fresh spinach
- Vegetable oil
- ¼ cup bread crumbs
- 1 medium onion, minced
- 2 cloves garlic, minced
- 1 Tbsp. butter
- ½ cup milk
- 2 Tbsp. butter
- 3 extra large eggs
- ⅓ cup grated Swiss cheese
- ⅓ cup fresh bread crumbs
- Nutmeg, several dashes
- ¼ tsp. salt
- ¼ tsp. white pepper
- 1 Tbsp. fresh lemon juice

Preheat oven to 350°. Remove stems and finely chop spinach; set aside. Lightly oil and coat insides of six ½-cup molds with the ¼ cup bread crumbs. Cook onion and garlic in the 1 tablespoon butter over low heat for 10 minutes, ***do not allow to brown***. Warm milk with the 2 tablespoons butter. Beat eggs; add onion-garlic mixture and Swiss cheese to eggs. While beating, slowly add warmed milk and butter to egg mixture. Add the ⅓ cup bread crumbs and spinach. Combine thoroughly. Season with nutmeg, salt, pepper and lemon juice to taste. Turn into prepared molds. Place molds in baking dish; carefully fill the dish with boiling water so that it comes ⅔ up the sides of molds. Bake for 30 minutes or until a knife inserted into center of timbales comes out clean. Turn out onto warm serving platter.

spinach delight

Serves: 6-8

- **2 10-oz. pkgs. frozen chopped spinach, cooked and drained**
- **1 lb. fresh mushrooms, sliced**
- **1 cup shredded sharp Cheddar cheese**

Place all ***well-drained*** spinach in lightly buttered 1½-quart casserole. Add ½ of the cheese. Layer all the mushrooms over cheese; add remaining cheese on top.* Bake at 350° for 1 hour.

Director's note: **Can be prepared to this point and refrigerated. Add a few minutes to baking time since casserole is cold.*

"upstage" spinach souffle

Serves: 6

- **2 10-oz. pkgs. frozen chopped spinach, cooked and drained**
- **1 env. onion soup mix**
- **½ pint sour cream**
- **½ cup cornflake crumbs**
- **2 Tbsp. butter** *or* **margarine, softened**

Mix together spinach, onion soup mix and sour cream. Place in buttered baking dish. Mix cornflake crumbs and butter. Sprinkle over casserole. Bake at 325° for 45 minutes to 1 hour.

quick's sauerkraut

A favorite of Gordon Symond's Scottish grandmother, Marie Quick.

- **2 lbs. sauerkraut**
- **2 cups water**
- **¼ cup sherry**
- **½ can of** *stale* **beer**
- **15 oz. sour cream**
- **½ cup poppy seeds**
- **½ cup sesame seeds**
- **Cooked sliced sausage** *or* **pork**

Place drained sauerkraut in steamer or boil in 2 cups water until tender. Drain and place in frying pan; add sherry and stale beer. Saute slowly for 10 minutes or until liquid is diminished by half. Place sauerkraut in bowl; fold in sour cream. Add poppy and sesame seeds. Garnish with sliced sausage or pork.

apple stuffed squash

Serves: 4

- 2 acorn *or* small butternut squash
- 3 tart apples, pared, cored and diced
- ¼ cup butter, melted
- ½ cup maple syrup *or* honey
- Melted butter
- Salt

Cut squash in half lengthwise; remove seeds and fiber. Place in baking pan, cut side down; pour in boiling water to the depth of ½-inch. Bake at 400° for 20 minutes. Mix apples with the ¼ cup melted butter and maple syrup. Turn squash cut side up. Brush with additional melted butter; sprinkle with salt. Fill squash with apple mixture. Cover pan with foil; bake for 30 minutes or until apples and squash are tender.

harvest squash

Serves: 4

- 2 acorn squash
- Salt
- 2 Tbsp. butter
- 1 20-oz. can pineapple chunks, drained
- ¼ cup honey
- 2 Tbsp. dark rum
- ½ tsp. pumpkin pie spice
- ½ cup chopped walnuts, toasted (opt.)

Cut squash in half lengthwise; remove seeds and fiber. Sprinkle with salt. Place in baking pan, cut side down. Bake at 350° for 40 minutes. Turn squash cut side up. Divide butter and place in hollows of squash, spreading evenly. Pierce squash with fork. Combine pineapple, honey, rum, spice and walnuts. Spoon mixture into squash. Bake 15 minutes more or until tender.

sherried tomatoes

Serves: 6-8

- 4 large ripe tomatoes
- ¼ cup dry sherry
- ½ tsp. salt *or* seasoned salt
- ¼ tsp. pepper
- 1 tsp. oregano
- 8 Tbsp. mayonnaise
- ¼ cup grated Parmesan cheese

Preheat over to 300°. Cut tomatoes in half horizontally. Place in baking dish, cut side up; prick with fork. Sprinkle with sherry slowly so tomatoes absorb it. Sprinkle with salt, pepper, and oregano. Place in oven for 5 minutes. Remove from oven and increase temperature to broil. Top tomatoes with mayonnaise; sprinkle with cheese. Broil until lightly browned. Serve immediately.

fish house tomatoes

Serves: 1

Good with veal or lamb as well as fish.

1 medium tomato* per person
2 tsp. brown sugar
2 Tbsp. butter
2 tsp. finely chopped Bermuda onion
Salt and pepper to taste

Preheat oven to 350°. Cut a slice from top of tomato; place in shallow baking dish. Cover tomato with combined remaining ingredients. Bake at least 1½ hours, basting 2 or 3 times after first half-hour. Tomato is done when basting juice becomes the consistency of syrup. Add hot water if juice becomes too thick or black. If using hothouse tomatoes, core and fill with ingredients, instead of placing on top.

Director's note: **Ingredients are for each tomato. Recipe multiplies easily.*

tomatoes provencal

Serves: 6

6 firm ripe tomatoes
1 cup parsley, minced
2 cups fresh bread crumbs
1 Tbsp. oregano
1 Tbsp. thyme
4 Tbsp. fresh basil
4 large cloves garlic, minced
4 large shallots, minced
Salt and pepper to taste
½ cup plus 1 Tbsp. olive oil
Parmesan cheese (opt.)

Preheat oven to 350°. Cut ⅓ of the tomato off the top. Remove all seeds from bottom part of each tomato, leaving pulp intact. Salt lightly. Place upside down on paper towels; drain about 1 hour. Combine all ingredients except oil, tomatoes and cheese. Add the ½ cup oil in light stream, stirring until mixture is moist but not wet. Place ½ teaspoon oil in each of the 8 tomatoes. Top each tomato with mixture. Place tomatoes in buttered non-aluminum baking pan. Cover tomatoes with buttered wax paper. Bake for 20 to 25 minutes until cooked but firm. If desired, remove wax paper during last 3 to 4 minutes of cooking and sprinkle tomatoes with Parmesan cheese.

ENCORE! ratatouille

Serves: 8-10

- **6 zucchini, cut into bite-size pieces**
- **1/4 lb. mushrooms**
- **1 medium eggplant, peeled and cubed**
- **2 small bell peppers, diced**
- **2 onions, sliced**
- **1/4 cup olive oil**
- **2 cloves garlic, minced**
- **2 tsp. salt**
- **1 tsp. basil**
- **1/2 cup parsley**
- **3 large tomatoes**
- **Swiss cheese, grated**

Simmer all ingredients except tomatoes for 30 minutes. Drain some of liquid. Place mixture in 9 x 13-inch baking dish.* Add tomatoes, cut into wedges. Cover with thick layer of grated Swiss cheese. Bake at 350° for 30 minutes.

Director's note: **Can be prepared to this point the day before serving and refrigerated. Finish preparation just before baking.*

chinese tofu

Serves: 4

- **1 lb. tofu**
- **1/4 cup tamari**
- **1 6-oz. can sliced water chestnuts**
- **2 cups fresh green vegetables, chopped**
- **1 clove garlic, minced**
- **1/2 cup chopped onion**
- **2 Tbsp. vegetable oil**
- **1 2.8 oz. pkg. wholewheat ramen noodles**
- **1 1/2 cups hot water**
- **4 oz. Monterey Jack cheese**

Drain tofu on paper towels; cut into 1/2-inch cubes. Marinate tofu in tamari for 10 minutes. In large frying pan or wok, saute tofu and vegetables, including garlic and onion, in hot oil. Break noodles into small chunks; add to vegetables along with water. Cook, covered, 5 to 6 minutes until noodles are tender. Top with cheese; heat until cheese melts.

Director's note: *Tofu and tamari can be purchased in Oriental markets or the produce or gourmet sections of supermarkets.*

"Tell me what you eat, and I will tell you what you are."
Anthelme Brillat-Savarin

zucchini jumba

Serves: 10

Good for a summer barbecue.

- **4 medium zucchini**
- **1 to 2 green peppers**
- **10 medium raw potatoes**
- **½ cup vegetable oil**
- **2 cups grated Romano cheese**
- **Salt and pepper to taste**
- **1 Tbsp. parsley**
- **2 tsp. basil**
- **4 tomatoes**

Slice zucchini ¼-inch thick. Slice green peppers. Chop potatoes, leaving skins on. Pour ¼ cup of the oil into 9 x 13-inch baking dish. Add zucchini, green pepper and potato. Add remaining ¼ cup oil, cheese, salt, pepper, parsley and basil. Cut tomatoes into quarters; squeeze a bit over the casserole to produce some juice, then add. Cover dish with foil; bake at 350° for 1 to 1½ hours. Uncover and bake another 45 minutes until brown and almost "fried."

Director's note: *Can be made ahead and reheated.*

zucchini casserole

Serves: 6-8

- **6 slices bacon, chopped**
- **1 onion, chopped**
- **2 lbs. zucchini**
- **8 oz. Cheddar cheese, shredded**
- **1 8-oz. can tomato sauce**

Fry bacon and onion together. Slize zucchini ¼-inch thick. Cook in small amount of water for 2 minutes; drain. In 1½-quart baking dish, layer in the following order, ***drained*** zucchini, bacon, onion and cheese. Top with tomato sauce. Bake at 350° for 30 to 40 minutes.

zucchini italiano

Serves: 4

- **2 medium zucchini**
- **1 medium onion**
- **1 env. Good Seasons Italian Salad Dressing Mix**
- **¼ cup vegetable oil**
- **2 Tbsp. red wine vinegar**
- **Parmesan cheese**

Slice zucchini and onion. Place in shallow, 1-quart baking dish. Add salad dressing mix, oil, vinegar and as much Parmesan cheese as you like. Mix thoroughly. Sprinkle more Parmesan cheese on top. Bake at 350° for 30 to 45 minutes until zucchini is crisp-tender.

Understudies

Pasta

Rice

Sauces

Photo on p. 213:
The Comedy of Errors, 1980 - Marcus Smythe (Antipholus), Yolande Bavan (Adriana), Kevin Shumway (Antipholus Alternate), Kensyn Crouch (Egeon)

armenian pilaff

Serves: 6

Nice side dish. Would complement any number of main dishes.

- **1 large handful of thin noodles**
- **2 Tbsp. butter**
- **1 cup long grained rice**
- **2 Tbsp. butter**
- **1 tsp. salt**
- **2 cups chicken broth**

Using a heavy pan, brown noodles in 2 tablespoons butter over high heat until very brown. Wash and drain rice. Add rice, 2 tablespoons butter and salt to pan. Stir fry about 3 minutes. Add chicken broth. Cover pan and bring to full boil. Reduce heat to simmer for 20 minutes. Turn off heat. Leave pan on burner at least 10 to 15 minutes. Do not remove cover.

linguine with broccoli, cauliflower and mushrooms

Serves: 8

- **1 cup Ricotta cheese**
- **⅓ cup grated Romano cheese**
- **1 tsp. salt**
- **1 medium head cauliflower, trimmed and cut into florets**
- **1 bunch broccoli, trimmed and cut into florets**
- **1 cup olive oil**
- **6 cloves garlic, minced**
- **1 lb. mushrooms, thickly sliced**
- **2 tsp. salt**
- **½ tsp. crushed red pepper**
- **1 lb. linguine**
- **Grated Romano cheese**

Combine Ricotta and Romano cheeses; set aside. In large pot of boiling, salted water, cook cauliflower and broccoli about 7 minutes. Remove vegetables with slotted spoon, reserving liquid for cooking linguine. Heat olive oil in large frying pan. Lightly brown garlic; stir in mushrooms, salt and red pepper; saute about 5 minutes. Stir in broccoli and cauliflower; continue cooking 10 minutes. Bring cooking liquid to rapid boil, adding water if needed. Add linguine, stirring with fork to prevent sticking. Cook al dente, about 10 to 12 minutes. Drain well. Reheat vegetable mixture; stir in linguine.* Top with cheese mixture. Dust with more Romano cheese.

Director's note. **Combine vegetable mixture and linguine; place in baking dish. Top with cheese mixture. Bake at 350° for 20 minutes or until heated through.*

pasta primavera

Serves: 4-8

- **1 medium onion, minced**
- **1 clove garlic, minced**
- **½ cup unsalted butter**
- **1 lb. thin asparagus, diagonally sliced ¼-inch thick (leave tips intact)**
- **½ lb. mushrooms, sliced**
- **1 small bunch broccoli, cut into florets**
- **1 medium zucchini, sliced ¼-inch thick**
- **1 carrot, thinly sliced**
- **1 cup heavy cream**
- **½ cup chicken stock**
- **2 tsp. basil**
- **1 cup frozen tiny peas, thawed**
- **2 oz. cooked ham, chopped**
- **5 scallions, chopped**
- **Salt and pepper**
- **1 lb. fettucine, cooked al dente, drained**
- **1 cup grated Parmesan cheese**

In large frying pan, saute onion and garlic in butter until onion is transparent. Add asparagus, mushrooms, broccoli, zucchini and carrot. Cook about 2 minutes.* Add cream, stock and basil. Boil mixture until liquid is slightly reduced, about 3 minutes. Stir in peas, ham and scallions; cook 1 minute more. Season to taste. Add pasta and cheese, tossing until thoroughly combined and heated through. Garnish with any reserved vegetables. Serve immediately. Serves 4 to 6 as main course; 6 to 8 as first course.

Director's note: **Can be prepared to this point the day before needed. The rest can be done about ½ hour before serving.*

spanish noodles

Serves: 4

- **2 slices bacon**
- **1 lb. ground beef**
- **2 cups uncooked noodles**
- **Salt and pepper to taste**
- **½ green pepper, minced**
- **1 medium onion, minced**
- **3 cups canned tomatoes**
- **½ cup chili sauce**

Dice bacon and fry crisp. Add meat; brown well. Place all ingredients in large kettle, being careful that noodles are well covered. Cover tightly; cook until steam comes from top. Reduce heat and simmer about 45 minutes. Stir well to mix all ingredients.

"supporting player" casserole

Serves: 8-10

A delicious and "supportive" dish for any meal.

1 cup small curd cottage cheese
1 pint sour cream
1 Tbsp. Worcestershire sauce
⅓ cup finely chopped onion
Salt
8 oz. fine noodles, cooked
Parmesan cheese, grated

Mix cottage cheese with 1 cup of the sour cream. Add Worcestershire sauce, onion and salt to taste. Combine with cooked noodles. Place in 1½-quart baking dish.* Spread with the remaining 1 cup sour cream. Sprinkle generously with Parmesan cheese. Bake at 350° for 45 minutes.

Director's note: **Can be prepared to this point in advance. Finish preparation just before baking.*

noodle pudding

Serves: 12

A different accompaniment to meat and poultry.

1 lb. wide noodles
½ cup margarine
½ tsp. salt
1 cup sugar
1 cup raisins
2 tsp. cinnamon
1 pint sour cream
4 eggs, beaten
1½ lbs. small curd cottage cheese (not diet style)
Cinnamon-sugar mixture

Boil noodles 9 minutes; drain. Add margarine, salt, sugar, raisins, cinnamon, sour cream, eggs and cottage cheese. Mix well. Pour into 9 x 13-inch baking dish. Sprinkle top liberally with cinnamon-sugar mixture. Bake at 325°, uncovered, for 45 minutes to 1 hour or until knife inserted into center comes out clean.

"No man can be a patriot on an empty stomach."
William Cowper Brann

fritzie's noodle pudding

Serves: 10-12

A delicious and very special dish! Well worth the time it takes to prepare. Serve with meat or poultry.

- **½ lb. dried apple bits**
- **2 cups cider *or* apple juice**
- **1 8-oz. pkg. wide noodles**
- **½ cup corn *or* safflower oil**
- **6 medium apples, diced**
- **½ cup sugar (more if apples are sour)**
- **4 eggs, beaten**
- **4 tsp. cinnamon**
- **½ lb. white raisins**
- **1 10½-oz. bottle maraschino cherries and juice**
- **1 cup coarsely chopped walnuts**
- **2 tsp. vanilla**

Soak dried apple bits in cider for 1 hour.

Cook noodles al dente; drain. In large bowl, pour oil over noodles. Mix in soaked apple bits and remaining ingredients. Place in buttered 9 x 13-inch baking dish.* Sprinkle Crumb Topping over all. Bake in preheated 350° oven for 1 hour.

Crumb Topping

- **2 cups Ritz cracker crumbs *or* 1 cup cracker and 1 cup vanilla wafer crumbs**
- **2 Tbsp. sugar**
- **½ cup butter, melted**
- **½ cup chopped walnuts**
- **1 tsp. vanilla**

To make crumbs: either place enough crackers in blender to produce 2 cups crumbs, turn on and off until the right texture, or place crackers in plastic bag and roll with rolling pin. Add sugar, butter, nuts and vanilla. Mix thoroughly.

Director's note: **Casserole may be frozen at this point or refrigerated and baked when desired, even the next day. Sprinkle on Crumb Topping just before baking.*

lumache al provolone

Serves: 6-8

(Shells with Provolone sauce)

- **8 Tbsp. butter**
- **1 Tbsp. grated lemon peel**
- **1 pinch saffron**
- **1 lb. shell-shape pasta**
- **Freshly ground pepper**
- **½ lb. mild Provolone cheese, cut into ½-inch cubes**
- **Lemon slices**
- **Parsley sprigs**

Preheat oven to 400°. Melt butter in large baking dish. Add lemon peel and saffron, which has been softened in several drops of water. Cook gently 1 minute. Meanwhile, cook pasta al dente. Drain; toss pasta in the butter-lemon sauce. Season with pepper. Add Provolone and toss again. Bake 5 minutes until cheese melts. Garnish with lemon slices and parsley sprigs.

spaghetti carbonara

Serves: 4

Contributed by Arthur Storch, Producing Director of Syracuse Stage.

- **4 eggs**
- **¼ cup heavy cream *or* milk**
- **4 Tbsp. butter *or* margarine**
- **12 oz. spaghetti, cooked and drained**
- **¼ cup chopped parsley**
- **½ lb. bacon, crisply cooked and crumbled**
- **1 cup grated Parmesan *or* Romano cheese**
- **Pepper**

Have eggs, cream and butter at room temperature. Beat eggs and cream together. Toss spaghetti with butter. Add parsley, egg mixture, bacon, and grated cheese; toss well. Sprinkle with pepper to taste.

Suggested wines:

Italian Gavi
Italian Pinot Grigio

"A big butter and egg man."
Texas Guinan, describing a lavish spender or theatrical 'angel'
Title of George S. Kaufman play 1925

stuffed shells

Serves: 4-6

- **1 1-lb. box jumbo shells**
- **2 lbs. Ricotta cheese**
- **8 oz. Mozzarella cheese, grated**
- **⅓ cup grated Romano cheese**
- **2 eggs, beaten**
- **1 Tbsp. parsley**
- **½ tsp. salt**
- **Dash pepper**
- **Spaghetti sauce**

Cook shells in boiling, salted water, for 12 to 14 minutes. Drain well. Meanwhile, combine all cheeses, eggs, parsley, salt and pepper. Fill shells with cheese mixture. Place in shallow baking pan in single layer. Cover with spaghetti sauce; bake at 350° for 1 hour.

rice and noodle casserole

Serves: 12-15

- **1 8-oz. pkg. fine noodles, uncooked**
- **1½ cups butter *or* margarine, melted**
- **2 cups uncooked instant rice**
- **2 10½-oz. cans onion soup**
- **2 10¾-oz. cans chicken broth**
- **1 Tbsp. soy sauce**
- **1 cup water**
- **2 4 to 5-oz. cans mushrooms, undrained**

Slightly brown noodles in butter; add rice and mix well. Add soup, broth, soy sauce, water and mushrooms. Turn into 9 x 13-inch baking pan. Bake at 350° for 1 hour.

risotto a la milanese

Serves: 4

- **1 10¾-oz. can chicken broth**
- **½ cup finely chopped onion**
- **4 Tbsp. butter**
- **1 cup uncooked rice**
- **½ cup water**
- **⅓ cup dry white wine**
- **2 Tbsp. butter**
- **½ cup freshly grated Parmesan cheese**

Heat chicken broth; set aside. In large saucepan, saute onion in the 4 tablespoons butter until tender, but not brown. Add rice; cook, stirring occasionally, until rice is golden, about 5 minutes. Add chicken broth, water and wine; bring to a boil. Reduce heat; simmer, covered, 30 minutes or until all liquid is absorbed. Just before serving, stir in the 2 tablespoons butter and the cheese.

rice casserole

Serves: 4-6

Wonderful with beef or chicken.

- **1 10¾-oz. can cream of mushroom soup**
- **1 10½-oz. can consomme**
- **1 cup uncooked rice**
- **¼ cup butter *or* margarine**

In a 5-cup, covered baking dish, mix soups together. Add rice and mix again. Cut up butter in small chunks and stir into rice mixture. Cover and bake at 350° for 30 to 45 minutes. Remove the cover, ***stir thoroughly*** and bake, ***uncovered***, for 15 to 20 minutes more.

wild rice and mushrooms

Serves: 6-8

A wonderful dish for a buffet supper.

- **1 6-oz. box long grain wild rice mixture (not instant)**
- **1 Tbsp. grated onion**
- **1 Tbsp. chopped parsley**
- **1 Tbsp. chopped green pepper**
- **1 Tbsp. chopped chives**
- **¼ cup butter**
- **½ lb. fresh mushrooms, thinly sliced**
- **Salt, pepper, nutmeg**

Prepare rice according to package directions; set aside. Saute onion, parsley, green pepper and chives in butter. Add mushrooms; cook over low heat for 5 minutes, stirring frequently. Season to taste with salt, pepper and nutmeg. Combine with cooked rice. Serve immediately or place in casserole and keep in warm oven until ready to serve.

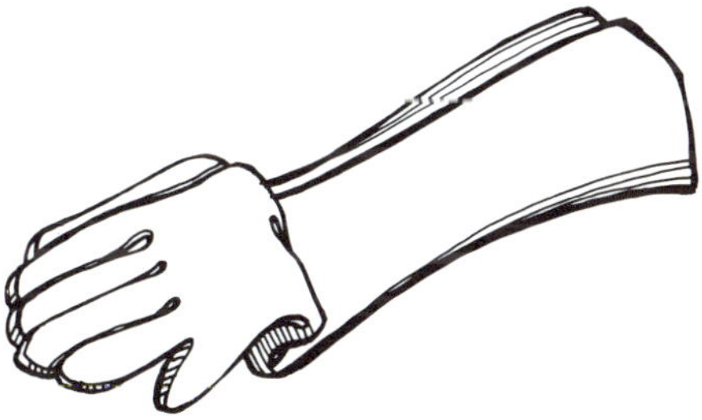

clam sauce for pasta

Serves: 4

- 1 Tbsp. chopped chives
- 1 Tbsp. chopped parsley
- 1 clove garlic, minced
- 1 Tbsp. butter
- 1 Tbsp. vegetable oil
- 1 Tbsp. cornstarch
- ½ cup water *or* chicken broth
- 2 6½-oz. cans minced clams

Saute chives, parsley and garlic in butter and oil. Combine cornstarch and water; add to chive mixture. Stir over low heat until thickened. Add minced clams with juice; continue to cook until desired thickness is obtained. Serve hot with favorite pasta.

pasta sauce

Serves: 4

- ½ cup chopped onion
- ½ cup chopped mushrooms
- 1 clove garlic, minced
- 2 Tbsp. butter
- ½ tsp. oregano
- ¼ cup chopped fresh parsley
- ¼ tsp. tarragon (opt.)
- 1 lb. Italian sausage (casing removed), crumbled
- 1 cup heavy cream

Saute onion, mushrooms and garlic in butter until tender. Add oregano, parsley, tarragon and sausage. Cook over low heat until sausage is done. Add cream and heat through. Serve over a pound of freshly cooked, drained hot pasta (linguine is especially nice). Mix well.

pesto sauce

- 1 cup olive oil
- 3 Tbsp. butter
- 1 clove garlic
- 12 blanched walnut halves
- 12 blanched almond halves
- 1 Tbsp. pine nuts
- ½ cup Romano cheese
- ½ cup grated Parmesan cheese
- 1 cup fresh Italian parsley
- 2 cups fresh basil leaves, coarsely chopped

Starting with olive oil, place all ingredients in order listed in blender. Blend well. Pour sauce over 1 pound of cooked spaghetti; toss well.

Grand Finale

Pies

Tarts

Crusts

Desserts

Photo on p. 223:
Loved, 1979 - Jeffrey Ware (Arthur), Dina Merrill (Amy)

apple sour cream pie

Serves: 6

Try fresh peaches instead of apples in this scrumptious pie.

½ cup sugar
2 Tbsp. cornstarch
⅛ tsp. salt
½ tsp. cinnamon
½ cup sour cream
6 cups sliced apples
1 9-inch unbaked pie shell

Combine sugar, cornstarch, salt and cinnamon; stir in sour cream. Add apples; mix well. Turn into unbaked pie shell. Bake at 425° for 30 to 40 minutes until apples are almost tender. Remove from oven; sprinkle with Crumb Topping. Return to oven; bake 10 minutes more.

Crumb Topping

⅔ cup brown sugar
½ cup flour
4 Tbsp. butter

Blend ingredients well.

concord grape pie

Serves: 6

4 cups Concord grapes
¾ cup sugar
1½ Tbsp. lemon juice
1 Tbsp. grated orange rind
1 Tbsp. quick cooking tapioca
Pastry for 2 crust 9-inch pie
1 Tbsp. butter *or* **margarine**

Preheat oven to 400°. Slip skins from grapes. Bring pulp to a boil; press through sieve to remove seeds. Add skins. Add sugar, lemon juice, orange rind and tapioca. Fill pastry-lined pie plate; dot with butter. Cover with lattice top crust. Bake for 40 to 50 minutes.

pecan glazed apple pie

Serves: 6

Gorgeous and delicious! Somewhat tricky to remove from pan, but definitely worth the trouble.

Pastry

- **3 cups flour**
- **4 Tbsp. confectioners sugar**
- **½ tsp. salt**
- **⅔ cup shortening**
- **2 egg yolks**
- **8 Tbsp. water**

Sift flour, sugar and salt together; cut in shortening. Blend egg yolks and water; gradually add to flour mixture. Arrange Pecan Glaze in pie plate. Roll out ½ of pastry for bottom crust and place over pecans. Turn Filling into crust. Roll out remaining pastry; top pie, crimping edges together. Prick top with fork and bake in preheated 450° oven for 10 minutes. Reduce heat to 350°; bake for 40 minutes more. Cool pie until filling stops bubbling. Place serving plate over pie. ***Invert carefully.*** Remove pie plate. Top with whipped cream, if desired.

Pecan Glaze

- **¼ cup butter, softened**
- **¾ cup pecan halves**
- **⅔ cup brown sugar**

Spread butter evenly over bottom and sides of 9-inch glass pie plate. Press pecans, round side down, into butter to form a shell. Pat brown sugar over pecans.

Filling

- **½ cup raisins**
- **2 Tbsp. bourbon**
- **7 cups sliced apples**
- **2 Tbsp. lemon juice**
- **1 Tbsp. flour**
- **½ cup sugar**
- **1 tsp. cinnamon**
- **½ tsp. nutmeg**
- **Dash of salt**
- **1 tsp. grated lemon peel**
- **Whipped cream (opt.)**

Plump raisins in bourbon for several hours; drain and set aside.

Combine drained raisins with remaining ingredients, except whipped cream.

"No matter what conditions
Dyspeptic come to feaze,
The best of all physicians
Is apple pie and cheese!"
Eugene Field

impossible pie

Serves: 6

- **1 cup packaged coconut**
- **3 eggs**
- **¼ cup butter**
- **½ cup flour**
- **½ tsp. baking powder**
- **1 cup sugar**
- **¼ tsp. salt**
- **1 tsp. vanilla**
- **1 tsp. grated lime rind**
- **2 cups milk**
- **1 Tbsp. coconut flavored rum *or* rum flavoring**
- **Whipped cream**

Preheat oven to 350°. Place ingredients in blender; mix slightly. Turn blender on to blend thoroughly. Pour into buttered pie plate. Bake for 1 hour. Serve with whipped cream.

best-ever lemon meringue pie

Serves: 6

- **1⅓ cups sugar**
- **½ cup cornstarch**
- **¼ tsp. salt**
- **1¾ cups water**
- **4 eggs, separated**
- **2 Tbsp. butter *or* margarine**
- **1 Tbsp. grated lemon rind**
- **½ cup lemon juice (4 lemons)**
- **1 8-inch baked pie shell**
- **¼ tsp. cream of tartar**
- **½ cup sugar**

Combine the 1⅓ cups sugar, cornstarch and salt in saucepan; gradually stir in water. Cook over medium heat, stirring constantly, until mixture comes to a boil and is thickened. Boil 1 minute. Remove from heat. While stirring briskly, gradually add about ½ cup hot mixture to beaten egg yolks. Slowly stir back into remaining mixture in saucepan. Cook, stirring constantly, over low heat for 2 minutes (do not overcook); remove from heat. Stir in butter, lemon rind and juice; pour into cooled pastry shell. Cover with transparent wrap; refrigerate until cold, about 3 hours. When well chilled, beat the 4 egg whites with cream of tartar until soft peaks form. Gradually add the ½ cup sugar, beating until stiff and glossy. Spoon meringue onto cold pie filling;* spread so it touches crust all the way around. Brown quickly in preheated 425° oven for 3 to 5 minutes.

Director's note: **Meringue can be spooned onto greased and lightly floured cookie sheet in large puffs. Bake at 425° for 3 to 5 minutes; cool. When cool, remove carefully with spatula and place on chilled pie.*

shaker lemon pie

Serves: 6

Contributed by Allan Stevens who played in MAN AND SUPERMAN (1980).

2 large lemons
2 cups very fine granulated sugar
Pastry for 9-inch, 2 crust pie
4 eggs, well beaten

Wash and dry lemons. Slice into paper-thin crosswise slices. Remove all seeds. Place lemon slices in a bowl; add sugar. Gently toss slices so that all are coated with sugar. Let stand at room temperature for 2½ hours, stirring occasionally.

Preheat oven to 450°. Prepare pastry. Roll out ½ the pastry and line a 9-inch pie plate. Combine the beaten eggs with the lemon mixture; pour into lined pie plate. Roll out remaining pastry and place over filling. Trim pastry; fold top crust edges under bottom crust and flute edges. Cut several slashes in top crust to allow steam to escape. Bake 15 minutes. Reduce temperature to 350° and bake 30 to 35 minutes more or until crust is golden brown. Serve warm.

lemon sponge pie

Serves: 6

Contributed by Marjorie Lovett who played in A STREETCAR NAMED DESIRE (1977) and MAN AND SUPERMAN (1980).

2 eggs, separated
Juice and grated rind of 1 lemon
1 cup sugar
½ tsp. salt
2 Tbsp. flour
1 Tbsp. butter, melted
1 cup milk
1 8 *or* 9-inch unbaked pie shell

Preheat oven to 450°. Beat egg yolks until thick and lemon-color; add lemon juice and rind, sugar, salt and flour. Mix thoroughly; add melted butter and milk. Beat egg whites until stiff and glossy; fold into lemon mixture. Pour into pie shell. Bake for 10 minutes. Reduce heat to 325°; bake 30 minutes more or until center is firm.

key lime pie

Serves: 8

Contributed by Eydie Alyson who played in DAMES AT SEA (1980).

Crumb Crust

- **1½ cups graham cracker crumbs**
- **¼ cup sugar**
- **¼ cup finely chopped almonds**
- **¼ cup butter, melted**

Preheat oven to 375°. Combine crumbs, sugar, almonds and butter; blend well. Pat mixture onto bottom and sides of 10-inch pie plate. Bake for 8 to 10 minutes. Remove and cool. Reduce temperature to 350°. Pour Filling into Crumb Crust. Bake 15 minutes; cool. Spread cooled pie with whipped cream. Decorate with lime slices, if desired.

Filling

- **6 egg yolks**
- **1¼ cups sweetened condensed milk**
- **¾ cup *fresh* lime juice**
- **2 tsp. grated lime rind**
- **1 cup heavy cream, whipped, sweetened to taste**
- **Lime slices (opt.)**

Beat egg yolks in small bowl. Gradually add condensed milk, stirring constantly. Add lime juice and rind.

Director's note: *Instead of whipped cream topping, a meringue could be made of remaining 6 egg whites, if preferred.*

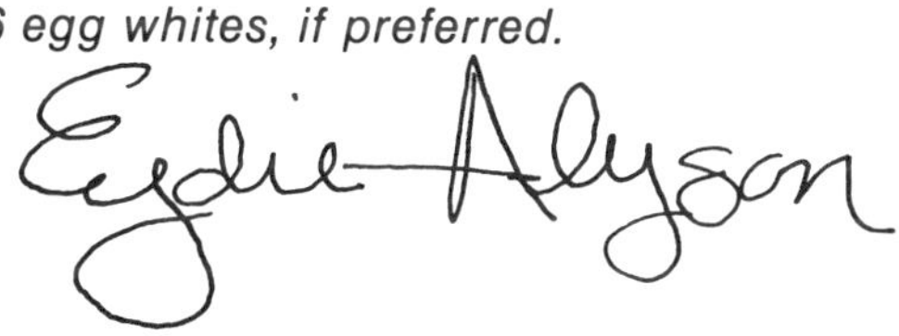

"prop shop" peanut pie

Serves: 6

- **2 Tbsp. butter *or* margarine melted**
- **½ cup sugar**
- **3 eggs, beaten**
- **½ cup light corn syrup**
- **½ cup dark corn syrup**
- **1 tsp. vanilla**
- **1 cup chopped salted *or* unsalted peanuts**
- **1 9-inch unbaked pie shell**

Preheat oven to 375°. Combine butter, sugar, eggs, corn syrups and vanilla; mix until well blended. Pour into pie shell; sprinkle with peanuts. Bake for 10 minutes. Reduce heat to 350°; bake for 35 to 40 minutes more.

green tomato mincemeat

An interesting substitute for traditional mincemeat pie filling.

- **3 lbs. green tomatoes**
- **2 oranges**
- **1 lemon**
- **2 lbs. raisins, chopped**
- **3 lbs. apples, chopped, more if desired**
- **4 cups brown sugar**
- **2 Tbsp. salt**
- **1 cup suet**
- **1 cup vinegar**
- **2 Tbsp. cinnamon**
- **1 Tbsp. ground nutmeg** *or* **1 nutmeg, grated**
- **2 tsp. cloves**

Wash and chop tomatoes; drain well and measure juice. Add water to equal this amount to tomatoes; discard juice. Scald mixture; drain and measure liquid. Add water to tomatoes again equal to the amount drained. Scald and repeat process for a third time. Drain liquid and discard. Meanwhile, extract juice from oranges and lemon; reserve. Cook rinds in clear water; drain. Chop rinds finely or grind. To tomatoes, add raisins, chopped apple, brown sugar, salt, suet, vinegar, spices, chopped rinds and reserved juices. Cook entire mixture until clear. Pour into hot, sterile canning jars and seal. Use to make pies when desired.

walnut-butterscotch pie

Serves: 6-8

Yummy! Much like pecan pie.

- **1 6-oz. pkg. butterscotch chips**
- **¼ cup water**
- **3 Tbsp. butter**
- **¾ cup light corn syrup**
- **3 eggs**
- **2 Tbsp. brown sugar, packed**
- **1 tsp. vanilla**
- **¼ tsp. salt**
- **1 9-inch unbaked pie shell**
- **1¼ cups chopped walnuts**
- **Whipped cream (opt.)**

Preheat oven to 375°. In top of double boiler, combine butterscotch pieces, water and butter. Heat over hot water until melted. Stir in corn syrup. Beat eggs with brown sugar, vanilla and salt until blended. Stir in the hot mixture; turn into pie shell. Scatter walnuts over top. Bake about 35 minutes until set. Cool thoroughly before cutting. Top with whipped cream, if desired.

ambrosia chiffon pie

Serves: 6-8

- **½ cup sugar**
- **½ tsp. salt**
- **1 env. unflavored gelatin**
- **1 cup orange juice**
- **3 eggs, separated**
- **1 tsp. grated orange peel**
- **½ tsp. grated lemon peel**
- **⅓ cup sugar**
- **1 cup diced orange sections**
- **⅓ cup flaked coconut**
- **1 9-inch baked pie shell**
- **1 cup heavy cream, whipped**
- **Orange sections for garnish**

In top of double boiler, combine the ½ cup sugar, salt and gelatin. Stir in orange juice and lightly beaten egg yolks. Cook over hot, not boiling, water until mixture thickens slightly. Stir in orange and lemon peels. Remove mixture to large mixing bowl. Chill until partially set, stirring occasionally. Beat egg whites until soft peaks form. Add the ⅓ cup sugar gradually; continue beating until stiff and glossy. Fold egg whites into chilled mixture. Add orange sections and coconut. Chill again until mixture mounds slightly when spooned. Pour into baked pie shell; chill until set. Just before serving, top with whipped cream and orange sections.

Elmire, *Tartuffe*

bridge club pie

Serves: 6

When the slam goes down one, serve this!

1 pkg. Dream Whip (2 env.)
8 oz. cream cheese, softened
1 cup sugar
1 8 *or* 9-inch baked pie shell
Sliced banana
1 21-oz. can cherry *or* blueberry pie filling

Prepare Dream Whip according to package directions. Blend with cream cheese and sugar; beat well. Pour into baked pie shell; top with sliced banana and pie filling.

Director's note: *Sweet 'n Low can be substituted for sugar according to package directions.*

frozen mud pie

Serves: 8-10

Even better than your childhood "mudpuddle" variety!

Crust

1½ cups vanilla wafer crumbs
¼ cup sugar
¼ cup butter *or* margarine, room temperature

Preheat oven to 375°. Mix ingredients; press into 10-inch springform pan or 10-inch pie plate. Bake for 5 minutes. Cool. Pour "Mud" over crust; cool. Pile ice cream Filling on top of "Mud". Smooth each layer. Freeze. Before serving, top with sweetened whipped cream. Decorate with grated chocolate, if desired.

Mud

6 1.45-oz. Hershey bars, with almonds (6 to a box)
1 heaping tsp. instant coffee
¼ cup water

Melt candy; stir in coffee and water. Cool slightly.

Filling and Topping

1 pint of either coffee *or* mocha ice cream
1 pint vanilla ice cream
1 pint chocolate ice cream
Sweetened whipped cream *or* non-dairy whipped topping
Grated chocolate (opt.)

Soften ice cream a little.

brandied date pie

Serves: 6-8

Good for the holidays in place of Plum Pudding.

Crust

1½ cups flour
½ tsp. salt
½ cup shortening
2 egg yolks, beaten

Preheat oven to 450°. Mix together flour and salt; cut in shortening; stir in egg yolks. Add several tablespoons cold water (4 to 6); blend dough until it handles well. Roll out dough to fit a 10 to 11-inch pie plate. Bake shell until golden brown. Let cool. Chill. Pile brandied date filling into shell; refrigerate.

Filling

1 cup cut-up dates
½ cup brandy
1 env. unflavored gelatin
¼ cup cold water
1 cup milk
2 eggs, separated
¼ cup sugar
⅛ tsp. salt
1 cup heavy cream, whipped

Soak dates in brandy overnight.

Soften gelatin in cold water. Cook milk, egg yolks, sugar and salt over hot water in double boiler until mixture coats metal spoon. Stir in gelatin until dissolved. Cool. Fold in whipped cream and dates. Beat 2 egg whites until stiff peaks form; fold into mixture.

coffee ice cream pie

Serves: 6

1 egg
¾ cup sugar
3 Tbsp. flour
1½ tsp. baking powder
⅛ tsp. salt
1 tsp. vanilla
1 to 1½ cups chopped walnuts
½ cup chopped apple
Coffee ice cream
Whipped cream, garnish
Shaved chocolate, garnish

Preheat oven to 350°. Beat egg and sugar together. Add flour, baking powder and salt. Fold in vanilla, nuts and apple. Pat into buttered 9-inch pie plate. Bake for 25 minutes. Cool; crumble. Place ½ of crumbs in buttered 9-inch pie plate. Spread with layer of softened coffee ice cream. Spread remaining crumbs, then another layer of coffee ice cream. Freeze. Serve frozen, covered with whipped cream and shaved chocolate.

grapefruit chiffon pie

Serves: 6

1 env. unflavored gelatin
1 cup fresh grapefruit juice
4 eggs, separated
½ cup sugar
¼ tsp. salt
1 Tbsp. grated fresh grapefruit peel
¼ cup sugar
1 cup heavy cream, whipped
Toasted Coconut Pie Shell
Grapefruit sections (opt.)
Mint (opt.)

Soften gelatin in grapefruit juice; set aside. In top of double boiler, with electric mixer or beater, beat egg yolks well with the ½ cup sugar and salt. Gradually beat in gelatin mixture. Cook over boiling water until mixture starts to thicken, about 7 minutes, stirring constantly. Add grapefruit peel. Chill until mixture begins to thicken, about 1 hour, stirring occasionally. Beat egg whites until foamy; gradually add the ¼ cup sugar, beating until soft peaks form. Fold beaten egg whites and whipped cream into grapefruit-gelatin mixture. Spoon into Toasted Coconut Pie Shell. Chill 2 hours or until firm. Garnish with grapefruit sections and mint sprigs, if desired.

Toasted Coconut Pie Shell

2 cups toasted coconut*
6 Tbsp. butter *or* margarine, melted
¼ cup brown sugar, packed
1 Tbsp. grated fresh grapefruit peel

Combine all ingredients. Press firmly onto bottom and sides of 9-inch pie plate; chill.

Director's note: **To toast coconut, spread coconut in shallow pan. Place in 375° oven 8 to 10 minutes, stirring often for even toasting.* ***Watch closely, it burns easily.*** *Cool.*

mint chiffon pie

Serves: 6

1 6-oz. pkg. semisweet chocolate chips
1 Tbsp. butter *or* margarine
4 cups whole wheat flakes, crushed to make 3 cups crumbs
¼ cup sugar
2 env. unflavored gelatin
½ tsp. salt
2 cups milk
2 eggs, separated
1 tsp. vanilla
½ tsp. mint extract
Green food coloring
¼ cup sugar
1 cup heavy cream, whipped
Extra whipped cream, shaved chocolate (opt.)

Melt chocolate chips and butter over low heat; stir until smooth. Add cereal and mix carefully until crumbs are evenly coated. Press evenly onto bottom and sides of buttered 9-inch pie plate. Chill. In saucepan, combine ¼ cup sugar, gelatin and salt. Add milk and beaten egg yolks. Cook over low heat, stirring constantly (do not boil), until mixture coats metal spoon. Chill until mixture begins to set. Stir in vanilla and mint extract. Stir in green food coloring to desired tint. Beat egg whites until soft peaks form. Gradually beat in ¼ cup sugar; continue beating until stiff and glossy. Fold egg whites into gelatin mixture. Fold in the 1 cup whipped cream. Spoon mixture into chilled pie shell. Chill until firm. Serve with whipped cream and shaved chocolate, if desired.

easy lemon creme pie

Serves: 8

1 14-oz. can sweetened condensed milk
1 6-oz. can frozen lemonade concentrate, thawed
1 tsp. grated fresh lemon rind
1 8-oz. container non-dairy whipped topping
1 8-inch graham cracker crust
Graham cracker crumbs, lemon slices (opt.)

Mix condensed milk and lemonade together; add lemon rind. Fold in non-dairy whipped topping. Pour into prepared crust and refrigerate. Before serving, top with graham cracker crumbs and thin lemon slices, if desired.

"I ate umble pie with an appetite."
David Copperfield, Charles Dickens

girl scout mint cookie pie

Serves: 6

16 "Girl Scout" chocolate thin mint cookies
3 egg whites
Dash salt
¾ cup sugar
½ cup chopped nuts
½ tsp. vanilla
1 cup heavy cream, whipped
Shaved chocolate (opt.)

Preheat oven to 325°. Roll cookies between two sheets of wax paper to make fine crumbs.* Beat egg whites and salt until soft peaks form. Gradually beat in sugar until stiff and glossy. Fold in crumbs, nuts and vanilla. Spread in buttered 8-inch pie plate. Bake for 35 minutes. Cool and refrigerate for 3 hours. Cover with whipped cream and shaved chocolate.

Director's note: **Freeze cookies a few minutes for easy rolling.*

orange drambuie pie

Serves: 6

2 Tbsp. cornstarch
½ cup orange juice
5 egg yolks
¼ cup sugar
½ cup orange juice
1 env. unflavored gelatin
1 Tbsp. butter
⅓ cup Drambuie
¾ cup heavy cream, whipped
1 9-inch baked pie shell
½ cup orange marmalade
2 small navel oranges

Mix cornstarch with ½ cup orange juice. Add egg yolks and sugar; beat well; set aside. Pour remaining ½ cup orange juice into medium saucepan. Sprinkle gelatin over juice; stir over medium heat until gelatin is dissolved. Remove from heat. While stirring quickly, gradually add a few spoonfuls of hot juice to egg yolk mixture. Gradually return mixture to saucepan, stirring rapidly. Return to heat; cook 3 minutes, stirring constantly. Remove from heat; stir in butter until melted; add Drambuie. Cool quickly over bowl of ice, then place in refrigerator until completely cool. Fold whipped cream into cooled mixture; pour into pie shell. Melt marmalade over low heat. Slice ***unpeeled*** oranges into very thin slices. Dip each slice into melted marmalade. Starting at outside of pie, arrange slices in circular fashion, overlapping slices. Cover entire top of pie. Refrigerate until ready to serve.

strawberry daiquiri pie

Serves: 6

- **4 cups bite-size rice squares, crushed to 1 cup**
- **¼ cup sugar**
- **⅓ cup butter *or* margarine, softened**
- **2 env. unflavored gelatin**
- **⅓ cup milk**
- **20 large *or* 2 cups miniature marshmallows**
- **¼ cup sugar**
- **⅓ cup light rum**
- **1¾ cups chopped fresh strawberries**
- **16 oz. non-dairy whipped topping**
- **Red food coloring (opt.)**

Preheat oven to 350°. Combine cereal crumbs and ¼ cup sugar. Mix in butter until evenly distributed. Press evenly onto bottom and sides of buttered 9-inch pie plate. Bake 7 to 9 minutes, or just until lightly browned. Cool completely. Meanwhile, in saucepan soften gelatin in milk. Heat over low heat, stirring to dissolve gelatin. Add marshmallows; heat and stir until marshmallows are melted. Remove from heat; cool slightly. Combine ¼ cup sugar and rum; stir to dissolve sugar. Stir in the strawberries. Add to gelatin mixture. Chill, stirring occasionally, until mixture mounds when spooned. Beat on high speed of electric mixer until fluffy, 1 or 2 minutes. Beat in topping on low speed. Add red food coloring if desired. Spoon into cooled pie shell. Chill until set, about 2 hours.

frozen peanut butter pie

Serves: 6

S-o-o-o-o rich!

- **3 oz. cream cheese, softened**
- **1 cup confectioners sugar**
- **½ cup peanut butter**
- **½ cup milk**
- **1 8-oz. carton non-dairy whipped topping**
- **1 9-inch baked graham cracker shell**

Beat cream cheese until fluffy; beat in confectioners sugar, peanut butter, milk and topping. Blend well. Turn into baked graham cracker shell. Sprinkle cracker crumbs on top, if desired. Freeze until ready to serve.

In cooking, fat goes to the top. Afterward, it goes to the bottom.

pumpkin ice creme pie

Serves: 6

- **1 pint vanilla ice cream**
- **1 9-inch baked pie shell** *or* **graham cracker crust**
- **1 cup canned pumpkin**
- **¾ cup sugar**
- **½ tsp. ginger**
- **¼ tsp. nutmeg**
- **½ tsp. cinnamon**
- **½ tsp. salt**
- **1 cup heavy cream, whipped**

Spoon softened ice cream over bottom of pie shell. Place in freezer while preparing pumpkin mixture. Combine pumpkin, sugar, spices and salt; blend well. Fold in whipped cream. Remove pie from freezer. Spread pumpkin mixture evenly over ice cream. Freeze.

raspberry chiffon pie

Serves: 6

- **1 10-oz. pkg. frozen raspberries, thawed**
- **1 env. unflavored gelatin**
- **¼ cup sugar**
- **3 egg whites**
- **¼ tsp. cream of tartar**
- **⅓ cup sugar**
- **½ cup heavy cream, whipped**
- **1 baked 9-inch pie shell**

In saucepan, combine raspberries, gelatin and the ¼ cup sugar; bring to a full boil, stirring constantly. Place pan in cold water and cool until mixture mounds slightly when dropped from spoon. Beat egg whites until soft peaks form. Gradually add cream of tartar and the ⅓ cup sugar; continue beating until stiff and glossy. Fold into raspberry mixture. Fold in whipped cream. Spoon into pie shell. Chill several hours until set.

"segue" strawberry pie

Serves: 6

- **1 3-oz. pkg. strawberry gelatin**
- **1 4 to 5-oz. pkg. vanilla pudding and pie filling**
- **1¼ cups water**
- **1 quart strawberries, whole** *or* **sliced**
- **¼ cup orange liqueur**
- **1 8** *or* **9-inch baked pie shell**

In saucepan, combine gelatin and pie filling. Stir in water. Cook and stir over high heat until mixture comes to a boil. Remove from heat. Stir in strawberries and liqueur. Chill until slightly thickened. Pour into pie shell; refrigerate about 2 hours. Top with whipped cream, if desired.

ENCORE!

rum cream pie

Serves: 6

- 2⅔ cups crushed vanilla wafer cookie crumbs (50 wafers)
- ½ cup butter, melted
- 6 egg yolks
- 1 cup sugar
- 1 env. plus 1 tsp. unflavored gelatin
- ½ cup cold water
- 1 pint heavy cream, whipped
- ¼ cup rum

Combine crumbs and melted butter. Press into 10-inch pie plate. Bake at 375° for 10 minutes. Beat egg yolks; add sugar and beat thoroughly. In saucepan, soften gelatin in cold water; bring to a boil over low heat, stirring until completely dissolved. While stirring briskly, gradually add small amount of hot gelatin to egg mixture. Continue to add hot mixture slowly, beating at low speed until well mixed. Fold whipped cream into egg mixture; fold in rum. Refrigerate until mixture holds soft peaks; pile into cooled crust. Keep refrigerated.

three-layer pie

Serves: 6-8

Lovely to look at -- delightful to eat!

- ¾ to 1 cup sugar
- 3 cups milk
- 6 Tbsp. cornstarch
- Dash salt
- 3 eggs, separated
- 3 Tbsp. butter
- 2 tsp. vanilla
- ½ cup semi-sweet chocolate chips, melted
- ½ cup sliced fresh *or* frozen strawberries, well-drained
- Red food coloring (opt.)
- 6 Tbsp. sugar
- 1 9-inch baked pie shell

Combine the ¾ cup sugar, milk, cornstarch, salt and egg yolks. Beat for 1 minute. Cook over medium heat, stirring constantly, until mixture starts to thicken. Add butter; stir until mixture thickens. Remove from heat; add vanilla. Divide cooked mixture into 3 bowls. Stir melted chocolate chips into 1 bowl. Turn into cooled pie shell. Next, gently pour 1 bowl of plain mixture over chocolate. Fold strawberries and food coloring into remaining bowl. Gently pour into pie crust over white layer. Chill at least ½ hour. Beat egg whites until soft peaks form. Gradually beat in the 6 tablespoons sugar; continue beating until stiff and glossy. Spread meringue on pie. Bake about 3 to 5 minutes in preheated 425° oven until meringue is lightly browned.

anyberry tart

Serves: 6-8

Contributed by John Seidman, who played in THE MERCHANT OF VENICE (1982).

Pastry

- **1 cup flour**
- **6 Tbsp.** *frozen* **butter, cut-up**
- **1 egg yolk**
- **1 Tbsp. ice water**
- **⅛ tsp. salt**
- **2 Tbsp. sugar**

Combine all pastry ingredients in food processor.* Turn on and off rapidly for 5 seconds or so. Continue processing until dough forms a ball on the blades. Refrigerate for ½ hour. Roll out dough; line 8-inch tart pan and prick bottom of crust all over. Bake in preheated 425° oven for 10 to 12 minutes. Remove from oven and while still warm, trim edges neatly with a very sharp knife. Cool. Prepare Filling and arrange in cooled shell. Refrigerate. Thirty minutes before serving, remove from refrigerator. Remove pan sides, leaving tart sitting on pan bottom. Leave at room temperature.

Filling

- **8 oz. almond paste**
- **2 to 3 Tbsp. sour cream**
- **1 egg yolk**
- **2 Tbsp. unsalted butter**
- **¼ cup currant jelly**
- **2 Tbsp. water**
- **1 squeeze of lemon**
- **Pinch of sugar**
- **1 to 1½ pints fresh berries**

In food processor or mixer, cream together almond paste, sour cream, egg yolk and butter until very smooth. Spread on bottom of cooled shell. Heat jelly, water, lemon juice and sugar in small saucepan until melted. Arrange berries on almond cream base, covering it completely. Brush carefully with jelly glaze.

Director's note: **Both pastry and filling can be done without a food processor. Prepare pastry with a pastry blender and work quickly. The less the dough is handled, the flakier it will be.*

John Seidman

apple tart

Pate Sucree

1¾ cups flour	**10 Tbsp. butter *or* margarine**
1 tsp. salt	**2 Tbsp. shortening**
2 Tbsp. sugar	**¼ to ⅓ cup cold water**

Combine flour, salt and sugar. Cut in butter and shortening until crumbly. Add cold water and form dough into firm ball. Refrigerate at least 1 hour.* Roll dough and carefully place in tart pan. Prick bottom and sides of pastry with a fork. Lay the buttered side of a piece of wax paper on the pastry and weigh down with dry beans. Bake in preheated 450° oven for 10 minutes. Remove beans and bake 5 minutes more or until crust is firm and starting to brown. Paint inside of tart shell with 1 recipe of Apricot Glaze. Pour apple puree into tart shell. Cover edges with aluminum collar. Cover with apple slices, overlapping to form concentric circles. Reduce temperature to 400° and bake for 25 to 30 minutes. Prepare another recipe of Apricot Glaze; spread lightly over apple slices before serving.

Apple Filling

10 to 12 cooking apples	**2 Tbsp. butter**
2 Tbsp. water	**2 Tbsp. lemon juice**
⅓ to ½ cup sugar	**Cinnamon, nutmeg**
2 tsp. grated orange rind	

Pare, core and quarter 5 or 6 apples. Cook in covered saucepan with water until tender. Add more water if necessary. Add sugar to taste, orange rind and butter. Puree the mixture and cool. Pare, core and slice remaining 5 or 6 apples. Toss slices with lemon juice; sprinkle lightly with cinnamon and nutmeg.

Apricot Glaze

2 Tbsp. apricot preserves	**1 tsp. lemon juice**
2 Tbsp. water	

Combine ingredients; heat until liquid.

Director's note: **May be frozen at this point. Thaw and roll out.*

"A dessert without cheese is like a beautiful woman with only one eye."
Anthelme Brillat-Savarin

bavarian apple torte

Serves: 8

Crust

- **½ cup butter** *or* **margarine, softened**
- **⅓ cup sugar**
- **¼ tsp. vanilla**
- **1 cup flour**

Cream butter, sugar and vanilla. Blend in flour. Pat onto bottom of 9-inch springform pan. Pour Filling onto unbaked crust. Spread with Apple Topping. Bake in preheated 450° oven for 10 minutes. Reduce temperature to 400° and bake for 25 minutes more.

Cheese Filling

- **8 oz. cream cheese, softened**
- **1 egg**
- **¼ cup sugar**
- **½ tsp. vanilla**

Beat cream cheese with egg, sugar and vanilla until smooth.

Apple Topping

- **4 cups sliced apples**
- **⅓ cup sugar**
- **½ tsp. cinnamon**
- **¼ cup sliced almonds**

Toss apples with sugar and cinnamon and almonds.

Elmire, *Tartuffe*

dutch apple tart

Serves: 6

7 medium-size tart cooking apples
1 9-inch unbaked pastry shell
¾ to 1 cup sugar
2 Tbsp. flour
½ tsp. cinnamon
¼ cup cream
2 Tbsp. butter *or* **margarine**

Preheat oven to 400°. Pare, halve and core apples; slice 4 halves into pie shell, making an even layer. Mix sugar, flour and cinnamon; sprinkle ½ over sliced apples. Arrange remaining apple halves, cut side down, in single layer on top. Sprinkle with remaining sugar mixture. Pour cream in slowly near center; dot with butter. Bake about 1 hour or until apples are tender but still hold their shape (juices will thicken as pie cools). Remove from oven. With a fork, lightly press apple halves into juices. Serve warm or cold.

lindsertorte

Serves: 8

Really a tart or European pie.

2 cups butter
1 cup sugar
1 egg
1½ tsp. vanilla
6 oz. pecans
4½ cups flour
1 12-oz. jar raspberry preserves*

Preheat oven to 325°. Cream butter and sugar until light and fluffy. Beat in egg and vanilla. Grate pecans in a nut grinder to make fluffy ground nuts. Stir nuts into mixture; mix in flour. Divide dough in half. Press ½ of dough onto bottom and sides of 9 or 10-inch tart or pie pan. Allow dough to firm up in refrigerator or freezer for only a few minutes. Spread a thick layer of preserves on crust. Put remaining half of dough back into mixer; mix until soft consistency. Place in pastry bag with wide tube opening. Squeeze lattice strips over preserves attaching each strip to the dough on side of pan.** Bake for 30 to 35 minutes. Let cool 35 minutes; remove rim from pan.

Director's note: **Add ¼ teaspoon lemon juice and dash cinnamon if raspberry preserves are too sweet. **Dough may be patted out flat on lightly floured surface and cut into lattice strips.*

tzarina tart

Serves: 6

Crust

- **1¼ cups flour**
- **1 Tbsp. sugar**
- **½ cup butter *or* margarine, softened**
- **1 egg yolk**
- **2 Tbsp. milk *or* brandy**

Preheat oven to 400°. Sift together flour and sugar; cut in butter. With floured fingers, add egg yolk and milk. Press onto bottom and sides of 9-inch flan pan or pie plate. Spoon Filling into shell. Bake for 10 minutes. Reduce temperature to 325° and bake 30 minutes more. Serve warm (not hot) with whipped cream.

Filling

- **½ cup butter *or* margarine**
- **1¼ cups sugar**
- **2 eggs**
- **1 Tbsp. flour**
- **2½ to 3 cups sliced fresh strawberries**
- **Sweetened whipped cream**

Cream butter; add sugar gradually; beat until fluffy. Add eggs, 1 at a time, beating well after each addition. Beat in flour; fold in strawberries.

brown sugar pastry

- **½ cup butter *or* margarine**
- **1 cup flour**
- **¼ cup brown sugar, packed**
- **½ cup chopped pecans**

Place all ingredients in pie plate; do not mix. Bake at 400° for 15 minutes. Remove from oven; stir well with fork at once. Pat out into 9-inch pie shell.

Director's note: *Pastry is very rich -- best filled with ice cream or plain custard or pudding.*

gingersnap crust

- **1½ cups fine crumbs (24 gingersnaps)**
- **¼ cup butter, softened**

Mix well; press into pie plate and bake at 375° for 8 minutes. Cool.

pecan crust for ice cream pie

½ cup unsalted butter
1 cup flour
1 cup sugar
¾ cup chopped pecans

Melt butter and stir in flour, sugar and nuts. Cook and stir constantly over medium heat until mixture is golden and crumbly. Press onto buttered 9-inch glass pie plate. Freeze before filling with ice cream.

almond puff

½ cup butter
1 cup flour
2 Tbsp. water
½ cup butter
1 cup water
1 tsp. almond extract
1 cup flour
3 eggs
Chopped nuts

Preheat oven to 350°. Cut ½ cup butter into 1 cup flour; sprinkle the 2 tablespoons water over mixture; mix with fork. Shape into ball. Divide in half on ungreased baking sheet. Pat each half into a 3 x 12-inch strip. Place 3 inches apart. In saucepan, heat ½ cup butter and the 1 cup water to rolling boil. Remove from heat and quickly stir in almond extract and 1 cup flour. Stir vigorously over low heat until mixture forms a ball, about 1 minute. Remove from heat. Beat in eggs all at once. Divide mixture in half; spread over strips. Bake 60 minutes or until brown. Cool. Frost with Confectioners Sugar Glaze. Sprinkle with chopped nuts.

Confectioners Sugar Glaze

½ cup confectioners sugar
2 Tbsp. butter, softened
1 to 1½ tsp. almond extract
1 to 2 Tbsp. warm water

Mix glaze ingredients until smooth.

ENCORE! grandmother's apple crisp

Serves: 6-8

- **1 cup flour**
- **1 tsp. baking powder**
- **½ tsp. salt**
- **½ to 1 cup sugar***
- **1 egg, unbeaten**
- **7 or 8 apples, pared and sliced**
- **1 Tbsp. cinnamon**
- **⅓ cup butter, melted**

Preheat oven to 350°. Combine dry ingredients; add egg and beat with a fork until crumbly. Place apples in 2½-quart baking dish. Sprinkle with a little extra sugar, depending on the tartness of the apples, and a little of the cinnamon. Spread dry ingredients over apples. Pour melted butter over top, covering well. Sprinkle with remaining cinnamon. Bake for 30 to 40 minutes until apples are tender and pudding is bubbly.

Director's note: **Amount of sugar depends on how sweet a dough you like.*

amaretto baked apples

Serves: 6

- **6 large baking apples (Northern Spy, Ida Red *or* Rome Beauty)**
- **¼ cup butter**
- **⅓ cup brown sugar, packed**
- **½ cup chopped dates**
- **½ cup toasted chopped almonds**
- **¼ cup Amaretto**
- **¼ tsp. cinnamon**
- **½ cup apple juice *or* cider**
- **2 Tbsp. lemon juice**
- **2 Tbsp. brown sugar, packed**

Preheat oven to 375°. Core apples to within 1 inch of the bottom. Pare upper ⅓ of skin from each apple to prevent splitting. Cut butter into the ⅓ cup brown sugar until crumbly. Mix in almonds, dates, Amaretto and cinnamon. Fill apples with mixture. Place in shallow baking dish. Mix apple juice, lemon juice and the 2 tablespoons brown sugar. Pour over apples. Bake, uncovered, basting often with juices until tender, about 40 minutes. Serve with cream.

"An apple a day keeps the doctor away."
Anonymous

apple chehalis

Serves: 6

Eat it warm from the oven -- plain, with whipped cream or ice cream. Delicious!

1 egg, beaten
¾ cup sugar
½ cup flour
1 tsp. baking powder
Pinch salt
½ tsp. vanilla
¼ cup chopped nuts (opt.)
3 medium apples, pared and sliced very thin with a parer
1 tsp. sugar
⅛ tsp. cinnamon

Preheat oven to 350°. Combine egg, sugar, flour, baking powder, salt and vanilla. Fold in nuts and apple. Spread in buttered 8 or 9-inch pie plate. Mix sugar and cinnamon; sprinkle over top of pie. Bake for 20 to 30 minutes. Serve warm.

george's cherry pudding

Serves: 6-8

2 cups canned tart red cherries
¼ cup butter *or* **margarine**
½ cup sugar
1 tsp. vanilla
1 cup flour
1½ tsp. baking powder
½ cup milk
¼ cup brown sugar
¼ tsp. salt
1½ Tbsp. cornstarch
¼ cup sugar
2 drops red food coloring (opt.)

Preheat oven to 350°. Drain cherries, reserving liquid. Cream butter and the ½ cup sugar until light and fluffy. Add vanilla. Sift flour and baking powder together; add to creamed mixture alternately with milk. Spread drained cherries over bottom of buttered 8-inch square baking pan. Pour batter over cherries. Add enough water to reserved cherry juice to make 1¼ cups. Bring to a boil. Combine brown sugar, salt, cornstarch and the ¼ cup sugar. Stir in boiling juice and food coloring. Pour over batter in pan. Bake 45 minutes. Cool to lukewarm before serving.

chocolate fudge steamed pudding

Serves: 10-12

Pudding*

- **¾ cup milk**
- **½ cup sugar**
- **½ cup brown sugar**
- **¼ cup butter, melted**
- **2 Tbsp. cream**
- **1 Tbsp. rum**
- **1 tsp. vanilla**

Preheat oven to 350°. Combine pudding ingredients thoroughly; place in buttered 6 x 10-inch glass baking dish.

Cake

- **½ cup sugar**
- **½ cup flour**
- **3 Tbsp. cocoa**
- **¼ tsp. baking powder**
- **½ cup chopped nuts**
- **1 cup water**

Sift together sugar, flour, cocoa and baking powder. Spoon over pudding mixture. Sprinkle with nuts. Slowly and evenly add water Do not mix. Bake for 50 to 60 minutes. Serve warm or cold with whipped cream or ice cream.

Director's note: **If more pudding is desired, double pudding ingredients.*

date pudding

Serves: 8

- **3 eggs, separated**
- **1 cup sugar**
- **1 Tbsp. flour**
- **4 Tbsp. milk**
- **1 cup dates**
- **1 cup chopped nuts (pecans especially good)**
- **1 heaping tsp. baking powder**
- **Whipped cream (opt.)**

Preheat oven to 325°. Beat egg yolks, sugar, flour and milk; add dates and nuts. Beat egg whites until soft peaks form; add baking powder and beat to stiff peaks. Fold egg whites into date-nut mixture. Pour into 8 x 10-inch baking pan ***or*** 9 x 13-inch pan for thinner pudding. Place baking pan in pan of hot water. Bake for 45 minutes. Serve with whipped cream, if desired.

"The proof of the pudding is in the eating."
Miguel de Cervantes

fresh peach kuchen

Serves: 8-10

- **2 lbs. ripe peaches, peeled and sliced (about 6)***
- **2 Tbsp. lemon juice**
- **1½ cups flour**
- **½ cup sugar**
- **2 tsp. baking powder**
- **¼ tsp. salt**
- **2 eggs**
- **2 Tbsp. milk**
- **1 Tbsp. grated lemon peel**
- **¼ cup butter** *or* **margarine, melted**
- **¼ cup sugar**
- **½ tsp. cinnamon**
- **1 egg yolk**
- **3 Tbsp. heavy cream**
- **Whipped cream** *or* **vanilla ice cream (opt.)**

Preheat oven to 400°. Sprinkle peaches with lemon juice; toss to coat well. Sift dry ingredients together. In large bowl, using fork, beat eggs with milk and lemon peel. Add dry ingredients and melted butter, mixing until smooth, about 1 minute. Do not overmix. Turn batter into buttered, 9-inch springform pan or round baking pan. Spread evenly over bottom.

Combine sugar and cinnamon; mix well. Drain peach slices; arrange on batter in pinwheel fashion; fill in center in rows. Sprinkle with cinnamon-sugar. Bake for 25 minutes. Remove from oven. With a fork, beat egg yolk with cream; pour over peaches. Bake 10 minutes more. Cool 10 minutes on wire rack. Remove sides of springform pan or, if baking pan is used, serve from pan. Serve warm with whipped cream or ice cream, if desired.

Director's note: **2½ 10-ounce packages frozen sliced peaches, drained, may be substituted.*

Milo, *Sleuth*

queen of puddings

Serves: 6-8

A magnificent dessert! Worthy of its name.

- **2 cups ¼-inch white bread cubes, tightly packed (bread should be firm, not soft)**
- **3 Tbsp. sugar**
- **2⅔ cups milk**
- **2½ Tbsp. butter *or* margarine, melted**
- **¼ tsp. salt**
- **1¼ tsp. vanilla**
- **3 eggs, separated**
- **½ cup dried currants**
- **1 cup dark seedless raisins**
- **6 Tbsp. sugar**
- **⅓ cup currant jelly**

Preheat oven to 375°. Combine bread cubes, the 3 tablespoons sugar, milk, butter, salt and vanilla. Beat egg yolks slightly; stir into bread mixture. Add currants and raisins. Pour pudding into a buttered, deep 2-quart baking dish and set it in a larger pan. Pour warm water into the larger pan to a depth of 1 inch. Bake pudding for 70 to 80 minutes, or until set. Remove pudding from oven and increase temperature to 425°. Beat egg whites until soft peaks form. Gradually beat in the 6 tablespoons sugar; continue beating until stiff and glossy. Spread currant jelly over pudding. Cover with meringue. Bake 4 to 5 minutes, or until meringue is lightly browned. Remove dish carefully from pan of water. Serve warm.

rhubarb cobbler

Serves: 6

- **¾ to 1 cup sugar**
- **2 Tbsp. cornstarch**
- **¼ tsp. cinnamon**
- **1 lb. rhubarb, cut into 1-inch pieces (4 cups)**
- **1 Tbsp. water**
- **2 Tbsp. butter *or* margarine**
- **1 cup flour**
- **⅓ cup sugar**
- **1½ tsp. baking powder**
- **½ tsp. salt**
- **4 Tbsp. butter *or* margarine**
- **⅓ cup milk**
- **¼ cup chopped pecans**
- **1 tsp. shredded orange peel**

Preheat oven to 400°. In saucepan, combine the ¾ cup sugar, cornstarch and cinnamon. Add rhubarb and water. Cook and stir until mixture comes to a boil; cook 1 minute. Pour into 8-inch round or square baking dish; dot with the 2 tablespoons butter. Place in oven while preparing biscuits. Sift together flour, the ⅓ cup sugar, baking powder and salt. Cut in the 4 tablespoons butter. Stir in milk, pecans and orange peel. Drop large spoonfuls of dough on top of hot rhubarb mixture. Bake about 25 minutes.

tipsy bread pudding

Serves: 8-10

- **10 slices day old white bread, broken into pieces**
- **4 cups milk, scalded**
- **1 cup cream**
- **4 eggs**
- **1 cup sugar**
- **1 tsp. vanilla**
- **1 tsp. cinnamon**
- **½ tsp. nutmeg**
- **¼ cup butter, melted**
- **½ cup seedless raisins**

Preheat oven to 350°. Combine bread, milk and cream. In large bowl, beat eggs; add sugar and mix well. Stir in bread mixture. Add vanilla, cinnamon and nutmeg. Stir in butter and raisins. Pour into buttered, 2-quart baking dish. Set in pan of warm water about 1 inch deep. Bake for 1 hour or until knife inserted into center comes out clean. Serve warm with cool Tipsy Topping.

Tipsy Topping

- **3 egg yolks**
- **1 cup sugar**
- **1 tsp. vanilla**
- **1½ cups milk**
- **1 Tbsp. cornstarch**
- **¼ cup water**
- **1½ oz. brandy**

In saucepan, beat egg yolks; add sugar, vanilla and milk. Blend well. Cook until mixture comes to a boil. Blend cornstarch in water and stir into hot mixture. Cook until thick. Remove from heat and stir in brandy. Cool.

bananas foster

Serves: 4

Straight from Brennan's in Houston!

- **8 Tbsp. brown sugar**
- **4 Tbsp. butter**
- **4 ripe bananas, peeled and sliced lengthwise**
- **Dash cinnamon**
- **2 oz. banana liqueur**
- **4 oz. white rum**
- **4 large scoops vanilla ice cream**

Over low heat, melt brown sugar and butter in frying pan or flat chafing dish. Add bananas and saute, turning gently, until tender. Sprinkle with cinnamon. Pour liqueur and rum into pan and set aflame carefully.* Baste with liquid until flame burns out. Serve immediately over ice cream.

Director's note: **Safest way to flame liqueur is to warm in saucepan and flame with a long match. Pour over dish to be flamed.*

amaretto cream

Serves: 6-8

Gerard Maras, executive chef at Mr. B's Bistro and Bar in the French Quarter in NewOrleans, is from Baldwinsville, New York and worked at the Hotel Syracuse, the former Walter White's Steak and Ale House and the Poseidon Restaurant. The Palm Beach Country Club, Commander's Palace and other famous spots have enjoyed his talents. He was kind enough to contribute this recipe from Mr. B's for our cookbook.

2¼ cups milk
½ cup sugar
2 oz. cornstarch
3 eggs
3 cups heavy cream
Amaretto liqueur
Toasted almonds (opt.)

Heat milk in large sauce pan. Sift sugar and cornstarch together until well mixed. Add eggs to cornstarch mixture; whip until well blended. When milk comes to a rolling boil, add egg mixture at once, stirring constantly, so custard will not burn. When custard becomes thick, remove from heat; pour into bowl to cool. When cool, whip cream and refrigerate. Whip custard; add Amaretto to taste and fold into whipped cream. Pour into serving glasses and refrigerate. Decorate top with a single toasted almond, if desired.

bourbon on a cloud

Serves: 6-8

This will put you in touch with the angels!

¾ cup sugar
1 env. unflavored gelatin
3 eggs, separated
¾ cup bourbon
⅓ cup chopped walnuts
1 cup heavy cream, whipped

Combine 6 tablespoons of the sugar with gelatin; mix well. Beat egg yolks slightly. Gradually add bourbon, stirring constantly. (Adding bourbon too fast will "cook" the egg yolks.) Add yolk mixture to gelatin. Cook over hot (not boiling) water, stirring constantly until mixture coats a metal spoon, about 10 minutes. Beat egg whites until foamy. Gradually add remaining sugar and beat until stiff and glossy. Fold in yolk mixture. Chill 20 minutes. Fold in walnuts and whipped cream. Turn into 4 or 5 cup mold which has been rinsed with cold water. Chill until firm. Unmold and garnish with strawberries or raspberries, if desired.

apricot buttercream squares

Serves: 12-16

Try fresh strawberries or peaches instead of apricots -- delicious, too!

- **1 11-oz. pkg. dried apricots (approx. 2 cups)**
- **¾ cup sugar**
- **6 Tbsp. butter, melted**
- **2½ cups fine graham cracker crumbs**
- **½ cup chopped walnuts**
- **6 Tbsp. butter, softened**
- **3 cups sifted confectioners sugar**
- **2 eggs**
- **1 cup heavy cream, whipped**

Cook apricots until very tender; drain. Add sugar to hot apricots; puree. Set aside to cool thoroughly. Mix melted butter thoroughly with 2 cups of the graham cracker crumbs and nuts. Press onto bottom of 9 x 13-inch baking pan. Cream butter and confectioners sugar (mixture will be crumbly). Add eggs, 1 at a time; beat until smooth. Spoon over crumbs in pan; smooth gently. Put small spoonfuls of cooled apricots over buttercream layer; top with smooth layer of whipped cream. Sprinkle with remaining ½ cup crumbs. Cover and chill at least 8 hours before serving. Cut into squares.

Director's note: *If substituting fresh fruit for apricots, do not puree, just place on cream filling -- top with whipped cream.*

kahlua chocolate mousse

Serves: 4

- **1 6-oz. pkg. semi-sweet chocolate chips**
- **2 tsp. instant espresso**
- **3 Tbsp. water**
- **3 egg whites**
- **¼ cup sugar**
- **1 Tbsp. Kahlua**
- **1 tsp. vanilla**
- **1 cup heavy cream, whipped**

In saucepan, stir chocolate chips, espresso and water over low heat until chocolate is melted and blended. Let cool to room temperature. Beat egg whites until soft peaks form. Gradually beat in sugar; continue beating until stiff and glossy. Fold Kahlua and vanilla into whipped cream; fold into cooled chocolate mixture. Fold in beaten egg whites. Chill.

Director's note: *For the real chocolate lover, substitute instant cocoa mix instead of instant espresso; substitute Bailey's Irish Cream Liqueur instead of Kahlua.*

chocolate cheese supreme

Serves: 4-6

- **1 6-oz. pkg. semi-sweet chocolate chips**
- **2 Tbsp. water**
- **8 oz. cream cheese, softened**
- **1 cup heavy cream**
- **1 Tbsp. sugar**
- **Maraschino cherries**

Melt chocolate chips in water. Beat cream cheese until smooth. Beat in melted chocolate and 1/4 cup of the heavy cream. Whip the remaining 3/4 cup heavy cream with sugar and fold 1/2 of this into cheese mixture. Spoon into stemmed glasses. Put a dollop of whipped cream on each and top with maraschino cherry. Chill at least 2 hours.

jean stapleton's chocolate fondue

- **6 1-oz. squares unsweetened baking chocolate**
- **1 1/2 cups sugar**
- **1 cup light cream**
- **1/2 cup butter**
- **1/8 tsp. salt**
- **3 Tbsp. creme de cacao (opt.)**

In top of double boiler, melt chocolate over simmering water. Stir in sugar, cream, butter and salt. Cook, stirring constantly, for 10 minutes. Add creme de cacao. Transfer to fondue pot and serve with "Dippers".

Dippers

Squares of pound cake or angel food cake
Marshmallows
Fruit chunks
Almonds

dina's delight!

Serves: 4-6

Contributed by Dina Merrill who played in LOVED (1979). Dina discovered this dessert when she was a guest of Mildred Eggers, wife of the Chancellor of Syracuse University.

1 12-oz. can Orange-Plus, frozen
½ pint heavy cream
3 to 4 Tbsp. brandy
Mint leaves
Orange zest

Five minutes before preparation, remove Orange-Plus from freezer. Whip cream until it holds stiff peaks. Spoon Orange-Plus into large bowl; fold in whipped cream, then brandy. Spoon into parfait glasses; return to freezer for at least 1 hour. Decorate with mint leaves or orange zest.

chocolate cookie ice cream

Serves: 8

3 egg yolks
1 14-oz. can sweetened condensed milk
2 Tbsp. water
4 tsp. vanilla
1 cup coarsely crushed chocolate sandwich cookies
2 cups heavy cream, whipped (not whipped topping)

Beat egg yolks; stir in condensed milk, water and vanilla. Fold in cookies and whipped cream. Pour into aluminum foil-lined 2-quart container (a 5 x 9-inch loaf pan works well). Cover; freeze 6 hours or until firm. To serve, scoop ice cream right from pan or remove, peel off foil and slice.

"Look here, Steward, if this is coffee, I want tea; but if this is tea, then I wish coffee."
Punch

"curtain call" chocolate mousse

Serves: 6-8

1 cup semi-sweet chocolate chips
1 1-oz. square unsweetened baking chocolate
¼ cup water
5 eggs, separated
3 Tbsp. brandy

In top of double boiler, melt the 2 chocolates and water over boiling water. Remove from heat. Add beaten egg yolks and brandy. Cool. Beat egg whites until stiff; fold into chocolate mixture. Turn into serving dish or individual dishes; chill for 8 hours.

english trifle

Serves: 6

1 pkg. lady fingers *or* **pound cake**
Raspberry jam
Sherry to taste
Egg Custard*
1 cup heavy cream, whipped
¼ cup chopped walnuts *or* **almonds**

Split lady fingers lengthwise. Spread raspberry jam on cut side. Arrange in serving bowl (a glass dish is especially attractive), jam side up, and spoon sherry over lady fingers. Allow it to be absorbed. Prepare Custard. Cool and pour over ladyfingers. Mix all together and spread flat, making sure sponge mixture is below custard. Chill. Before serving, top with whipped cream; sprinkle with walnuts.

Egg Custard*

4 eggs
⅔ cup sugar
1 tsp. flour
2½ cups milk, scalded
¼ tsp. salt
2 tsp. vanilla

Combine eggs, sugar and flour. Gradually stir in milk. Cook, stirring constantly, in double boiler over hot, not boiling, water until mixture coats metal spoon. Remove from heat immediately. Cool slightly; stir in salt and vanilla. Chill.

Director's note: *Trifle can be prepared in layers, if desired, alternating lady fingers and custard.*

"Strange to see how a good dinner and feasting reconciles everybody."
Samuel Pepys, November 9, 1665

easy ice cream

Great for the kids to make!

1½ cups strawberry jam
2 cups buttermilk

Stir ingredients together. Freeze until firm. Break up mixture; whip with mixer until light and fluffy. Refreeze.

fruit pizza

Serves: 8-10

1 17-oz. tube Pillsbury frozen sugar cookie dough
8 oz. cream cheese, softened
Fruits of your choice:
Bananas (dipped into pineapple juice)
Mandarin oranges
Peaches (dipped into pineapple juice, if fresh)
Grapes
Pineapple chunks
Strawberries (in season)
1 10-oz. jar apricot *or* peach preserves (or less)

Preheat oven to 350°. Slice cookie dough into ½-inch slices. Place on pizza pan. Pat together to form crust. Bake until light brown, about 12 minutes. Let cool. Spread cream cheese on baked crust. Arrange ***drained*** fruits on top in any pattern you like. Warm preserves; pour over top of fruit. Chill well; slice and serve.

marshmallow date roll

Serves: 8

18 graham crackers, finely crushed
¾ cup chopped dates
14 marshmallows, finely cut*
1 cup chopped nuts
¼ cup light cream *or* evaporated milk

Reserve ⅓ cup cracker crumbs. Mix remaining crumbs with rest of ingredients; form into a roll. Spread reserved crumbs on sheet of wax paper. Place marshmallow roll on paper; roll to coat with crumbs; wrap tightly in the paper. Refrigerate 24 hours. Slice and serve with whipped cream.

Director's note: **To cut marshmallows easily, use wet scissors.*

fred's favorite dessert

Serves: 18

Crust

1½ cup flour
¾ cup butter *or* margarine
¾ cup chopped nuts

Preheat oven to 350°. Mix crust ingredients and press into 9 x 13-inch pan; bake for 20 minutes. Cool. Spread Filling in layers. Refrigerate several hours before serving.

Filling

8 oz. cream cheese, softened
1 cup confectioners sugar
3 cups non-dairy whipped topping*
2 3 to 4-oz. pkgs. coconut cream pudding mix
1 20-oz. can cherry pie filling
Toasted coconut**

Cream the cream cheese; beat in confectioners sugar. Fold in 1 cup of the whipped topping. Spread on cooled crust. Prepare pudding according to package directions; cool and spread on top of cheese layer. Spread pie filling over pudding layer. Spread remaining 2 cups whipped topping on top of pie filling. Sprinkle with toasted coconut.

Director's notes: **An 8-oz. container of non-dairy whipped topping contains 3 cups. **To toast coconut, spread flaked coconut in shallow pan. Place in 375° oven for 8 to 10 minutes, stirring often for even toasting.* ***Watch closely, it burns easily.***

green grapes in cognac

Serves: 6

3 lbs. seedless green grapes
¾ cup honey
¾ cup cognac
1 Tbsp. lemon juice
1 to 2 cups sour cream

Wash and dry grapes thoroughly; remove from stems. Combine honey, cognac and lemon juice. Toss grapes with honey mixture. Chill 5 hours, stirring occasionally. Before serving, top with sour cream.

"It's a very odd thing
As odd as can be
That whatever Miss T eats
Turns into Miss T."
Walter de La Mare

ENCORE!

fruit torte

Serves: 10-12

½ cup shortening
½ cup sugar
4 eggs, separated
1 cup flour
1 tsp. baking powder
½ tsp. salt
5 Tbsp. milk
1 cup sugar
1 cup heavy cream, whipped
1 pint strawberries *or* fresh peaches

Preheat oven to 325°. Cream shortening and the ½ cup sugar. Beat in egg yolks. Combine flour, baking powder and salt. Add to mixture alternately with milk. Mix very well. Grease and flour 2 large pizza pans.* Spread cake dough on each pan. Beat egg whites until foamy. Gradually beat in the 1 cup sugar; continue beating until stiff and glossy. Spread ½ of meringue on top of each cake layer. Bake for about 15 to 25 minutes. Cool 15 minutes. Place 1 layer on cake dish, meringue side down; cover with whipped cream and fruit. Place second layer, meringue side up, on the fruit. Refrigerate for several hours (even overnight) before serving to allow flavors to blend.

Director's note: **Disposable aluminum pizza pans work very well. Each layer can be "popped off" easily.*

dutch lemon cream

Serves: 8

4 eggs, separated
½ cup sugar
¼ cup lemon juice
¾ cup dry white wine
Grated rind of ½ lemon

Refrigerate egg whites until needed. In small bowl, with mixer at medium speed, beat egg yolks with sugar until thick and fluffy. Add lemon juice and wine, blending well. Stir in lemon rind. Place in double boiler. Cook over boiling water, beating constantly with wire whisk until thickened. Refrigerate. Just before serving, beat egg whites until stiff; fold into egg-lemon mixture. Turn into individual serving dishes.

"button"

2 3-oz. pkgs. lemon gelatin
2 cups boiling water
1 cup cold water
2 cups sugar
Rind and juice of 2 lemons
2 13-oz. cans evaporated milk
Graham cracker crumbs

Dissolve lemon gelatin in boiling water. Add cold water. Refrigerate until slightly thickened. Whip evaporated milk;* add to mixture with sugar and lemon rind and juice. Whip all together until fluffy. Spread cracker crumbs in 9 x 13-inch pan to the depth of ⅛ inch. Spoon filling over crumbs. Sprinkle more crumbs on top. Chill until set, about 4 to 5 hours. Cut into squares to serve.

Director's note: **Chill evaporated milk and beaters while gelatin is thickening to insure whipping.*

frozen maple nut cream

Serves: 6-8

New York State maple syrup makes this recipe a special treat.

4 egg yolks
¾ cup maple syrup
2 cups heavy cream, whipped
Grapes, chopped nuts (opt.)

Beat egg yolks with electric mixer at high speed until light and fluffy, about 4 minutes. Heat syrup in top of double boiler until ***very hot***. While beating rapidly, gradually add a small amount of hot syrup to beaten egg yolks. Beat egg-syrup mixture into remaining maple syrup in top of double boiler. Place over hot, not boiling, water. Cook, stirring constantly, until mixture thickens. Cool over ice and water, stirring frequently. Fold whipped cream into cooled egg mixture. Turn into 4-cup mold that has been rinsed with cold water. Freeze overnight or until firm. Unmold; garnish with chopped nuts and grapes, if desired.

Director's note: *For an extra-pretty look, place chopped nuts in mold first and pour mixture on top of them.*

"Who riseth from a feast
With that keen appetite that he sits down?"
The Merchant of Venice, Shakespeare

devonshire peaches

Serves: 4

- **1 28-oz. can peach halves**
- **1 1-lb. can pitted, dark sweet cherries, drained**
- **2 Tbsp. butter**
- **½ cup sour cream**
- **½ cup brown sugar**

Drain peaches, reserving ½ cup syrup. Place peaches, cut-side up, in electric frying pan. Add reserved syrup and drained cherries to pan. Dot peaches with butter. Put on pan cover; heat with vent open on medium-low heat for 5 to 7 minutes. Remove cover. Spoon sour cream into peach centers; sprinkle with brown sugar. Cover and heat until sugar melts, about 3 minutes. Serve immediately.

burgundy pears

Serves: 6

- **⅓ cup sugar**
- **⅓ cup currant jelly**
- **½ cup pear juice**
- **1 29-oz. can pears, drained**
- **⅓ cup Burgundy wine**
- **Sour cream, cinnamon**

Heat sugar and jelly in pear juice until melted. Add pears and wine; warm over low heat.* Serve warm, topped with sour cream and dusted with cinnamon.

Director's note: **Can be prepared to this point and reheated over low heat when ready to serve.*

Little Boy, *A Christmas Carol*

cocoa riviera

Serves: 8

- **6 Royal Riviera pears**
- **1 Tbsp. butter**
- **2 cups Hot Fudge***
- **1 cup sour cream**
- **2 cups whipped cream**
- **3 bananas**

Wash and halve pears (do not pare). Melt butter in non-stick frying pan; saute pears for 4 to 5 minutes, but ***do not brown.*** Pour Hot Fudge Sauce into 10 or 12-inch square glass baking dish. Place pears in hot fudge. Fold sour cream into whipped cream. Pour over top of pears. Slice bananas and arrange over top. Place under broiler to brown bananas.

Hot Fudge*

- **1 12-oz. pkg. semi-sweet chocolate chips**
- **2 to 4 Tbsp. Kahlua**
- **¼ cup water**

Melt chips over low heat. Stir in Kahlua and water. Blend.

raspberry meringue squares

Serves: 9

- **1½ cups vanilla wafer crumbs, (about 30 wafers)**
- **4 Tbsp. butter** *or* **margarine, melted**
- **2 Tbsp. sugar**
- **4 egg whites**
- **½ cup sugar**
- **1 pint red raspberries, sweetened***
- **1 2-oz. pkg. dessert topping mix**
- **1 Tbsp. lemon juice**

Preheat oven to 325°. Combine crumbs, butter and the 2 tablespoons sugar; mix well. Press firmly onto bottom of 9-inch square baking pan. Beat egg whites until soft peaks form; gradually add the ½ cup sugar, beating until stiff and glossy. Swirl meringue over crumb crust. Bake for 12 to 15 minutes; cool. Spread berries over meringue. Prepare dessert topping mix according to package directions; gently stir in lemon juice. Spread over berries; chill. Cut into squares to serve.

Director's note: **Frozen berries may be substituted; drain well.*

frosty strawberry squares

Serves: 12-16

- 1 cup flour
- ¼ cup brown sugar
- ½ cup chopped walnuts
- ½ cup butter *or* margarine, melted
- 2 egg whites
- ⅔ cup sugar*
- 1 10-oz. pkg. frozen strawberries partially thawed*
- 2 Tbsp. lemon juice
- ½ pint heavy cream, whipped

Preheat oven to 350°. Mix flour, brown sugar, walnuts and butter. Spread evenly in 9 x 13-inch baking pan. Bake for 15 to 20 minutes. Turn crumbs over after 10 minutes and stir occasionally to brown. Remove ½ of crumbs and reserve for topping. Press remaining half evenly onto bottom of pan. In large bowl, combine egg whites, sugar, berries and lemon juice. Beat at high speed until stiff peaks form, about 10 minutes. Fold in whipped cream. Spoon mixture over crumbs in pan. Sprinkle reserved crumbs on top. Freeze at least 6 hours. To serve, remove from freezer; cut into squares; trim with whole, fresh berries. ***Do not thaw.***

Director's note: **2 cups sliced, fresh berries and 1 cup sugar may be used in place of frozen berries and ⅔ cup sugar.*

ENCORE!

strawberries romanoff

Serves: 4-6

- 5 egg yolks
- 1 cup sugar
- ½ cup sherry
- 1 cup heavy cream, whipped
- 1 quart strawberries, sliced and sugared slightly, if desired

Cook egg yolks and sugar in double boiler until yolks are cooked. Slowly stir in sherry and cook, stirring constantly until thick. Chill.* Just before serving, fold in whipped cream and strawberries. Serve in individual dishes.

Director's notes: **Can be prepared to this point and refrigerated. Once the berries and whipped cream are added, serve fairly soon. Do not add berry juice.*

"A dinner lubricates business."
William Scott, Lord Stowell

delectable strawberries

Serves: 4-6

- 1 quart fresh strawberries
- ¼ cup raspberry jam
- 2 Tbsp. sugar
- ¼ cup water
- 1 Tbsp. Kirsch
- ¼ cup slivered almonds

In saucepan, combine jam, sugar and water; simmer about 2 minutes. Add Kirsch and chill. Place strawberries in individual serving dishes. Pour sauce over top. Sprinkle with almonds.

ENCORE!

sherry buds

Serves: 14

- ½ lb. marshmallows
- ⅔ cup sherry
- 1 pint heavy cream, whipped
- Maraschino cherries

Dissolve marshmallows in ⅓ cup of the sherry over low heat. ***Cool.*** Fold whipped cream into sherry mixture. Slowly add and fold in remaining sherry. Spoon into fluted paper cups. Top with halved cherries. Freeze, covered, until needed.

tortoni

Serves: 6-8

- 1 quart vanilla ice cream, softened
- ½ cup toasted slivered almonds
- 2 Tbsp. chopped maraschino cherries
- 1 oz. milk chocolate, grated
- ¼ tsp. grated orange peel
- ¼ tsp. grated lemon peel
- ½ tsp. brandy flavoring *or* 2 Tbsp. brandy
- Nuts, cookie crumbs, cherries for decoration

Blend all ingredients except topping decorations into softened ice cream. Freeze in individual paper baking cups or small molds. Sprinkle nuts or cookie crumbs on top, or decorate with cherry pieces.

The Last Act

Cakes

Frosting/Glaze/Sauce

Cookies

Photo on p. 265:
Goodnight Grandpa, 1981 - Estelle Kemler (Mrs. Soloman), Joe DeSantis (Isaac), Earl Sydnor (Mr. Wilson), Fyvush Finkel (Sol), Sylvia Harman (Bertha)

applesauce cake

Serves: 12-15

- ½ cup butter *or* margarine
- 1¾ cups sugar
- 1½ cups applesauce
- 2 small eggs *or* 1 large egg
- 2½ cups flour
- ½ tsp. baking powder
- ¾ tsp. salt
- 1½ tsp. baking soda
- ¾ tsp. cinnamon
- ½ cup water
- 1 cup raisins
- ½ cup nuts

Preheat oven to 350°. Cream butter and sugar; add applesauce and egg. Beat thoroughly. Combine dry ingredients (reserve 2 tablespoons flour) and add to creamed mixture alternately with water. Mix thoroughly. Toss raisins and nuts with reserved flour; add to batter. Turn into greased and floured bundt pan. Bake for 50 to 60 minutes. Cool 10 to 15 minutes in pan on wire rack; remove and cool completely.

Director's note: *A 9 x 13-inch baking pan can be used.*

frosted apple cake

Serves: 12

- 2 cups flour
- 2 cups sugar
- 2 tsp. cinnamon
- 2 tsp. baking soda
- 1 tsp. salt
- ½ cup vegetable oil
- 2 eggs
- 2 tsp. vanilla
- 4 cups chopped apple
- ½ to ¾ cup chopped nuts
- ½ cup raisins

Preheat oven to 325°. Combine dry ingredients. Add oil, eggs and vanilla; mix well. Fold in apple, nuts and raisins; mix thoroughly at medium speed of mixer. Turn into greased and floured 9 or 10-inch bundt pan or tube pan or 9 x 13-inch baking pan. Bake 1 hour or until tester inserted into cake comes out clean. (Bundt or tube pan will require longer baking time.) Cool and frost.

Frosting

- 8 oz. cream cheese, softened
- ½ cup butter, softened
- 1 cup confectioners sugar
- 1 tsp. vanilla

Mix frosting ingredients; beat until creamy.

german apple cake with sauce

Serves: 12

2 cups flour
2 cups sugar
1 tsp. baking soda
½ tsp. salt
¾ cup chopped pecans
4 cups pared and chopped apple
2 eggs, beaten
1 cup vegetable oil
1 tsp. vanilla

Preheat oven to 350°. Sift dry ingredients. Add pecans and apple. Combine eggs, oil and vanilla. Add to dry ingredients; mix well. Batter will be stiff. Spread in greased 9 x 13-inch baking pan. Bake for 45 minutes or until done. Serve warm Brandy Sauce over cake.

Brandy Sauce

⅓ cup butter
1 cup sifted confectioners sugar
3 Tbsp. apricot brandy
3 egg yolks
½ cup heavy cream

Beat butter until soft in top of double boiler. Add confectioners sugar and beat until creamy. Slowly beat in brandy. Beat in egg yolks, 1 at a time. Add cream; cook until thickened.

mother's banana cake

Serves: 15

½ cup butter
1½ cups sugar
1 medium egg *or*
2 small eggs
1 cup mashed banana
2 cups sifted cake flour
1 tsp. baking powder
1 tsp. baking soda
½ tsp. salt
¾ cup buttermilk *or*
sour milk*
½ cup chopped walnuts
1 tsp. vanilla

Preheat oven to 375°. Cream butter and sugar thoroughly. Add egg and mashed banana. Mix well. Sift dry ingredients; add to mixture alternately with buttermilk. Add nuts and vanilla. Pour into greased and floured 9 x 13-inch baking pan. Bake for approximately 40 minutes.

Director's note: **To sour milk, add enough milk to 1⅓ tablespoons vinegar* ***or*** *1½ tablespoons lemon juice to make 1 cup.*

broken glass cake

Serves: 8-12

1 3-oz. pkg. lime gelatin
1 3-oz. pkg. lemon gelatin
1 3-oz. pkg. cherry *or* **raspberry gelatin**
Boiling water
1 env. unflavored gelatin
¼ cup cold water
1 cup pineapple juice
1 Tbsp. sugar
1 cup heavy cream, whipped

Dissolve each package of gelatin separately in 1½ cups of boiling water. Pour into separate pans; refrigerate overnight. Cut into cubes.

Sprinkle unflavored gelatin over ¼ cup cold water. Bring pineapple juice to a boil. Add sugar and gelatin; stir until dissolved. Set aside to cool. Meanwhile, prepare crust. Fold whipped cream into cooled pineapple mixture. Fold in cubed gelatin. Pour into springform pan; smooth and top with remaining crumbs. Press down lightly. Refrigerate overnight. Remove sides of springform; slice to serve.

Crust

24 graham crackers, finely crushed
½ cup sugar
¼ cup butter, melted

Combine cracker crumbs with sugar and melted butter. Line bottom of 10-inch springform pan with ½ inch of crumb mixture. Reserve remaining crumbs for topping.

Unicorn, *The Glass Menagerie*

carrot cake

Serves: 10-12

This is an old European recipe.

4 eggs
1 cup vegetable oil
2 cups flour
2 cups sugar
2 tsp. baking soda
1 tsp. salt
2 tsp. cinnamon
4 cups grated raw carrot (8 to 10 medium size)
½ cup chopped pecans
Pecan halves

Preheat oven to 350°. Beat eggs; slowly beat in oil. Combine dry ingredients; gradually add to mixture, beating until smooth. Stir in carrots and nuts. Turn into 3 greased and floured 8-inch cake pans. Bake for 25 to 30 minutes. Cool in pans 10 minutes. Remove and cool completely on wire rack. Frost and fill between layers with Cream Cheese Frosting. Decorate top with pecan halves. Store in refrigerator. Remove ½ hour before serving for best flavor.

Cream Cheese Frosting

4 Tbsp. butter, softened
6 oz. cream cheese, softened
1 tsp. vanilla
4⅓ cups confectioners sugar
1 tsp. maple flavoring

Blend butter and cream cheese. Gradually add sifted confectioners sugar, beating until smooth and creamy. Stir in vanilla and maple flavoring.

crustless cheese cake

Serves: 12-14

1 lb. cream cheese
1 lb. Ricotta cheese
½ cup butter
2 cups sugar
6 eggs
1 tsp. vanilla
2 Tbsp. lemon juice
3 Tbsp. flour
3 Tbsp. cornstarch
16 oz. sour cream

Preheat oven to 325°. Have all ingredients at room temperature. Beat cream cheese, Ricotta cheese and butter together. Add remaining ingredients except sour cream; beat well. Stir in sour cream. Spoon into greased 10 to 12-inch springform pan. Bake for 1½ hours. Cool in oven at least 2 hours.*

Director's note: **Can be left in oven overnight.*

cake 'n cheesecake

Serves: 8-10

Cake

1 cup flour	**⅔ cup sugar**
1 tsp. baking powder	**2 eggs**
½ tsp. salt	**1 Tbsp. milk**
½ cup butter	**1 tsp. vanilla**

Preheat oven to 325°. Sift together flour, baking powder and salt; set aside. Cream butter and sugar; add eggs, 1 at a time, beating well after each addition. Stir in milk, vanilla and dry ingredients. Turn into well greased 10-inch pie plate. Pour Cheese Filling into center. Bake for 45 to 50 minutes. Top with Sour Cream Topping while cheesecake is still warm.

Cheese Filling

8 oz. cream cheese, softened	**1 tsp. vanilla**
⅔ cup sugar	**2 eggs**
½ cup sour cream	

Cream the cream cheese and sugar. Add sour cream and vanilla. Add eggs, 1 at a time, beating well after each addition.

Sour Cream Topping

1 cup sour cream	**1 tsp. vanilla**
2 Tbsp. sugar	

Combine thoroughly.

Director's note: *Any pie filling may be substituted for Sour Cream Topping.*

ENCORE!

jel-oh! cake

1 1-lb. pkg. pound cake mix	**1 tsp. lemon flavoring**
1 3-oz. pkg. lemon gelatin	**4 eggs, separated**
¾ cup apricot nectar	**1 cup confectioners sugar**
¾ cup vegetable oil	**Juice of 1½ lemons**

Preheat oven to 300°. Combine cake mix, gelatin, apricot nectar, oil and lemon flavoring; mix well. Add egg yolks, 1 at a time, beating after each. Beat egg whites until stiff; fold into mixture. Pour batter into greased 9 x 13-inch baking pan. Bake for 1 hour. While hot, glaze with a mixture of the confectioners sugar and lemon juice.

chocolate cheesecake

Serves: 16

Crust

- **2 cups chocolate cookie crumbs***
- **½ tsp. cinnamon**
- **½ cup butter, melted**

Preheat oven to 350°. Mix cookie crumbs with cinnamon and butter. Press crumbs onto bottom and sides of 9-inch springform pan. Chill. Meanwhile, prepare Filling and pour into chilled shell. Bake for 45 minutes. Chill overnight. Remove from pan. Decorate with shaved chocolate.

Filling

- **1 cup sugar**
- **4 eggs**
- **24 oz. cream cheese, softened**
- **16 1-oz. squares semi-sweet chocolate**
- **1 tsp. vanilla**
- **2 Tbsp. cocoa**
- **3 cups sour cream**
- **¼ cup unsalted butter, melted**

Beat sugar with eggs until light and fluffy. Add cream cheese gradually, beating well after each addition. Melt chocolate; add to cheese mixture along with vanilla, cocoa and sour cream, beating constantly. Add melted butter. Mix well.

Director's note: **Two 8-ounce packages chocolate cookies will yield 2 cups crumbs.*

Kate, *She Stoops to Conquer*

chocolate ripple cheesecake

Serves: 12-16

Cracks in the top are normal in this scrumptious cheesecake.

Crust

- **¾ cup flour**
- **2 Tbsp. sugar**
- **¼ tsp. salt**
- **¼ cup butter *or* margarine**
- **1 1-oz. env. pre-melted unsweetened chocolate***

Preheat oven to 400°. Combine flour, sugar and salt. With pastry blender or fork, cut in butter until particles are fine. Stir in chocolate. Press mixture onto bottom of 9-inch springform pan. Bake 10 minutes. Remove from oven; increase temperature to 500°. Pour ½ of plain cheese Filling over baked crust. With a circular motion, drizzle ½ of chocolate Filling on top of plain Filling. Cover with remaining plain Filling, then rest of chocolate Filling. With spatula, cut through batter to marbleize the two. Bake at 500° for 12 minutes, then lower temperature to 200° and bake 1 hour. Remove from oven and cool away from drafts 2 to 3 hours. Then refrigerate at least 8 hours before serving. To cut, use sharp knife, which has been run under hot water.

Filling

- **24 oz. cream cheese, softened**
- **1 cup sugar**
- **¼ cup flour**
- **2 tsp. vanilla**
- **6 eggs**
- **1 cup sour cream**
- **2 1-oz. env. pre-melted unsweetened chocolate***

In large bowl, with electric mixer at low speed, blend cream cheese with sugar until smooth. Blend in flour and vanilla. Add eggs, 1 at a time, beating well after each; beat in sour cream. In small bowl, combine 1½ cups of this cheese mixture with chocolate.

Director's note: **Run envelopes of chocolate under hot water before opening, so the chocolate will squeeze out easily.*

"Praise is the best diet for us, after all."
Sydney Smith

grasshopper cheesecake

Serves: 8-10

Try this instead of Grasshopper Pie.

- **1½ cups chocolate wafer crumbs (about 26 wafers)**
- **¼ cup butter *or* margarine, melted**
- **24 oz. cream cheese, softened**
- **1½ cups sugar**
- **4 eggs**
- **1 egg yolk**
- **¼ cup plus 2 Tbsp. creme de menthe**
- **3 Tbsp. white creme de cacao**
- **4 1-oz. squares semi-sweet chocolate**
- **1 cup sour cream**

Preheat oven to 350°. Combine chocolate wafer crumbs and butter, stirring well. Press onto bottom of 9-inch springform pan; set aside. Beat cream cheese at medium speed of electric mixer until light and fluffy. Gradually add sugar, beating well. Add eggs, 1 at a time, beating well after each. Add egg yolk; beat well. Stir creme de menthe and creme de cacao into cream cheese mixture. Spoon into crumb crust. Bake for 55 to 60 minutes or until set. Cool thoroughly. Melt chocolate in top of double boiler; allow to cool slightly. Stir in sour cream. Spread chocolate mixture over top of cheesecake. Chill well before serving.

college kids' cake

Serves: 12

This is a super cake to send anywhere -- it stays fresh for weeks.

- **1¼ cups margarine**
- **1¾ cups sugar**
- **6 eggs**
- **½ tsp. butter flavoring**
- **½ tsp. coconut flavoring**
- **1 tsp. vanilla**
- **1 lb. vanilla wafers, crushed (approx. 3½ cups)**
- **2 cups flaked coconut**
- **1 cup chopped pecans**

Preheat oven to 300°. Cream margarine and sugar. Add eggs, 1 at a time, beating well after each addition. Beat in the flavorings. Add vanilla wafer crumbs, coconut and pecans; blend well. Bake for 1½ to 2 hours in well greased bundt or tube pan. Refrigerate overnight before slicing.

Director's note: *If this is to be mailed, wrap in foil while still hot and place in freezer immediately. When frozen, pack in freshly popped corn, leaving cake in foil; wrap securely. The kids will enjoy the popcorn, too.*

"ingenue's" cheesecake

Serves: 12-16

Crust

1 cup graham cracker crumbs
3 Tbsp. sugar
¼ tsp. cinnamon
3 Tbsp. melted margarine

Preheat oven to 350°. Mix crust ingredients; press onto bottom and up sides a little of 9-inch springform pan. Pour Filling into crust. Place on center rack of oven. Bake for 45 minutes or until set. Remove and let stand 20 minutes. Pour Topping over cake and smooth gently with spatula to cover cake. Bake for 10 minutes more. Let stand until cold, then chill. Before serving, spread cherry pie filling over top.

Filling

24 oz. cream cheese
1 Tbsp. lemon juice
1 cup sugar
¼ tsp. salt
5 large eggs

Beat cheese and lemon juice until creamy. Add sugar, salt and eggs. Beat at medium speed 10 minutes or until smooth, creamy and lemon-color.

Topping

1½ cups sour cream
2 Tbsp. sugar
½ tsp. vanilla
1 21-oz. can cherry pie filling

With spoon, beat sour cream, sugar and vanilla for 1 minute.

Director's note: *Will stay fresh 2 or 3 days in refrigerator or 1 month in freezer.*

hawaiian pineapple icebox cake

Serves: 10-12

½ cup butter *or* **margarine**
1 cup sugar
2 egg yolks
1 15-oz. can crushed pineapple, drained
½ cup chopped nuts
1 pint heavy cream, whipped
2 egg whites, stiffly beaten
1 lb. vanilla wafers, crushed

Cream butter and sugar; add egg yolks. Mix well. Add drained pineapple and nuts; set aside. Fold whipped cream into beaten egg whites. Place ¾ of vanilla wafer crumbs in 9 x 13-inch pan. Spread pineapple mixture over crumbs, then spread egg white mixture. Top with remaining crumbs. Chill at least 24 hours before serving.

chocolate mocha cake

Serves: 8-9

Grand! Lovely with French vanilla ice cream.

2 1-oz. squares unsweetened baking chocolate
2 tsp. butter
1 cup flour
2 tsp. baking powder
Pinch of salt
¾ cup sugar
1 tsp. vanilla
½ cup milk
½ cup chopped nuts (opt.)
½ cup brown sugar
½ cup sugar
4 tsp. cocoa
1 cup cold coffee

Preheat oven to 350°. Melt chocolate and butter together over low heat. Combine flour, baking powder, salt and the ¾ cup sugar; stir in the chocolate mixture. Add vanilla and milk. Combine thoroughly. Add nuts, if desired. Pour into greased 9-inch square baking pan. Mix brown sugar, the ½ cup sugar and cocoa. Sprinkle over batter. Pour cold coffee over all. Bake for 40 minutes or until done.

"scrooge's" chocolate cake

Serves: 15-18

Contributed by Alan Brasington who played in A CHRISTMAS CAROL (1981). A great chocolate cake lover, he says, "This has passed from my great-grandmother to grandmother to mother and I send it on to you."

¾ cup shortening
2 cups sugar
2 eggs
1 tsp. vanilla
2½ cups flour
2 tsp. baking soda
1 tsp. salt
½ cup cocoa
1 cup sour milk*
1 cup boiling water

Preheat oven to 350°. Cream shortening and sugar until fluffy. Add eggs, 1 at a time, beating thoroughly after each addition. Add vanilla. Sift dry ingredients together; add to creamed mixture alternately with sour milk. Stir in boiling water (batter will be very thin). Immediately pour batter into 2 greased and floured 9-inch cake pans or 9 x 13-inch baking pan. Bake for 30 minutes for layer cakes or 45 minutes for 1 large cake.

Director's note: **Add enough milk to 1⅓ tablespoons vinegar* ***or*** *1½ tablespoons lemon juice to make 1 cup.*

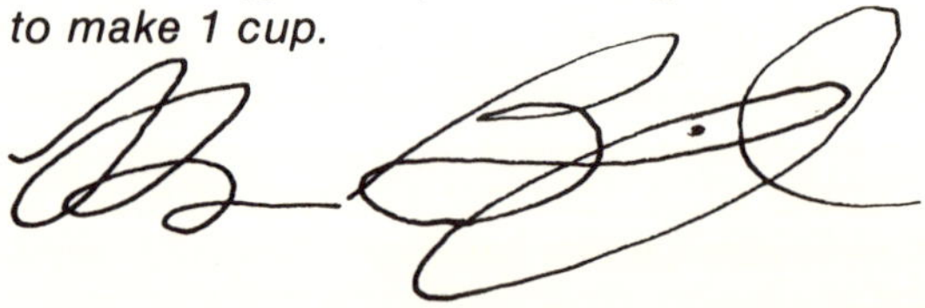

cranberry tea cakes

20-22 cakes

- ½ cup butter *or* margarine, softened
- 1 cup brown sugar, packed
- 2 eggs
- 1 tsp. cinnamon
- 1 tsp. nutmeg
- ½ tsp. salt
- ½ tsp. baking soda
- 1½ cups flour
- ½ cup sour cream
- ½ cup jellied cranberry sauce
- ½ cup chopped nuts

Preheat oven to 350°. Line 20 to 22 muffin cups with paper liners. Cream butter and brown sugar; mix well. Beat in eggs, cinnamon and nutmeg; blend thoroughly. Combine salt, baking soda and flour; stir in alternately with sour cream and cranberry sauce. Do not overmix. Fold in nuts. Fill muffin cups ⅔ full. Bake for 20 to 25 minutes. Cool completely. Frost with Buttermilk Frosting, if desired.

Buttermilk Frosting

- ½ cup butter, softened
- 1 egg yolk
- ½ tsp. vanilla
- 2 Tbsp. buttermilk *or* sour milk*
- 3 cups confectioners sugar

Combine all frosting ingredients; beat at medium speed until smooth.

Director's note: **To make sour milk, add 3 drops lemon juice to 2 tablespoons milk.*

chocolate truffle cake

Serves: 8

For the true chocolate connoisseur!

- 16 oz. semi-sweet chocolate
- ½ cup *unsalted* butter
- 1½ tsp. flour
- 1½ tsp. sugar
- 1 tsp. hot water
- 4 eggs, separated
- 1 cup heavy cream, whipped

Preheat oven to 425°. Grease bottom of 8-inch springform pan. Melt chocolate and butter in top of double boiler. Add flour, sugar and water; blend well. Add egg yolks 1 at a time, beating well after each addition. Beat egg whites until stiff and glossy. Fold into chocolate mixture. Turn into pan; bake 15 minutes. Cake will look very uncooked in center. Let cool completely (as cake cools, it will sink a bit in center). Then chill or freeze. Spread very thick layer of whipped cream over top of cake, smoothing with spatula. Cut cake while cold but let stand at room temperature about 15 minutes before serving.

hot fudge sundae cake

Serves: 9

Something different to take along and bake when you get there.

- 1 cup flour
- ¾ cup sugar
- 2 Tbsp. cocoa
- 2 tsp. baking powder
- ¼ tsp. salt
- ½ cup milk
- 2 Tbsp. vegetable oil
- 1 tsp. vanilla
- ½ cup chopped walnuts
- 1 cup brown sugar
- ¼ cup cocoa
- 1¾ cup hottest tap water
- Favorite flavor ice cream

In ungreased 9-inch square baking pan, mix together flour, sugar, the 2 tablespoons cocoa, baking powder and salt. Stir in milk, oil and vanilla with fork until smooth. Stir in nuts. Spread evenly in pan. Mix brown sugar and the ¼ cup cocoa; sprinkle on batter.* When ready to bake, pour hot water over batter. Bake in preheated 350° oven for 35 to 40 minutes. Let stand 15 minutes, no longer. Cut into squares. Place in serving dishes; top with ice cream and spoon sauce from baking pan over top.

Director's note: **Batter can be prepared to this point and refrigerated, even a day in advance.*

prairie beer cake

Serves: 14

Moist, dark and unusual tasting!

- 1 cup shortening
- 2 cups brown sugar, packed
- 2 eggs, well beaten
- 3 cups sifted flour
- ½ tsp. salt
- 2 tsp. baking soda
- 1 tsp. cinnamon
- ½ tsp. allspice
- ½ tsp. cloves
- 2 cups beer
- 1 cup chopped walnuts
- 2 cups finely chopped dates *or* prunes

Preheat oven to 350°. Cream shortening until soft; gradually add sugar, creaming until light and fluffy. Add beaten eggs; beat well. Sift together flour, salt, baking soda and spices. Reserve about 2 tablespoons dry mixture; beat remainder into batter. Slowly add beer and blend thoroughly. Toss nuts and fruit with reserved flour mixture to coat lightly. Fold into batter. Turn batter into greased and floured 10-inch tube pan (not bundt pan). Bake for 1 hour and 15 minutes or until tester inserted into cake comes out clean. Cool in pan 10 minutes, then carefully turn out to cool completely. Cover and refrigerate overnight. Serve plain, dusted with confectioners sugar or with a lemon glaze.

kentucky whiskey cake

An old family recipe -- handed down through four generations.

- **1 lb. red candied cherries, cut-up**
- **½ lb. golden raisins, cut in half** *or* **½ lb. chopped dates**
- **1 pint Kentucky Bourbon whiskey**
- **1½ cups butter**
- **2 cups sugar**
- **1 cup brown sugar**
- **8 eggs, separated**
- **5 cups flour, sifted before measuring**
- **1 lb. shelled pecans**
- **2 tsp. nutmeg**
- **1 tsp. baking powder**

Soak cherries and raisins in bourbon overnight.

Cream butter and both sugars until fluffy. Add egg yolks and beat well. Add soaked fruit with remaining liquid. Sprinkle a small amount of flour on the pecans; set aside. Add remaining flour, nutmeg and baking powder to batter. Beat egg whites to soft peaks; fold into batter. Add pecans. Turn into 10-inch greased tube pan lined with greased wax paper. Bake at 250° to 275° for 3 to 4 hours. Watch baking time.

When thoroughly cool, stuff center hole with cheesecloth soaked in bourbon. Place in tightly covered container or wrap in heavy aluminum foil. Keep very cool. Refrigerate, if necessary. Do not eat for at least 2 weeks after baking.

Director's note: *Stays fresh for 2 months in refrigerator. Can be frozen at any time -- even after 2 months.*

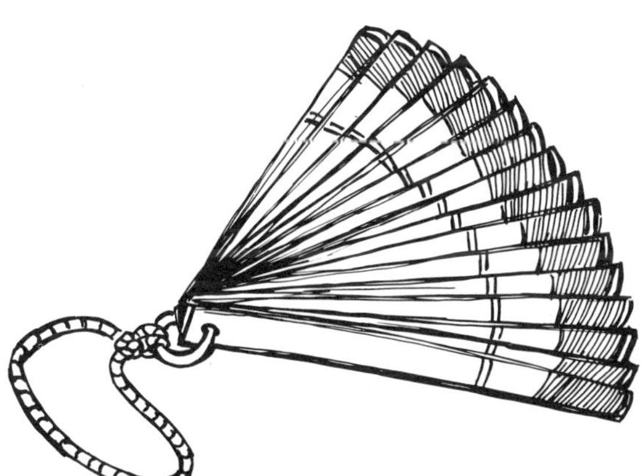

marble spice cake

1 loaf

A southern loaf cake.

- **½ cup butter**
- **1 cup sugar**
- **2 eggs**
- **2 cups sifted cake flour**
- **2 tsp. baking powder**
- **¼ tsp. salt**
- **⅔ cup milk**
- **1 tsp. instant coffee**
- **1 tsp. powdered, unsweetened cocoa**
- **1 tsp. cinnamon**
- **½ tsp. nutmeg**
- **½ tsp. cloves**
- **2 Tbsp. light *or* dark molasses**

Preheat oven to 375°. With mixer, cream butter; add sugar and beat 1 to 2 minutes. Add eggs, 1 at a time. Increase speed to high and beat another 1 to 2 minutes. Sift together flour, baking powder and salt. On lowest speed, alternately add flour mixture in 3 additions and milk in 2 additions, scraping bowl often and beating ***only*** until smooth after each addition. Remove about ½ the batter; set aside. To remainder, add instant coffee, cocoa, cinnamon, nutmeg, cloves and molasses; beat only until smooth. Alternately spoon large tablespoonfuls of both batters into buttered and lightly floured 5 x 9-inch loaf pan. Bake 65 minutes or until tester inserted into center of loaf comes out clean. Cool in pan 10 minutes. Remove and cool completely on wire rack.

Director's note: *Easily doubled to make 2 loaf cakes.*

sour cream pound cake

Serves: 16-20

Delicious with fresh strawberries or vanilla ice cream!

- **6 eggs, separated**
- **1 cup butter**
- **3 cups sugar**
- **1 cup sour cream**
- **¼ tsp. baking soda**
- **3 cups flour**
- **Pinch salt**
- **1 tsp. vanilla**
- **1 tsp. almond extract**

Preheat oven to 300°. Beat egg whites until stiff but not dry; set aside. Cream butter and sugar; beat in egg yolks. Combine sour cream and baking soda. Add flour and salt to the creamed mixture alternately with sour cream. Fold in beaten egg whites and flavorings. Spoon batter into greased and floured 10-inch tube or bundt pan. Bake for 1½ hours.

oatmeal cake

Serves: 12

- 1½ cups boiling water
- 1 cup quick oats
- ½ cup shortening
- 1 tsp. salt
- 2 eggs
- 1½ cups flour
- ¼ tsp. nutmeg
- 1 tsp. cinnamon
- 1 tsp. baking soda
- 1 cup brown sugar
- 1 cup sugar

Preheat oven to 350°. Pour boiling water over oats and let stand. Combine all ingredients except oats; mix thoroughly. Add oats and mix again. Bake in greased and floured 7 x 11-inch baking pan for 30 to 40 minutes. While cake is still warm, pour Frosting over it.*

Frosting

- 6 Tbsp. butter, melted
- ½ cup brown sugar
- 1 cup coconut
- ½ cup chopped nuts
- 1 tsp. vanilla
- ¼ cup evaporated milk

Mix ingredients together. Place in pie or cake pan and brown under broiler.

Director's note: **For a crispier frosting, spread uncooked frosting on cake after it is baked and return to oven to brown.*

toni's cake

Serves: 12-15

- 1 2-layer yellow cake mix
- 4 eggs
- ½ cup vegetable oil
- 1 16-oz. can mandarin oranges with juice

Preheat oven to 350°. Combine cake mix, eggs and oil. Blend in oranges and juice. Pour into greased and floured tube pan or 9 x 13-inch baking pan. Bake for 45 minutes or until done. Cool slightly and remove from pan. When completely cooled, slice in half crosswise; spread frosting in the middle; replace top. Frost top and sides of cake; decorate with coconut.

Frosting

- 1 20-oz. can crushed pineapple with juice
- 1 3¾-oz. pkg. instant vanilla pudding mix
- 1 8-oz. container non-dairy whipped topping
- Coconut (opt.)

Mix pineapple, pudding and topping thoroughly.

plum jelly roll

Serves: 8-10

This is a foolproof jelly roll recipe.

- **Three drinking glasses, all the same size**
- **4 eggs**
- **Sifted flour**
- **Sugar**
- **½ tsp. salt**
- **½ tsp. cream of tartar**
- **1 tsp. vanilla** *or* **lemon extract**
- **Confectioners sugar**
- **1 cup plum jelly**

Preheat oven to 375°. Break eggs into first glass. Spoon sifted flour into second glass, to reach same level as eggs. Spoon sugar into third glass to reach same level as others. Beat eggs with salt, cream of tartar and vanilla until thick. Add sugar gradually, beating at least 4 minutes. Add flour in 3 portions, folding by hand quickly and thoroughly. Spread batter in wax paper-lined 11 x 15-inch jelly roll pan. Bake for 15 minutes. Invert immediately on towel (not terry cloth), which has been sprinkled with confectioners sugar. Peel off wax paper. Roll up in towel. Let cool to room temperature. Unroll and spread with plum jelly, softened with fork. Roll again.

Director's note: *To adjust the size of jelly roll, change number of eggs as follows:*

From **2** to **5** eggs,
Use same amount of flour and sugar as eggs
⅛ tsp. *each* salt and cream of tartar for ***each*** egg used
¼ tsp. flavoring for ***each*** egg used
Beat eggs with sugar at least 1 minute ***per*** egg

orange sour cream cake

Serves: 8

Delightful flavor, not overly sweet. A great breakfast cake. For dessert, whipped cream is a nice topping.

- **½ cup butter**
- **1 cup sugar**
- **2 eggs**
- **1 cup sour cream**
- **1 cup raisins**
- **1 whole orange, ground in food chopper, including juice**
- **2½ cups cake flour**
- **1 tsp. baking soda**

Preheat oven to 350°. Cream butter and sugar. Beat in eggs and sour cream. Fold in raisins, orange and juice. Sift flour and baking soda into mixture; blend well. Pour into greased and floured 9-inch square baking pan. Bake for about 35 minutes.

pineapple-carrot-coconut-walnut cake

2 loaves

Contributed by David Tabor, who played in A CHRISTMAS CAROL (1981). This cake is very rich -- he prefers it without icing.

- **1½ cups vegetable oil**
- **2 cups sugar**
- **4 eggs**
- **2¾ to 3 cups presifted flour**
- **2 tsp. baking soda**
- **1 tsp. cinnamon**
- **½ tsp. salt**
- **1 tsp. vanilla**
- **1 20-oz. can unsweetened crushed pineapple, well-drained**
- **2 cups grated carrots**
- **1 4 to 6 oz. can finely chopped walnuts**
- **1 3½-oz. can unsweetened coconut**

Preheat oven to 350°. Beat oil, sugar and eggs together. Add dry ingredients; blend thoroughly. Add remaining ingredients; mix well. Turn into two 5 x 9-inch greased and floured loaf pans. Bake for approximately 60 to 70 minutes.

Cream Cheese Frosting

- **8 oz. cream cheese, softened**
- **½ cup butter, softened**
- **1 Tbsp. cocoa**
- **1 1-lb. box confectioners sugar**

Combine cream cheese and butter. Blend in cocoa and sugar; mix well.

Director's note: *Can be baked in well oiled 10-inch tube pan for 1 hour and 20 minutes instead of loaf pans. Fold in 2 cups banana slices in place of carrots for a different flavor; do not beat. Try Butterscotch Glaze (p. 284) instead of Cream Cheese Frosting.*

"Would ye both eat your cake and have your cake?"
John Heywood

glazed prune cake

Serves: 12-14

- **1 cup vegetable oil**
- **1½ cups sugar**
- **3 eggs**
- **1 tsp. vanilla**
- **1 cup cut-up cooked pitted prunes**
- **1 cup chopped pecans** *or* **walnuts**
- **2 cups sifted cake flour**
- **1 tsp. baking soda**
- **¼ tsp. salt**
- **1 Tbsp. cinnamon**
- **2 tsp. nutmeg**
- **2 tsp. allspice**
- **1 cup buttermilk**

Preheat oven to 350°. Beat together oil and sugar. Beat in eggs, 1 at a time; add vanilla. Sprinkle some of the flour over prunes and nuts, coating well; set aside. Sift remaining flour with dry ingredients; add to mixture alternately with buttermilk, ⅓ at a time. Fold in prunes and nuts. Turn into ***ungreased*** 9-inch tube pan with removable bottom. Bake for 65 to 70 minutes or until done. About 15 minutes before cake is done, prepare Butterscotch Glaze. Lift cake (still on pan bottom) out of pan to loosen. Set back in pan. While glaze is hot, pour slowly over cake in pan. Allow to soak in. Cool cake completely before removing from pan.

Butterscotch Glaze

- **1 cup sugar**
- **½ cup buttermilk**
- **½ tsp. baking soda**
- **¼ cup butter**
- **¼ cup light corn syrup**
- **½ tsp. vanilla**

Combine all ingredients in deep saucepan (it boils over easily). Stirring constantly, bring to a full boil; boil 10 minutes.

Director's note: *Cake will stay fresh several days in refrigerator. Can be baked in 9 x 13-inch pan for 40 to 45 minutes.*

frozen tia maria mousse cake

Serves: 10-12

Chocolate lovers' delight! Only small servings are necessary, but you'll want more!

- **3 cups chocolate wafer crumbs (12-oz. wafers)**
- **½ cup plus 2 Tbsp. butter, melted**
- **1 cup semi-sweet chocolate chips**
- **¼ cup boiling water**
- **¼ cup sugar**
- **4 large eggs, separated**
- **¼ cup Tia Maria**
- **¼ tsp. cream of tartar**
- **¼ cup sugar**
- **1 pint heavy cream, whipped**

Preheat oven to 375°. Lightly butter sides of 9-inch springform pan. Mix chocolate crumbs and butter; press firmly against bottom and sides of pan. Bake 8 minutes. Cool. In top of double boiler, melt chocolate with boiling water and ¼ cup sugar. Remove from heat; beat in egg yolks. Return and cook over hot water 1 minute. Add Tia Maria; blend thoroughly. Set aside to cool completely. Beat egg whites with cream of tartar until soft peaks form. Add ¼ cup sugar gradually; beat until stiff and glossy. Fold into chocolate gradually. Fold whipped cream into chocolate mixture. Spoon into crumb shell. Cover with plastic wrap. Freeze several hours or overnight.

white frosting

For your favorite chocolate cake.

- **4 Tbsp. flour**
- **1 cup milk**
- **8 Tbsp. butter**
- **8 Tbsp. vegetable shortening**
- **1 cup sugar**
- **1 tsp. vanilla**
- **Dash salt**

Blend flour into milk with wire whisk. Stir on low heat, cooking like pudding, until mixture thickens. Cover; set aside to cool. Cream butter with shortening. Add sugar, vanilla and salt; beat and add cooled mixture. Blend thoroughly.

Director's note: *Enough frosting to cover the tops and sides of a 9-inch, 2-layer cake, which has been split crosswise to make 4 thin layers.*

zucchini cake

Serves: 10

- 2 eggs
- ¾ cup sugar
- ½ cup vegetable oil
- ½ cup all-bran cereal
- 1½ tsp. grated orange peel
- 1 tsp. vanilla
- 1 cup unbleached flour
- 1 tsp. baking powder
- ½ tsp. baking soda
- 1 tsp. cinnamon
- ½ tsp. nutmeg
- 1 cup shredded zucchini
- ½ cup chopped walnuts

Preheat oven to 325°. Beat eggs, sugar and oil until well combined. Stir in cereal, orange peel and vanilla. Combine dry ingredients; add to mixture with zucchini and nuts. Mix well. Spread evenly in greased 6 x 10-inch glass baking dish. Bake for 35 minutes or until tester inserted near center comes out clean. Cool completely. Frost with Orange Cream Cheese Frosting.

Orange Cream Cheese Frosting

- 3 oz. cream cheese, softened
- 1 Tbsp. butter *or* margarine, softened
- ½ tsp. grated orange peel
- 1½ cups sifted confectioners sugar
- Milk, if needed

In small bowl, beat cream cheese, butter and orange peel until light and fluffy. Gradually add sugar, beating until fluffy and of spreading consistency. If mixture is too thick to spread, add 1 to 2 teaspoons milk.

maple frosting

Enough frosting for two 8 or 9-inch layers or one 9 x 13-inch cake.

- 2¾ cups confectioners sugar
- ½ tsp. salt
- 1 egg
- ¼ cup maple syrup
- ½ cup shortening
- 2 tsp. vanilla

Mix confectioners sugar, salt and egg. Blend in syrup. Add shortening and vanilla, mixing until smooth and creamy. Add more sugar to thicken or water to thin frosting, if required, until of spreading consistency.

birds' nest cookies

3½ dozen

1 cup butter *or* margarine, softened
½ cup brown sugar, packed
2 eggs, separated
½ tsp. vanilla
¼ tsp. salt
2 cups flour
1¼ cups finely chopped nuts
Jam *or* jelly

Preheat oven to 350°. Cream butter until light and fluffy; gradually add brown sugar. Add egg yolks; mix well. Blend in vanilla, salt and flour. Shape dough into 1-inch balls; dip each into unbeaten egg white, then nuts. Place on ungreased cookie sheets, 1 inch apart. Bake 5 minutes; quickly make a deep, wide depression with your finger or bowl of teaspoon in each cookie. Bake 8 minutes longer. Cool, fill depression with jam.

butter pecan turtle cookies

4 dozen

Crust

2 cups flour
1 cup brown sugar, packed
½ cup butter, softened
1 cup pecan halves

Combine flour, brown sugar and butter. Mix at medium speed, scraping sides of bowl often, 2 to 3 minutes, until particles are fine. Pat firmly into ungreased 9 x 13-inch baking pan. Place pecan halves evenly over unbaked crust.

Caramel Layer

⅔ cup butter
½ cup brown sugar
1 cup semi-sweet *or* milk chocolate chips

Melt butter in heavy pan; mix in sugar. Cook over medium heat, stirring constantly, until entire surface of mixture begins to boil. Boil ½ to 1 minute, stirring constantly. Pour caramel evenly over pecans and crust. Bake in center of oven at 350° for 18 to 22 minutes or until caramel is bubbly and edge of crust is light golden brown. Remove from oven. Immediately sprinkle with chocolate chips. Allow to melt slightly, 2 to 3 minutes. Slightly swirl with fork, leaving some whole for marbled effect. Do not spread chips. Cool completely; cut into bars.

"costume shop" cookies

- ½ cup butter *or* margarine
- 1 8-oz. pkg. chopped dates
- 1 egg, slightly beaten
- 1 cup sugar
- ¾ cup chopped walnuts
- 2 cups Rice Krispies
- Coconut

Melt butter in saucepan; add dates, egg and sugar. Boil for 6 minutes over medium heat, stirring constantly.

Pour hot mixture over walnuts and Rice Krispies; mix well. Cool slightly. Wet hands with cold water; form mixture into bite-size balls. Roll in coconut. They freeze well.

disappearing marshmallow brownies 1 dozen

Great for mailing to your college students. Wrap each bar individually.

- ½ cup butterscotch chips
- ¼ cup butter *or* margarine
- ¾ cup flour
- ⅓ cup brown sugar
- 1 tsp. baking powder
- ¼ tsp. salt
- ½ tsp. vanilla
- 1 egg
- 1 cup miniature marshmallows
- 1 cup semi-sweet chocolate chips *or* peanut butter chips
- ¼ cup chopped nuts (opt.)

Preheat oven to 350°. Over low heat, melt butterscotch chips and butter; cool. Add flour, brown sugar, baking powder, salt, vanilla and egg; beat well. Fold in marshmallows, chocolate chips and nuts. Spread in greased 9-inch square baking pan. Bake for 20 minutes. ***Do not overbake.*** The center will be jiggly, but gets firm as it cools.

magnificent fudge brownies

2 dozen

Cake

- **2 cups flour**
- **1½ cups sugar**
- **1 tsp. salt**
- **1 tsp. baking powder**
- **½ tsp. baking soda**
- **1 tsp. vanilla**
- **½ cup vegetable oil**
- **3 1-oz. squares unsweetened baking chocolate, melted***
- **1⅓ cups milk**
- **2 eggs**

Preheat oven to 350°. Combine dry ingredients; beat in remaining ingredients at medium speed for 3 minutes. Pour ½ of batter into greased 9 x 13-inch baking pan. Pour all Cream Cheese Filling over batter. Pour remaining batter on top. Bake for 35 to 40 minutes. Cool completely; frost with Chocolate Frosting.

Cream Cheese Filling

- **6 oz. cream cheese**
- **5 Tbsp. butter *or* margarine**
- **⅓ cup sugar**
- **2 eggs**
- **2 Tbsp. flour**
- **¾ tsp. vanilla**

Soften cheese and butter; blend well. Add remaining ingredients; beat thoroughly.

Chocolate Frosting

- **¼ cup milk**
- **1 1-oz. square unsweetened baking chocolate, melted***
- **¼ cup butter *or* margarine**
- **2½ cups confectioners sugar**
- **1 tsp. vanilla**

Boil milk, chocolate and butter. Stir and cook until smooth. Remove from heat; add sugar and vanilla. Beat until blended and creamy.

Director's note: **1 envelope premelted unsweetened chocolate may be substituted for each 1 ounce square of baking chocolate.*

canadian butter tarts

22 tarts

- **⅓ cup butter, melted**
- **⅓ cup corn syrup**
- **⅓ cup brown sugar**
- **1 egg, beaten**
- **½ tsp. vanilla**
- **⅓ cup raisins**
- **⅓ cup walnuts**
- **Pastry for 22 small tart tins *or* use prepared tart shells**

Preheat oven to 375°. Combine all ingredients thoroughly; spoon into unbaked tart shells. Bake for 20 to 25 minutes.

magic vanishing brownies

These were named by grandchildren who ate them so fast they vanished like magic!

Brownie Layer

- **3 1-oz. squares unsweetened baking chocolate**
- **½ cup butter *or* margarine**
- **1 cup sugar**
- **2 eggs, slightly beaten**
- **¾ cup flour**
- **¼ tsp. salt**
- **¼ tsp. baking powder**

Preheat oven to 350°. Melt chocolate and butter; stir sugar and eggs into chocolate until blended. Add dry ingredients to chocolate mixture, stirring until just blended. Spread into greased 8-inch square pan. Bake for 20 minutes. When completely cool, spread Mint Cream on top. Chill for 1 hour. Spread with Chocolate Glaze.

Mint Cream

- **1½ cups confectioners sugar**
- **3 Tbsp. soft butter *or* margarine**
- **2 Tbsp. milk *or* light cream**
- **¾ tsp. peppermint extract**

Mix thoroughly.

Chocolate Glaze

- **2 oz. semi-sweet chocolate chips**
- **2 Tbsp. butter**

Melt chips and butter in saucepan.

chocolate truffles

1 dozen

- **6 1-oz. squares semi-sweet chocolate**
- **¼ cup sifted confectioners sugar**
- **3 Tbsp. butter**
- **3 egg yolks, slightly beaten**
- **1 Tbsp. brandy**
- **2 1-oz. squares semi-sweet chocolate**
- **½ tsp. cinnamon**

In top of double boiler over hot, not boiling, water, melt 6 squares chocolate with sugar and butter. Remove from heat. While stirring rapidly, add small amount of hot mixture to slightly beaten egg yolks; return to hot mixture, stirring well. Blend in brandy. Chill without stirring for 1 to 2 hours. Shape into 1-inch balls. Finely grate 2 squares chocolate; mix in cinnamon. Roll balls in grated mixture. Store in refrigerator.

saucepan brownies

2 dozen

- ½ **cup butter** *or* **margarine**
- **4 1-oz. squares unsweetened baking chocolate**
- **2 cups sugar**
- **2 tsp. vanilla**
- **4 eggs**
- **1 cup ground oat flour***
- ½ **cup all purpose flour**
- **1 tsp. baking powder**
- ½ **tsp. salt**
- ½ **cup chopped nuts (opt.)**

Preheat oven to 325°. In large saucepan, over low heat, melt butter and chocolate together, stirring occasionally. Cool slightly. Add sugar and vanilla, blending well. Add eggs, 1 at a time, beating well after each addition. Stir in remaining ingredients, mixing until dry ingredients are just moistened. Pour into greased and floured 9 x 13-inch baking pan. Bake for 35 to 40 minutes or until edges begin to pull from sides of pan.

Director's note: **To make oat flour: put 1¼ cups quick or old fashioned oats into blender; cover and blend 1 minute. This makes 1 cup of oat flour.*

chocolate covered peanut butter balls

6 dozen

The chocolate-peanut butter lover's treat. Well worth the time it takes to make them.

- ½ **cup butter** *or* **margarine, melted**
- **2 cups confectioners sugar**
- **1 16-oz. jar crunchy peanut butter**
- **4 cups Rice Krispies**
- ¾ **pkg. semi-sweet chocolate chips, melted**
- **Paraffin wax***

Mix all ingredients except chocolate and paraffin. Form into large ball. Refrigerate 2 hours. Roll dough into 1-inch balls. Melt chocolate with ½ stick paraffin. Dip balls into chocolate.** Place on wax paper to harden. Cover well and refrigerate to store.

Director's note: **Paraffin can be purchased in supermarkets. **For dipping: use a fork, rather than a spoon -- it lets the excess chocolate drip off. Spear with a toothpick if you don't mind holes in the finished product.*

chocolate date bars

15 bars

Chocolate Layer

- **½ cup butter *or* margarine**
- **½ cup semi-sweet chocolate bits**
- **1⅓ cups flour**
- **¼ cup sugar**
- **1 Tbsp. milk**

Preheat oven to 350°. Melt butter with chocolate; stir in flour, sugar and milk. Pat into 9-inch square baking pan; bake for 10 minutes. Spread Date Layer over Chocolate Layer. Bake for 20 to 25 minutes more. Cool; cut into bars.

Date Layer

- **⅓ cup sugar**
- **2 Tbsp. flour**
- **½ tsp. baking powder**
- **2 eggs**
- **1 cup finely snipped dates***
- **½ cup chopped walnuts**

In small bowl, combine sugar, flour and baking powder. Add eggs; beat until fluffy. Fold in dates and walnuts.

Director's note: **To cut dates easily, use scissors dipped into hot water.*

dark chocolate drop cookies

6 dozen

- **¼ cup butter *or* margarine**
- **2½ 1-oz. squares unsweetened baking chocolate**
- **1 cup sugar**
- **½ tsp. salt**
- **1 egg**
- **1 tsp. vanilla**
- **1¾ cups sifted cake flour**
- **1½ tsp. baking powder**
- **½ cup milk**
- **½ cup chopped pecans *or* walnuts**

Preheat oven to 375°. Melt butter and chocolate in top of double boiler over simmering water. Remove from heat; cool. In large bowl, cream chocolate mixture, sugar and salt. Beat egg into creamed mixture until light and smooth. Add vanilla. Combine flour and baking powder. Add to creamed mixture alternately with milk, blending well after each addition. Stir nuts into batter. Drop by teaspoonfuls onto ungreased cookie sheet. Bake about 8 minutes. Remove to cooling rack. Store in airtight container with wax paper between layers.

chocolate-peanut butter bars

No calories at all!

Peanut Butter Layer

- **1 cup butter *or* margarine, melted**
- **⅔ cup graham cracker crumbs**
- **1 cup peanut butter**
- **4 cups confectioners sugar**

Combine Peanut Butter Layer ingredients. Spread in ungreased 9 x 13-inch baking pan. Pour chocolate mixture over top. Refrigerate for at least 3 hours. Cut into very small pieces.

Chocolate Layer

- **1 cup sugar**
- **⅓ cup milk**
- **5 Tbsp. butter *or* margarine**
- **1 6-oz. pkg. semi-sweet chocolate chips**
- **Dash vanilla**

In small saucepan, combine sugar, milk and butter. Stir and boil for 1 minute. Remove from heat; add chocolate chips and vanilla. Stir until well blended and smooth.

cheesecake cookies

3 dozen

- **⅔ cup brown sugar, packed**
- **1 cup chopped walnuts**
- **2 cups flour**
- **⅔ cup butter, melted**
- **16 oz. cream cheese, softened**
- **½ cup sugar**
- **2 eggs**
- **2 Tbsp. lemon juice**
- **4 Tbsp. cream *or* milk**
- **2 tsp. vanilla**

Preheat oven to 350°. Mix brown sugar, nuts and flour. Stir in the melted butter; mix until light and crumbly. Reserve ¾ cup of this mixture for topping. Firmly press remainder into greased 9 x 13-inch baking pan. Bake for 12 to 15 minutes. Beat cream cheese until smooth. Add sugar and mix thoroughly. Beat in the eggs, lemon juice, cream and vanilla. Pour this mixture onto baked crust. Top with reserved crumbs. Bake for about 25 minutes more. Cool thoroughly; cut into 2-inch squares.

Director's note: *Can be baked a day in advance and refrigerated.*

"Candy
Is dandy
But liquor
Is quicker."
Ogden Nash

kourabiedes

4 dozen

A delicate short cookie covered with powdered sugar -- always found in Greek homes.

- **1 lb. unsalted butter**
- **½ cup confectioners sugar**
- **3 egg yolks**
- **1 Tbsp. orange rind**
- **Juice of ½ orange, strained**
- **1 Tbsp. vanilla**
- **2 Tbsp. brandy**
- **¾ cup finely chopped walnuts**
- **4½ cups flour***
- **2 tsp. baking powder**
- **Confectioners sugar**

Preheat oven to 350°. Cream butter; add confectioners sugar and blend well. Add egg yolks, orange rind, juice, vanilla, brandy and walnuts. Combine flour and baking powder. Slowly add to mixture until a soft dough forms. Shape dough with floured hands into small balls; flatten slightly to ½-inch thickness. Place on cookie sheet. Bake for 20 to 30 minutes or until lightly browned. Place baked Kourabiedes on wax paper covered with confectioners sugar. When cool, sift confectioners sugar over tops of cookies and roll entire cookie in sugar to cover.

Director's note: **More flour may be needed depending on the size of egg yolks and orange. Cookies will stay fresh for weeks if tightly covered and stored in a cool place.*

Nora, *A Doll's House*

ENCORE!

liquor balls

100 cookies

These keep a long time -- if you hide them well!

- **2 12-oz. boxes vanilla wafers, finely crushed**
- **2 cups cocoa**
- **2 cups liquor***
- **1 tsp. salt**
- **8 Tbsp. light corn syrup**
- **6 cups chopped pecans** *or* **walnuts**
- **5 cups confectioners sugar**

In very large bowl, mix crushed wafers and cocoa. Stir in liquor, salt, corn syrup, nuts and 4 cups of the sugar. Mixture will be a bit sticky. Roll into 1-inch balls, dusting your hands with sugar from time to time. Rolls balls in remaining sugar and let stand on cookie sheets overnight, covered lightly with plastic wrap. Store in tightly covered containers.

Director's note: **Almost any kind of liquor is fine (rum, whiskey or bourbon) or a combination of rum and a liqueur.*

crescent cookies

- **1 lb. unsalted butter**
- **½ cup confectioners sugar**
- **4 cups sifted cake flour**
- **2 egg yolks**
- **1 shot whiskey**
- **Extra confectioners sugar**

Preheat oven to 325°. Thoroughly mix ingredients except extra sugar. Using large, walnut-size pieces of dough, form each into a crescent shape. Place on ungreased cookie sheet. Bake for 20 to 25 minutes (cookies should still be white on top). Sift confectioners sugar over cookies while still warm.

forgotten cookies

3½-4 dozen

- **2 large** *or* **jumbo egg whites**
- **¾ cup sugar**
- **½ tsp. almond** *or* **vanilla extract**
- **1 6-oz. pkg. butterscotch** *or* **semi-sweet chocolate chips**

Preheat oven to 375°. Beat egg whites until stiff. Beat in sugar gradually (be sure sugar is completely dissolved). Add flavoring; stir in chips. With teaspoon, spoon onto foil-lined or greased cookie sheet. Place in ***preheated oven***, close door and count slowly to 10. Turn off oven. Leave in closed oven for at least 5 hours.

lemon layer bars

1 cup flour
½ cup butter *or* margarine, melted
¼ cup confectioners sugar
1 cup sugar
2 Tbsp. flour
½ tsp. baking powder
2 eggs
2 Tbsp. fresh lemon juice
Grated rind of ½ lemon

Preheat oven to 350°. Combine the 1 cup flour, butter and confectioners sugar. Press into 8-inch square pan. Bake for 12 to 15 minutes. Combine sugar, flour and baking powder; add eggs and lemon juice and rind. Beat for 2 minutes at medium speed. Pour over baked crust; bake for 15 minutes more. Dust with confectioners sugar. Cut while slightly warm.

caramel pecan brownies

1 dozen

⅔ cup vanilla caramels, (12 caramels)
2 Tbsp. milk
2 eggs
¾ cup sugar
½ tsp. vanilla
⅓ cup butter *or* margarine, melted
¾ cup flour
½ tsp. baking powder
½ tsp. salt
½ cup chopped pecans

Preheat oven to 350°. Cook and stir caramels and milk over low heat until caramels are melted; set aside. Beat eggs; gradually beat in sugar. Blend in caramel mixture, vanilla and butter. Sift dry ingredients; stir into caramel mixture. Fold in pecans. Turn into greased and floured 9-inch square baking pan. Bake for 20 to 25 minutes. Cool; cut into bars.

scottish shortbread

4 pans

The real thing -- "melt in your mouth" good!

1 lb. butter (no substitutes)
1 cup superfine sugar
4 cups sifted flour
Pinch salt

Preheat oven to 400°. Cream butter and sugar until fluffy. Using your hands, gently work flour and salt into creamed mixture. (Over-working dough will make it tough.) Divide into 4 equal parts. Pat each part into 8-inch square or 9-inch round pan. With a fork, prick each shortbread thoroughly. Reduce heat to 350° and bake for 20 to 25 minutes until edges are light brown, but top is still white.

joe froggers

1½ dozen

Traditional molasses cookie from colonial times.

- 4 cups flour
- 1½ tsp. ginger
- ½ tsp. cloves
- ½ tsp. nutmeg
- ¼ tsp. allspice
- 1½ tsp. salt
- 2 Tbsp. rum
- ⅓ cup water
- 1 cup dark molasses
- 1 tsp. baking soda
- ½ cup butter
- 1 cup sugar

Combine flour, spices and salt. Mix rum and water. Combine molasses and baking soda. Cream butter and sugar. Add dry ingredients to creamed mixture alternately with rum mixture, beating after each addition. Stir in molasses mixture. Chill dough for several hours or overnight. On well-floured surface, roll dough ¼-inch thick; cut with 4-inch cutter or 1-pound coffee can. Bake on greased cookie sheet in preheated 375° oven for 10 to 12 minutes. Let stand a few minutes; remove from cookie sheet.

molasses sugar cookies

4 dozen

- ¾ cup shortening
- 1 cup sugar
- ¼ cup dark molasses
- 1 egg
- 2 tsp. baking soda
- 2 cups sifted flour
- ½ tsp. cloves
- ½ tsp. ginger
- 1 tsp. cinnamon
- ½ tsp. salt
- Sugar

Preheat oven to 375°. Melt shortening over low heat; remove and cool. Add sugar, molasses and egg; beat well. Sift remaining dry ingredients; add to molasses mixture. Mix well; chill thoroughly. Roll chilled dough into 1-inch balls; roll in sugar. Place on greased cookie sheet 2 inches apart. Bake for 8 to 10 minutes.

"Crosspatch, draw the latch,
Set by the fire and spin:
Take a cup and drink it up,
Then call your neighbors in."
Anon. Nursery Rhyme

old fashioned fruit cookies

12 dozen

- **1½ lbs. mixed fruit (citron, orange and lemon peels, cherries, pineapple, etc.)**
- **1 lb. dates**
- **1 12 to 16-oz. pkg. figs**
- **1 lb. nuts**
- **1 cup butter**
- **1 cup sugar**
- **2 eggs, beaten**
- **4 Tbsp. brandy** *or* **water***
- **2 cups flour**
- **1 tsp. baking soda**
- **1 tsp. salt**
- **1 tsp. cloves**
- **1 tsp. cinnamon**
- **1 tsp. allspice**

Preheat oven to 350°. Place mixed fruit on paper towels to dry as much as possible. Chop fruit, dates and figs, a few at a time, in food processor with a sprinkling of the flour. Chop quickly so flour keeps pieces separate. Chop nuts. Cream butter and sugar. Beat in eggs and brandy. Sift remaining flour with baking soda, salt, cloves, cinnamon and allspice. Add, in several portions, to creamed mixture. Stir in fruit and nuts. Dough will be very stiff. Drop by teaspoonfuls onto greased cookie sheet. Bake about 12 minutes.

Director's notes: *Cookies don't spread much, so can be placed close together. Dough can be mixed ahead and refrigerated. Freezes well after baking. *Wine can be substituted.*

maids of honor

2 dozen

Drew rave reviews from the sewing circle.

- **½ cup butter**
- **¾ cup sugar**
- **2 eggs**
- **2 cups flour**
- **¼ tsp. salt**
- **2 tsp. baking powder**
- **1½ cups raspberry jam**
- **½ cup chopped nuts**
- **Whipped cream**

Preheat oven to 375°. Cream butter and sugar. Add eggs; beat until light. Sift dry ingredients; add to creamed mixture. Form small balls between hands and put into small cupcake tins. Make a deep hole in center by pushing up around edges. Mix jam and nuts together; fill tarts. Bake about 12 minutes until lightly browned. Top with whipped cream when serving.

Director's note: *Flour your hands when working with dough. Paper liners may be used.*

pecan pie tarts

2 dozen

- ½ cup butter, softened
- 3 oz. cream cheese, softened
- 1 cup sifted flour
- 2 eggs, well beaten
- 1½ cups brown sugar
- Pinch salt
- ½ tsp. vanilla
- 1 cup broken pecans
- Pecan halves

Preheat oven to 350°. Blend butter and cream cheese; mix in flour as you would for pie crust until well blended. Divide into 24 balls; press onto bottom and up sides of small tart pans. Stir together (don't beat) eggs, brown sugar, salt and vanilla. Place broken pecans in bottom of tart shells; fill with filling. Top with pecan half. Bake for 20 to 25 minutes. These freeze very well.

yummy raisin cookies

5 dozen

- 2 cups seedless raisins
- 1 cup water
- 1 cup shortening
- 2 cups sugar
- 3 eggs
- 1 tsp. vanilla
- 1 cup chopped nuts
- 4 cups flour
- 1 tsp. baking powder
- 1 tsp. baking soda
- 1 tsp. salt
- 1½ tsp. cinnamon
- ¼ tsp. nutmeg
- ¼ tsp. allspice

Boil raisins and water together for 5 minutes or until liquid is decreased to ½ cup. Cool.

Preheat oven to 375°. Cream shortening; add sugar and blend well. Add eggs, 1 at a time, beating well after each addition. Add vanilla, nuts and cooled raisin mixture. Add sifted dry ingredients; blend well. Drop by teaspoonfuls onto greased cookie sheet. Bake for 9 minutes.

variety cookies

6 dozen

Dough can be frozen in unbaked rolls; slice and use when desired.

- **1 cup butter *or* margarine**
- **1 cup brown sugar**
- **1 cup sugar**
- **2 eggs**
- **3 cups flour**
- **1 tsp. salt**
- **½ tsp. baking soda**
- **1½ tsp. vanilla**
- **Nuts, dates, semi-sweet chocolate chips (opt.)**

Preheat oven to 375°. Cream butter and sugars together. Add eggs; blend well. Add remaining ingredients. Drop by teaspoonfuls onto greased cookie sheet. Bake for 8 to 10 minutes.

Director's note: *Recipe can be doubled easily.*

walnut dreams

9 dozen

Obscenely rich!

Crust

- **1 cup butter, softened**
- **½ cup sugar**
- **2 cups flour**

Preheat oven to 350°. Cream butter and sugar. Gradually add flour, blending well after each addition. Spread evenly in greased 12 x 18-inch jelly roll pan. Bake for 15 minutes. Pour Filling over hot Crust. Continue baking until set, about 15 to 17 minutes. Cool completely. Spread with Frosting. Let set. Cut into squares.

Filling

- **1 lb. brown sugar**
- **2 cups chopped walnuts**
- **¼ cup flour**
- **4 eggs**
- **1 tsp. salt**
- **1 tsp. baking powder**
- **1 tsp. vanilla**

Combine filling ingredients; blend well.

Frosting

- **2 cups confectioners sugar**
- **3 Tbsp. milk**
- **2 Tbsp. butter, melted**
- **Almond extract**

Combine Frosting ingredients; blend until smooth.

Director's note: *Best stored in airtight container in refrigerator. Can be kept as long as 2 weeks and will still be fresh.*

Backdrop

Accompaniments/ Potpourri

Photo on p. 301:
K-2, 1982 - Jay Patterson (Harold), Michael Tolaydo (Taylor)

ENCORE!

chilled carrots

Serves: 10

2 lbs. carrots
1 medium green pepper, diced
1 medium onion, diced
1 10¾-oz. can cream of tomato soup
½ cup vegetable oil
1 cup sugar
¾ cup vinegar
1 tsp. prepared mustard
1 tsp. Worcestershire sauce
Salt and pepper to taste

Slice carrots approximately ⅛ inch thick. Cook in lightly salted water until crisp-tender; drain. Combine carrots and remaining ingredients. Marinate for 24 hours. Drain before serving.

dilly onion rings

Serves: 4-6

Great accompaniment for almost everything.

1 large mild onion
⅓ cup sugar
2 tsp. salt
1 tsp. dried dill weed
½ cup white vinegar
¼ cup water

Cut onion into thin slices; separate into rings. Combine remaining ingredients; stir until sugar dissolves. Pour over onion rings. Cover and refrigerate at least 5 hours, stirring occasionally.

marinated tomatoes

Serves: 8-12

6 to 8 tomatoes, peeled and sliced
⅔ cup olive oil
1 cup cider vinegar
¼ cup chopped scallions
¼ cup chopped parsley
1 tsp. salt
¼ tsp. freshly ground pepper
2 tsp. thyme
1 clove garlic, minced
2 to 3 Tbsp. sugar, to taste

Place sliced tomatoes in shallow glass dish. Combine remaining ingredients; pour over. Refrigerate at least 6 hours or overnight. Remove tomatoes from marinade to serve.

Director's note: *Add more sliced tomatoes to left-over marinade and refrigerate. It will stay fresh for a few days.*

swedish cucumbers

Serves: 6-8

A delicious "extra" for any meal.

- **2 medium cucumbers**
- **3 medium onions**
- **½ cup white vinegar**
- **½ cup sugar**
- **½ tsp. salt**

Do not peel cucumbers, but score with tines of fork; slice paper-thin. Slice onions and separate into rings; combine with cucumber. Combine vinegar, sugar and salt; stir over low heat until sugar dissolves. Bring to a boil; pour over cucumber and onion. Refrigerate at least 4 hours or overnight.

cinnamon apples

A family tradition at Thanksgiving and Christmas, but delicious for everyday, too.

- **Firm apples i.e. Ida Red**
- **Red hot cinnamon candies**
- **Water**

Pare apples; cut in half; remove core. Place close together in baking pan, cut side up. Sprinkle with cinnamon candies. Add about ½ inch water to pan. Bake at 375° for 30 minutes. Turn apples over and continue baking until they are really red. Place in large bowl to cool. Serve cold.

cranberry-orange apples

Serves: 8

Luncheon guests raved about this!

- **½ cup sugar**
- **½ cup orange juice**
- **1 Tbsp. grated orange peel**
- **1 Tbsp. cornstarch**
- **⅛ tsp. salt**
- **4 large cooking apples, pared and cored**
- **1 14-oz. jar cranberry-orange relish**

Cook sugar, orange juice, orange peel, cornstarch and salt, stirring constantly until mixture is thickened. Cut each apple in half. Arrange halves, cut-side up, in 8 x 12-inch baking dish. Spoon relish over apples; spoon orange juice mixture over relish. Cover dish with foil; bake at 350° for 55 minutes or until apples are tender.

brandied cranberries

Marvelous gift for friends.

- **4 cups fresh cranberries**
- **2 cups sugar**
- **⅓ cup brandy**

Wash cranberries; place in 9 x 13-inch glass baking dish. Sprinkle sugar over top. Cover with foil; bake at 300° for 1 hour. Remove from oven; stir carefully. Let cool slightly. Add brandy. Store in covered container in refrigerator.

ENCORE!

curried fruit

Serves: 6-8

- **1 1-lb. can peach slices**
- **1 1-lb. can pear slices**
- **1 1-lb. can pineapple chunks**
- **2 Tbsp. butter, melted**
- **¼ cup brown sugar**
- **1 tsp. curry powder**
- **1 1-lb. can pitted dark sweet cherries**

Combine fruits, except cherries, in baking dish. Stir together butter, brown sugar and curry. Pour over fruits. Bake at 325° for 15 minutes. Gently stir in cherries. Bake for 15 minutes more. Serve warm.

brandied peaches

- **1 29-oz. can peach halves**
- **1½ cinnamon sticks**
- **5 whole cloves**
- **2 Tbsp. brandy**

Drain syrup from peaches into small saucepan. Add cinnamon sticks and cloves. Bring to a boil; lower heat and simmer 5 minutes. Stir in brandy; pour syrup over peaches in bowl. Cover and chill to blend flavors.

escalloped pineapple

Wonderful with baked ham.

- **1 20-oz. can crushed pineapple, undrained**
- **4 cups soft bread crumbs**
- **1 cup sugar**
- **1 tsp. vanilla**
- **1 cup half-and-half**
- **4 Tbsp. butter *or* margarine, melted**

Preheat oven to 350°. Combine ingredients well. Place in buttered, 2-quart casserole. Bake for 50 to 60 minutes.

Director's note: *Can be prepared in advance, refrigerated and baked just before serving.*

rhubarb and pineapple jam

Some husbands won't eat their breakfast toast without it.

- **3 lbs. fresh rhubarb**
- **2 1-lb. cans crushed pineapple in unsweetened juice**
- **4 lbs. sugar**
- **¼ cup lemon juice** *or* **brandy (opt.)**

Wash and cut rhubarb into 1-inch pieces. Place in saucepan with juice drained from pineapple. Cook slowly until tender, approximately 15 minutes. Add pineapple and sugar to rhubarb mixture. Stir well until it boils. Continue stirring for 20 minutes or until setting point is reached. Pour into hot, sterilized jars and seal.

cranberry-currant walnut sauce

Serves: 8

Delicious with poultry and ham.

- **1 lb. fresh cranberries**
- **1¼ cups sugar**
- **1 cup red currant preserves**
- **1 cup water**
- **1 cup coarsely chopped walnuts**
- **2 Tbsp. grated fresh orange peel**

In large saucepan, combine cranberries, sugar, preserves and water; bring to a boil. Reduce heat; simmer, uncovered, for 20 minutes. Skim foam; remove from heat. Stir in walnuts and orange peel. Refrigerate, covered, at least overnight.

rum raisin sauce

- **1½ cups water**
- **1 cup raisins**
- **¾ cup sugar**
- **2 Tbsp. cornstarch**
- **1 Tbsp. grated orange peel**
- **¼ tsp. salt**
- **½ cup water**
- **½ cup dark rum**
- **2 Tbsp. butter** *or* **margarine**

In large saucepan, heat the 1½ cups water and raisins to boiling. Reduce heat to low; cover and simmer 10 minutes or until raisins are tender. Combine sugar, cornstarch, orange peel, salt and the ½ cup water. Gradually stir into hot raisin mixture. Cook, stirring constantly, until sauce is thickened. Stir in rum and butter; cook until butter melts.

Director's note: *Sauce may be refrigerated in covered container for 1 month. Delicious over ice cream, desserts or ham.*

tzatziki

A versatile concoction from our marketing department at Syracuse Stage. Great with freshly baked bread, on rice, with shish kabob or cold meat.

1 clove garlic
1 tsp. olive oil
1 cup yogurt
½ cup sour cream
1 cucumber
Salt and pepper

In small bowl, crush garlic. Add oil, yogurt and sour cream. Pare, seed and dice 1 cucumber; add to mixture in bowl. Add salt and pepper to taste. Chill at least 2 hours before serving.

Director's note: *This keeps well for days if covered tightly with plastic wrap.*

"homemade" sweet dill pickles

1 quart dill pickles
½ cup water
½ cup vinegar
1 tsp. celery seed
1 tsp. mustard seed
1 cup sugar
1 cup brown sugar

Remove pickles from jar, discarding juice. In saucepan, combine remaining ingredients; cook 5 minutes. Meanwhile, cut pickles lengthwise and pack back into jar. Pour in cooked mixture; seal jar. Refrigerate and use after 1 week.

pepperoni rolls

12 rolls

Kids who are away from home love to find these in their "care" packages. Great dorm or camp snacks.

Bread dough for 1 loaf of bread
1 stick of pepperoni

Buy ready-to-use white or Italian bread dough; defrost if necessary. Meanwhile, cut the pepperoni into thirds, then cut each third lengthwise into 4 sticks. Cut thawed dough into 12 equal portions, pulling each piece into a rough oblong. Wrap each piece of pepperoni in piece of dough, making a neat, well-sealed roll. Place on greased cookie sheet about 3 inches apart. Let rise for 45 to 60 minutes or until double in bulk. Bake at 350° for 25 to 30 minutes or until golden brown. Serve hot or cold. Can be frozen after baking.

a theatrical seasoning

8 oz. salt
2 oz. granulated garlic
2 oz. black pepper
1 tsp. cayenne pepper
1 tsp. thyme
1 tsp. oregano
2 oz. paprika
1 Tbsp. granulated onion

Blend all ingredients. Store in cool, dry place.

teriyaki sauce

1½ cups

¾ cup vegetable oil
½ cup soy sauce*
2 Tbsp. honey
1½ tsp. ginger
2 Tbsp. vinegar
1 tsp. garlic powder
2 scallions, sliced

Blend all ingredients. Place meat in marinade. Cover and refrigerate. Marinate, turning once or twice, steak - 2 to 2½ hours, chicken - 1½ hours, hamburgers - 1 hour. Refrigerate sauce after use. Sauce can be used over and over.

Director's note: **For extra taste, use soyu sauce from a Chinese store.*

grandma brown's new york state fair sandwich

Grandma Brown's Beans originated in Mexico, New York in the 1930's and is still a family owned and operated business.

This sandwich was the hit of the 1950 New York State Fair when over 100,000 were sold.

Simply take a slice of your favorite bread, add a layer of beans (and catsup if you wish), then top off with another slice of bread.

Variation: Place a slice of cheese on bread, cover with baked beans and fried bacon strips. Place another slice of cheese and bread on top; grill until golden brown. Serve piping hot.

S.R.O.

Daphne's
the Steak House on the Green

tournedos anastasia

Serves: 1

- 2 4-oz. fillets of beef
- 2 tsp. butter
- ½ oz. black caviar
- 1 oz. sour cream
- Dash Worcestershire sauce
- 2 Tbsp. Dijon mustard
- Pinch tarragon
- Dash white pepper
- 1 oz. brandy
- 1 oz. heavy cream
- 1 slice bread, cut for toast points

In small frying pan, heat butter until it bubbles; add fillets and saute both sides until desired doneness of meat is reached. Remove meat, pour off butter. Add caviar, sour cream, Worcestershire sauce, mustard, tarragon and white pepper. Blend sauce with spoon; add brandy; flame and add heavy cream. On heated plate, place toast points in squares. Place one fillet on each square and pour sauce down middle. Serve immediately.

Director's note: *Daphne's suggests garnishing with a carrot flower and red cabbage.*

Photo on p. 309:
Man and Superman, 1980 - Innes-Fergus McDade (Violet), Allan Stevens (Hector)

Pascale

WINE BAR & RESTAURANT

poitrine de veau farci a la tin-tin

- 1 veal breast
- 6 oz. sweetbreads, blanched and peeled
- 4 strips bacon, cooked
- 3 to 4 fresh pheasant livers (duck livers, if not available)
- 1 10-oz. bag spinach
- 3 cloves garlic
- ¾ lb. Italian sweet sausage
- 2 eggs
- ½ cup bread crumbs
- ¼ cup pesto verde
- ½ cup Pignolia nuts
- 1 cup dry Marsala
- Salt and pepper
- Arrowroot

Cut breast meat from veal ribs in 1 piece; set aside. Trim meat from between ribs. Combine with all ingredients except pesto, pignolias, Marsala, salt, pepper and arrowroot in a food processor; chop medium fine to make a forcemeat. Lay out breast flat on work table; spread with pesto in thin even layer, then spread on forcemeat. Saute pignolias lightly until golden; sprinkle over forcemeat. Roll breast lengthwise; tie with twine. Place on rack in roasting pan; pour Marsala over. Cover, place in 300° oven for 1 hour, basting frequently with Marsala. Remove cover, increase temperature to 350° and continue cooking for 5 minutes. Remove to warm platter. Deglaze pan with veal stock (made from the veal rib bones); season with salt and pepper; thicken slightly with arrowroot. Slice breast and serve with sauce.

Nikki's
CONTINENTAL DINING

escallops de saumon

Serves: 4

- **4 8-oz. fillets of fresh salmon**
- **Court Bouillon***
- **12 oysters steamed on the half-shell**
- **1 bunch fresh spinach leaves, wilted****
- **12 oz. white wine sauce*****

Poach salmon in Court Bouillon, covered. Cool until they almost flake (seams will separate when pressure is applied). Remove and drain on towels; keep hot. To serve, place fillets of salmon on individual serving plates; surround each with 3 oysters. Top salmon with 3 to 4 leaves of spinach and spoon 3 ounces of White Wine Sauce over salmon and oysters.

Court Bouillon*

- **1 cup fish stock**
- **1 cup white wine sauce**
- **½ cup sliced mushrooms**
- **1 bay leaf**
- **Pinch thyme**
- **2 tsp. salt**
- **4 Tbsp. butter**

Combine all ingredients in shallow straight-sided pan with cover. Bring to a boil. Lower heat to a simmer once fish has been added.

Wilted Spinach**

- **1 bunch fresh spinach**
- **2 cups water**
- **1 tsp. salt**
- **2 Tbsp. butter**

Wash and de-stem spinach leaves. Drop leaves into boiling, salted butter-water just before serving, until leaves are slightly wilted.

White Wine Sauce***

- 1 tsp. minced shallots
- 1/8 cup clarified butter
- 2 cups white wine
- 1 cup sliced mushrooms
- 1 bay leaf
- 3 cups heavy cream
- Salt to taste
- White pepper to taste
- Dash Tabasco
- Juice of 1 lemon
- 1 cup butter, softened

In small saucepan, combine shallots in clarified butter. Cook until shallots take on a small amount of color. Add wine, mushrooms and bay leaf. Reduce to 1/3 of original volume. Add heavy cream. Reduce down to 2/3 volume until it thickens on its own, being careful sauce does not separate. Season with salt, pepper and Tabasco. Strain through fine sieve. Cool sauce slightly; whip in softened butter, a piece at a time, incorporating well after each. Hold in warm area.

BARBUTO'S

rolotini ala florentine barbuto's

Serves: 6

- 12 slices veal scallopini, about 6 x 3 x 1/4 inch
- 12 thin slices prosciutto ham
- 12 sticks Mozzarella cheese, 2 1/2 x 1/2 x 1/2 inch
- 2 cups cream sherry
- Juice of 2 lemons
- 1/2 tsp. garlic salt
- Dash paprika
- 1/2 cup butter

Pound veal pieces until thin. Top each piece with a slice of prosciutto. Place a cheese stick at one end of each piece of meat and roll up, tucking in ends to enclose cheese. Fasten with wooden picks. Place rolls in baking dish. In saucepan, mix sherry, lemon juice, garlic salt and paprika. Heat, then pour over veal rolls. Dot with butter. Cover with foil and bake at 350° for 25 minutes. Turn rolls and cook for 30 minutes more or until tender.

Brae Loch
Inn

scottish thistle

Serves: 1

This drink was created by H. Grey Barr, owner of The Brae Loch Inn. He explains its significance: "The green creme de menthe depicts the stem; the frozen daiquiri, the pulp and the parfait amour, the thistle."

1 tsp. green creme de menthe
2 oz. light rum
1 oz. lemon juice
1 oz. simple syrup
1 full cup ice
1 tsp. parfait-amour

Place the creme de menthe in the bottom of a 20-ounce stemmed glass (Bolla Grande). In a blender, combine rum, lemon juice, simple syrup and ice. Blend until the consistency of a frozen daiquiri. Carefully pour or spoon the daiquiri on top of the creme de menthe. Make an indentation on the top with a spoon; fill with parfait-amour.

Simple Syrup
Boil for 5 minutes, 1 part water to 2 parts sugar. Can be refrigerated and used when needed.

STERIO'S TRADEMARK INN

tenderloin steak pizzaiola

Serves: 6

- 2¾ lbs. tenderloin, trimmed and cut into slices about ½-inch thick (3 slices per person
- ½ cup oil
- ½ tsp. black pepper
- 1 tsp. chicken base
- ½ tsp. oregano
- 1 clove garlic, minced
- 1¼ cups sherry
- 2⅛ cups Marinara Sauce*
- Provolone cheese (3 slices per serving)
- Grated cheese
- Bread crumbs
- Parsley

Heat oil in small frying pan; saute meat quickly (30 to 45 seconds). Drain oil; add seasonings, sherry and Marinara Sauce. Simmer tenderloin slices until cooked to your preference. Remove meat from sauce; arrange on warm platter. Bring sauce to a rolling boil, reduce by half and ladle over tenderloin slices. Place Provolone slices evenly in 'x' pattern across center of meat. Sprinkle with grated cheese, bread crumbs and fresh parsley. Place under broiler just long enough for cheese and bread crumbs to reach a golden brown color. Serve.

Marinara Sauce*

- 2 lbs. diced tomatoes in juice
- ½ tsp. onion powder
- ⅓ bay leaf
- ⅛ tsp. black pepper
- ¼ tsp. salt
- ½ cup water
- 3 Tbsp. oil
- 3 cloves garlic, minced
- 2 tsp. fresh parsley, chopped

Put tomatoes, spices and water in a pot; bring to a slow simmer. Cook, uncovered, for about ½ hour. Heat oil in saucepan; quickly brown garlic. Add parsley to keep garlic from burning. Pour into tomato-spice mixture. Bring sauce to a boil; remove from heat.

STERIO'S LANDMARK RESTAURANT

veal piccata with glace de viande

Serves: 6-8

- **3 lbs. veal top round (allowing 6 oz. per serving)**
- **1/8 cup vegetable oil**
- **Flour**
- **4 medium cloves garlic, minced**
- **Sweet vermouth (2½ oz. per serving)**
- **⅓ cup fresh lemon juice**
- **Glace de Viande Sauce * (2 oz. per serving)**
- **Artichoke hearts (2 per serving)**
- **¾ lb. butter, cut into cubes**
- **Parsley**

Have butcher cut 2 to 3-ounce medaillons across the grain of the veal round. Place veal slices between plastic wrap and pound until about 1/8-inch thick. Heat oil; flour veal medaillons. Saute garlic and veal until golden brown, ***do not overcook***. Remove to serving platter and keep warm. Pour off oil, leaving bits and pieces that stick to pan. Deglaze pan with vermouth; allow to reduce to ½ the original amount, scraping bits and pieces off bottom. Add lemon juice and Glace de Viande; reduce sauce until slightly thick. Place artichokes in sauce; add butter cubes. This will thicken sauce more and give it a nice creamy appearance. Simmer very gently; do not boil. Add chopped, fresh parsley; taste and adjust seasonings. Arrange artichokes around veal and top with sauce.

Glace de Viande* (Veal Demi-glaze)

Prepare a day or two in advance.

- **2 lbs. veal leg bones**
- **1 large bay leaf**
- **Juice of 1 lemon**
- **3 cups mirepoix (2 onions, 3 stalks celery and a medium carrot, chopped)**
- **1 cup dry vermouth**

Bring all ingredients except dry vermouth to a boil; simmer gently for approximately 8 hours, skimming surface from time to time. Reduce to ¼ the original volume. Strain through cheese cloth. Return stock to clean pot; add dry vermouth. Simmer until reduced to ½ volume of liquid. Cool and refrigerate. When cold this should be golden beige in color and thick like gelatin. This sauce can also be frozen.

Artichoke Hearts

- **2 cans artichoke hearts**
- **Flour**
- **1 to 2 eggs, beaten**
- **Parsley, minced**
- **Vegetable oil**

Roll hearts in flour; dip in egg mixed with a little parsley. Drop in hot oil; brown on all sides. Drain on paper towels; set aside to use as garnish. Can be prepared in advance and refrigerated.

Director's note: *Rice pilaf or tiny roasted potatoes and a fresh vegetable such as carrots or sauteed snowpeas should be served with this dish for a good color combination.*

THE SHERWOOD INN

scallops louisianne

Serves: 1

At the Sherwood Inn, this is served in an "au gratin" boat.

- **5 oz. scallops**
- **2 Tbsp. butter**
- **2 artichoke hearts, quartered**
- **2 mushrooms, quartered**
- **1 Tbsp. chopped shallots**
- **Salt and pepper**
- **2 oz. dry white wine**
- **3 oz. heavy cream**

Heat butter in frying pan. Add artichoke hearts and mushrooms; saute about 1 minute. Add shallots and cook until softened. Add scallops; season with salt and pepper; saute about 1 minute. Add wine; allow to come to a boil. Reduce mixture slightly. Add cream and allow to boil, swirl and thicken.

PHOEBE'S GARDEN CAFE

baked vegetable melange

Serves: 6

- 2 medium zucchini
- 1 medium green pepper
- 2 medium tomatoes
- 2 medium carrots
- 2 stalks celery
- 1 large onion
- 12 oz. mushrooms
- 4 Tbsp. butter
- ½ tsp. basil
- ½ tsp. oregano
- 1 tsp. salt
- ½ tsp. white pepper
- 1 cup tomato juice
- 6 1-oz. slices Provolone cheese
- 6 1-oz. squares puff pastry
- 1 egg

Preheat oven to 375°. Medium dice all vegetables except mushrooms, which are sliced. In frying pan, melt butter; add vegetables. Saute about 5 to 8 minutes. Add seasonings and tomato juice; simmer about 5 minutes. Portion the mixture into six 8-ounce baking crocks. Cover each crock with a slice of Provolone and then a square of puff pastry. Brush the pastry with an egg wash (egg beaten with a little water). Bake for 25 to 30 minutes or until the pastry tops are golden brown. Serve immediately!

POSEIDON RESTAURANT

moussakas

Serves: 6-8

(Baked eggplant with minced veal and Bechamel Sauce)

3 to 4 lbs. eggplant
Salt
Olive oil
2 oz. butter
2 lbs. finely minced veal
2 Tbsp. grated onion
2 ripe tomatoes, chopped
1 Tbsp. chopped parsley
¼ tsp. cinnamon
¼ tsp. nutmeg
1 wineglass red wine
1½ pts. Bechamel Sauce
2 oz. grated cheese (Kefalotiri *or* Parmesan)
3 eggs, well beaten

Slice the eggplants crosswise, about ½ inch thick; sprinkle liberally with salt. Allow to drain in a colander for at least 30 minutes. Rinse well and pat dry. Brush both sides lightly with olive oil; bake at 350° until nicely browned on both sides. In another pan, melt butter and saute veal, onion and tomatoes. Add parsley, spices, salt and pepper to taste; moisten with wine and a little water, if necessary. Cook slowly for 20 minutes. Remove from heat and stir in 2 tablespoons of the Bechamel Sauce. Butter a 9 x 13-inch pan and fill with alternate layers of eggplant and veal, beginning and ending with eggplant. Sprinkle each layer with a little grated cheese; reserving enough cheese for top. Add a grate of nutmeg and the eggs to the Bechamel Sauce and pour over the dish. Sprinkle with the remainder of the grated cheese. Bake at 375° for 1 hour, or until top is golden brown.

THE HORNED DORSET INN

horned dorset mushroom soup

Serves: 10

1 cup butter
1½ lbs. very fresh button mushrooms, thinly sliced
Several reconstituted imported mushrooms, thinly sliced
1 large onion, thinly sliced
3 Tbsp. flour
1 quart chicken broth
4 Tbsp. sesame seeds
Butter
Salt, pepper, leaf thyme
1 pint heavy cream
Parsley

In frying pan, melt ½ cup of the butter. Add mushrooms and onion; saute slowly over low heat until soft. Cool; puree in food processor. Melt remaining ½ cup butter; make a roux by gradually adding the flour to the melted butter. Allow to bubble; cook slowly. In large pot, combine puree and cooked roux. While stirring, gradually add chicken stock to achieve desired consistency. Saute sesame seeds in a little butter until light brown. Add to soup. Season to taste with salt, pepper and leaf thyme. Just before serving, add heavy cream to taste. Garnish with plenty of fresh, finely chopped parsley (excluding stems).

veal oscar

Serves: 2

½ lb. veal medaillons, sliced from the saddle *or* fillet (at least ⅜-inch thick pounded to ¼-inch thickness)
10 small fresh asparagus spears
Meat from 8 Alaskan King Crablegs
2 cups clarified butter
1 egg yolk
Juice of 1 fresh lemon
2 tsp. whole leaf tarragon

Slowly saute veal medaillons, ***turning once*** and not overcooking. Steam asparagus until intensely green and crisp. Put crabmeat in small baking dish with enough clarified butter to cover; warm gently in medium oven. Arrange medaillons of veal on warm plate in star fashion. Overlay veal alternately with crablegs and asparagus spears. Coat with Bearnaise Sauce that has been made by slowly whipping (with hand whip) clarified butter into the egg yolk, finishing with the lemon juice and tarragon leaf that has been soaked in 2 tablespoons clarified butter. Consistency should be thick but not gloppy.

Tonino's Trattoria

bucatini alla tonino's

Serves: 12

The most famous of all pasta dishes is "Bucatini All' Amatriciana" or "Alla Marticiana," the origin of which is said to be "Amatrice," a little village between Lazio and the Abruzzo. The sauce is based on "Guanciale," (meaning to be free of all anxiety or simply stated, a very light sauce, easy to digest but very satisfying) diced and mixed with tomatoes, onions, olive oil, prosciutto, bacon and sauteed with the finest of dry white wine. This can be eaten with spaghetti or tagliatelle, but we at Tonino's, through our many experimentation sessions, have added some of our special seasonings and use only "Bucatini" (the large spaghetti with a hole in it) and found it to be the finest combination of them all, hence the name, "Bucatini Alla Tonino's."

10 Tbsp. olive oil
2 large onions, diced
10 oz. Prosciutto
6 oz. bacon, diced
1 cup dry white wine
6 lbs. canned pear tomatoes
Salt and pepper to taste
3 lbs. Bucatini Homemade Pasta Alla Tonino's
1½ cups grated Pecorino-Romano cheese

Heat oil; saute onions over low heat until soft. Add Prosciutto and bacon; fry slowly for a few minutes. Moisten with white wine; continue cooking until it evaporates a little. Chop and add tomatoes to pan. Season to taste with salt and pepper. Cook over brisk heat for not more than 15 minutes.

Bring a pan of salted water to a fast boil; lower the bucatini into the water, stir well and cook until just tender. Drain and dress the bucatini immediately with the hot sauce. Sprinkle with grated cheese and serve.

Curtain Call

Contributors

Recipes were contributed by Stage Guild members, Syracuse Stage subscribers and friends. Encore recipes are favorites from our first cookbook, Theatrical Seasonings.

Sally Alden
Betty Amann
Lee Amond
Jeanne Amrose
Bea Andrews
Lucille Anthony
Mary Armstrong
Rosemary Armstrong
Shirley Arones
Ann Atwater
Mary Ayer
Nancy Bartella
Barbara Beckos
Suzanne Beeching
M. Janet Berberian
Karen Berg
Ivy Besdin
Abigail Beutler
Marty Bieling
Mary Jane Bisesi
Shirley Blanding
Rosalind Bodow
Carol Boll
Laura Bongiovanni
Betty Born
Jenifer Breyer
Alice Broberg
Kathy Brown
Pamela Burdick
Shirley Burghard
Rona Butler
Rosemary Ciliberto
Gerardine Clark
James A. Clark
Jessica Cohen
Connie Colleran
Irene Collins
Helen Cornell
Pat Covell
Bonnie Coward
Vicki Crescenzi
Lucille Curley
Pauline Curt
Patricia D'Amico
Ellen Daniels
Carol Decker
Patricia DeClue
Linda DeFrancisco
Janet Dellas
Davelle DeMarco
Roe Dill
Pat Druger
Mary Durkin
Rita Durkin
Marti Eggers
Mildred Eggers
Jean Eschner
Cynthia Evans
Liz Fabel
Nancy Falcone
Nancey Farrell
Patricia Fatti
Molly Fitzpatrick
Dorothy Flanigan
Isabel Fleming
Amy Foster
Marilou Fredenburg
Ellie Freeman
Liz Freeman
Ruth Funk
Diane Galko
Phyllis Gammon
Sandy Gardinier
Nan Gartner
Pam Gatschet
Vivian Geiger
Bunny Geisler
Ann Marie Geiss
Marilyn Giancola
Jeannine Golden
Fred Goldie
Sheila Goldie
Marjorie Good
Karen Goodman
Barbara Grabowski
Tony Grabowski
Patti Haggerty
Elizabeth Hahn
Helen Hale
Linda Heacock
Sharon Heberlig
Margaret Heffernan
Gay Henegar
Suzanne Hickman
Ruth Hiller
C. vonHessert Hodge
Kathleen Horsman
Ruth Howard
Marilyn Husted
Phillip Ikins
Mercedes Irwin
Arlene Jerry
June Jesmain
Natalie Jivoff
Jane Keegan
Dottie Kelly
Peggy King
Frances Kip
Frances Knapp
Mary Knoepfle
Joan Krawchenko
Doris Kuckhoff
Jane Kyle
Arlene LaRue
Judith Laughlin
Lenore Lee
Gelene Lewis
Susan Lint
Marilyn Lintel
Betty Lourie
Janet Lower
Barbara MacKay
Frances MacKay
Phyl Malys
Kamal Maniktala
Marie Margosian
Marie Matchuk
Judith McCumber
Sally McDonald
Marilyn McKnight
Betty Jane McPhail
Dottie McVinnie
Mary Meers
Ann Melvin
Marge Merle
Denise Micek
Norma Milback
Stacy Milcos
Michele Milin
Andrea Miller
Denise Ruth Minnard
Nancy Mitchell
Kay Moore
Mary Anne Morrell
Jeanne Morris
Ann Mullin
Alice Murphy
Betty Murray
Joyce Nims
Patricia Numann
Diane O'Brien
Elayne O'Brien
Betty O'Hara
Fred O'Hara
Pat Orzell
Lib Palmer
Nan Palumbo
Nick Palumbo
Janice Pedersen
Bonnie Percival
Helen Perrone
Ursula Pettengill
Betty Pfeiffer
Ann Pierce
Amy Poltenson
Judy Poltenson
Carol Porter
Marjorie Pratt
Nancy Priest
Caryl Randolph
Eva Reidl
Pam Reussow
Suzanne Riester
Carrie Rood
Shannon Roscini
Peg Rose
Janet Rouen
Sharon Royce
Carole Russell
Ruth Sager
Nancy Salmonsen
Rosanne Sammons
Barbara Sassaman
Mardee Schaefer
Betty Schmidt
Mary Jane Schneider
Sheila Schwartz
Richard Scolaro
Marilyn Sechrist
Joan Shay
Elaine Shende
Loretta Shirtz
Virginia Shurtleff
Marilyn Sims
Kit Sine
Sylvia Slater
Sara Smiley
Diane Smith
Fritzie Nusbaum Smith
Helen Soulier
Lois Spitzer
Margaret Spriggs
Elaine Stepanian
Carol Stewart
Arthur Storch
Marie Sturge
Elizabeth Swaine
Gordon Symonds
Carol Taylor
Sue Teachout
Peggy Theis
Eileen Thompson
Inez Thompson
Sara Townsend
Sally Tully
Anne Vaccaro
Ursula Venier
Connie Vianese
Edith Viau
Dodie Vlassis
Elizabeth Volan
Mary Watson
Dorothy Weber
Jane Wein
Sandra Wells
Mary Wildridge
Hazel Zogg

Photo on p. 322:
A Christmas Carol, 1981 - Alan Brasington (Scrooge)

Index

Each recipe in this book has been tested for accuracy and excellence. We regret that we were unable to include many recipes which were submitted, due to similarity or availability of space.

Photo on p. 324: *Cat on a Hot Tin Roof*, 1982 - Walter Flanagan (Big Daddy), Margaret Phillips (Big Mama)

Glossary

Amplifiers - sound equipment

Aside - a piece of dialogue that other actors on stage are supposed not to hear

Break-a-leg - theater parlance for "good luck"

Button - an action term for the punctuation at the end of a scene; a sharp, clear ending

Center stage - the center of the stage

Curtain call - when the actors take a bow at the end of a play

Exposition - the dialogue that explains what has happened prior to the play's beginning; the relationship of the people in the play

Fast curtain (or slow curtain) - the director's term for the speed that the house (main) curtain is raised or lowered to emphasize whatever is going to happen or has happened on stage

Follow spot - spotlight that "follows" an actor as he moves around the stage

Green room - the room where actors wait to go on stage (lounge)

House-to-half - the direction to dim the house lights to half shortly before the play begins (curtain time)

In the wings - the areas of the stage beyond the main stage

Ingenue - leading young girl in the play

Magic time - the time between house-to-half and curtain going up when the excitement builds in the audience

Prompter side (British) - stage right, where the prompter sits

Proppy - a show with lots of things (props) in the set

Prop - anything used on stage, i.e. furniture, accessories, parts of the costume that are separate from the garment

2nd man - the second most important man in a play

Segue (seg-way) - a lead into something else -- where one thing blends into another, almost imperceptibly

Supporting player - any role surrounding a leading player

Saturday night supper - Stage Guild's volunteer program where the cast and crew are provided with dinner between the matinee and evening performances on Saturday

Stage Manager - the person who is in charge of the show once it opens. He sees to it that the technical aspects are ready, actors are rehearsed, calls all cues (sound, lighting, actors), rehearses understudies, and orchestrates everything that happens on stage during every performance.

Slow fade - sound or lights brought down slowly

S.R.O. - standing room only

Two-hander - two one-act plays

Tormentor - curtain that hangs at the sides of the stage

Teaser - curtain that goes across the top of the stage

Upstage - all stage directions are from the actors point of view - hence, upstage is toward the back of the stage, away from the audience

Understudies - actors who study a lead's part and are ready to go on stage should the lead be unable to perform